£3.00
26/11

WOMAN'S WEEKLY
Knitting for Children

WOMAN'S WEEKLY
Knitting for Children

edited by Marion Smith

HAMLYN

The designs in this book were originally
featured in *Woman's Weekly* magazine.

Published 1985 by
Hamlyn Publishing
a division of The Hamlyn Publishing Group Limited
Bridge House, London Road, Twickenham, Middlesex

Reprinted 1985

I S B N 0 600 50071 3

Printed in Spain by Cayfosa. Barcelona
Dep. Leg. B-18321-1985

Contents

Introduction

Following the popularity of the *Woman's Weekly Knitting Book* featuring designs for all the family, I have been asked once again to gather together some of the most requested patterns that have appeared in *Woman's Weekly* magazine during the last few years.

On this occasion we felt babies', toddlers' and children's garments would prove to be a most useful collection, so I have selected designs from babies' top-to-toe layettes through to children's sweaters and cardigans.

As before, I have chosen mainly standard yarns, such as 3-ply, 4-ply and double knitting, plus the odd speciality yarn. These are all yarns that will stay fresh and crisp, even after the constant washing required for children's wear.

Baby garments are always very popular with our readers, being attempted by both beginners and experienced knitters, as they are mainly quick to knit with an effective result at very little cost.

For the more experienced I have included several lacy and cable patterns, some with a touch of simple embroidery.

Many of the patterns have a little contrast colour introduced for added interest, plus the ever-faithful simple stocking stitch with a band of motifs knitted in, such as the duck sweater or our smashing train jersey suitable for both boys and girls. Our finger puppet sweaters have also proved very popular, giving the toddlers an opportunity to use their imagination.

I do hope you find at least one of your favourite designs within the following pages, plus several more that will tempt you to take up your knitting needles and happily click away the hours.

Marian Smith

Helpful Hints

SELECTING YOUR YARN

It is very important to obtain the yarn stated in the pattern, especially when a speciality yarn is used. Unfortunately, much time, effort and money can be wasted if this point is disregarded. Obviously, retailers cannot stock all the yarns and makes available, but do try to find the correct yarn whenever possible as results cannot be guaranteed when a substitute yarn has been used. (I have included a list of spinners' addresses on page 140 who will be pleased to supply either a local stockist or a postal service.)

In many cases where standard yarns such as 4-ply, double knitting and some Aran weights are substituted, the results are successful, but it is always advisable to buy just one ball of the proposed yarn and knit a tension sample before buying the full amount the pattern requires. If the correct tension is obtained and the resulting fabric is acceptable, then the garment will knit up to measurements similar to those stated in the pattern. However, do remember that yarn amounts differ, especially if a man-made fibre is used in place of 100 per cent wool, as wool weighs heavier and so has fewer metres to the ball. It is not advisable to substitute speciality yarns as no two yarns are exactly the same in weight or finish and, in many cases, the fabric is very difficult to unravel once it has been knitted up and often the surface of the yarn can be damaged in the process.

TENSION

The way to achieve successful results and a well fitting garment lies in obtaining the correct tension. This term is used to describe the number of stitches and rows which are produced to a certain measurement using a given size of needles, the specified yarn and a particular stitch pattern.

Before starting any pattern, knit up a sample square using the stated yarn and needles and enough stitches to measure at least 10 × 10 cm (4 × 4 in) according to the instructions given at the start of each pattern. If the finished square measures less than it should, it is working up too tightly and you should try again using a size larger needles. If it is larger, then the knitting is too loose and the square should be knitted again with a smaller size of needles. Also check your tension at regular intervals during the process of knitting your garment to make sure that you maintain the same tension throughout.

SIZES

Many of the patterns in this book are given in a range of sizes but this may create a certain amount of confusion, especially where a large number of sizes is included. It is advisable for knitters to first go through the instructions and underline all the figures which relate to the size to be worked.

JOINING NEW YARN

When possible, it is always advisable to join in a new ball of yarn at the beginning of a row. The ends are then woven into the seams when the garment is being made up. If the yarn has to be joined in the middle of the row, the 'splice' method is satisfactory in most cases. Unravel each end to be joined and cut away half of the strands from each end; overlay the remaining strands of the two ends from opposite directions and twist them together to obtain a similar thickness to that of the original yarn. Knit the next few stitches very carefully until the 'join' has been passed.

CHANGING COLOURS

When more than one colour is used in a row, it is necessary to weave in the loose strands at the back unless the colours are changed regularly every three or four stitches. In this latter case remember to strand the yarn not in use lightly across the back or the work will become puckered and will not lie smooth. Also remember when working adjacent blocks of colours to twist the yarn just used round that of the next colour to be used to avoid leaving a gap.

The 'weave in' method is used to avoid long strands on the wrong side of the garment that can easily catch and pull and distort the pattern when more than three or four stitches of one colour are worked before changing to another colour. For right side rows, the yarn not being used is lightly held in the left hand at the back of the knitting. To catch this up, insert the right-hand needle into the next stitch and under this back yarn, then knit the stitch in the usual way. The next stitch is then knitted excluding the back yarn, and you will find that the yarns not in use are neatly held in the back of the knitting. This procedure is repeated every four or five stitches. The same method works equally as well on wrong side rows, when the free yarn is lightly held in front of the work.

When knitting in stripes, strand yarn not in use

up the side of the knitting, by twisting it with the yarn in use every few rows to catch threads to the sides.

PICKING UP STITCHES

This is needed mainly for neck edges but also sometimes for front bands. Work with the right side of the fabric facing, unless otherwise stated. Divide the selected edge into several equal sections using pins as markers, then pick up an equal number of stitches from each section to obtain an evenly spaced edging.

If picking up from a straight edge, insert the needle either between or into the centre of the stitches along the edge of the fabric, take the yarn around the needle and draw a loop through. Continue inserting the needle into the same position along the remainder of the edge to obtain a neat join. A curved edge is worked in a similar way, but the needle is inserted into the centre of each stitch where possible.

PRESSING AND AFTER CARE

If the yarn used requires pressing then block out each piece of the garment with the wrong side of work uppermost, using plenty of pins and taking care to keep the shape of the knitting. Many patterns give information on pressing, but always check carefully with the instructions given by the manufacturers on the ball band, as once a yarn has been pressed wrongly and the fabric has gone 'flat', no amount of work will return it to its original state of elasticity. This also applies to the washing. Many of the modern yarns are machine washable, and easily maintained, but there are also a number of speciality yarns that are hand washable only. It is useful to include a ball band when giving a hand-knitted garment as a gift, so that after-care instructions are passed on for future use.

THE MAKING UP

There are several ways to seam pieces of the garment together and everyone has their own preferences, so I will mention three of the most popular methods. In each case you should use a blunt-ended wool needle and either the original yarn or a finer quality in the same shade.

Back stitch seam This is worked with the two right sides together and about 5 mm (¼ in) from the edges and is ideal for joining shaped edges. Insert the needle down through the two pieces and bring it up two stitches to the left, pulling the yarn through, *take the needle back across the front of the work to the right and insert it at the end of last stitch worked, then bring it up four stitches to the left; repeat from * to end.

Invisible seam This is worked in the centre of or between stitches with the right sides of the work facing and the pieces laid side by side. *Insert the needle under a stitch on one edge and pull the yarn through, then insert the needle under an adjacent stitch on the other edge and pull the yarn through; repeat from * taking a stitch from each side and drawing yarn up tightly between each stitch to form an invisible join.

Invisible seam

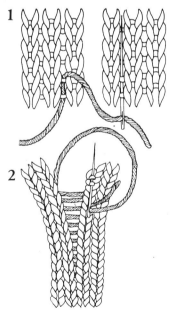

Flat seam This is worked with right sides together. *Insert the needle into an edge stitch of the first side, through the adjacent stitch on the second side and draw the yarn through, insert the needle into the next stitch to the left on the second side and through the adjacent stitch on the first side and draw the yarn through; repeat from * to end.

Babies

Layette with Lacy Panels

Illustrated on pages 19, 22 and 23

MATERIALS: *Allow the following quantities in 100 g balls of Emu Treasure 3-ply and 4-ply: Angel top: 1 ball 4-ply and 3 buttons. Matinee Jacket: 1 ball 4-ply and 3 buttons. Dress: 1 ball 4-ply and 3 buttons. Leggings: 1 ball 4-ply and shirring elastic. Cardigan: 1 ball 4-ply and 4 buttons. Vest: 1 ball 4-ply. Bonnett: 1 ball 4-ply and 1 metre of ribbon. Helmet: 1 ball 4-ply and 1 button. Bootees: 1 ball 4-ply and 1 metre ribbon. Bonnet, Helmet and Bootees can all be knitted from 1 ball of 4-ply. Christening robe: 3 balls 4-ply and 3 buttons. Shawl: 4 balls 3-ply. For all pieces: A long pair of No. 10 ($3\frac{1}{4}$ mm) knitting needles for 4-ply garments and a long pair of No. 8 (4 mm) needles for 3-ply shawl; 3 skeins green and 2 skeins yellow stranded embroidery thread.*

TENSION: *Work at a tension of 27 stitches and 36 rows to measure 10 × 10 cm over the stocking stitch, using No. 10 ($3\frac{1}{4}$ mm) needles and 4-ply, and 29 stitches and 36 rows to measure 10 × 10 cm, over the pattern using No. 10 ($3\frac{1}{4}$ mm) needles and 4-ply, and 26 stitches and 40 rows to measure 10 × 10 cm, over the pattern using No. 8 (4 mm) needles and 3-ply, to obtain following measurements: Angel top and Matinee jacket: Length 26 cm ($10\frac{1}{4}$ inches); side seam 16 cm ($6\frac{1}{4}$ inches); sleeve seam 15 cm (6 inches). Dress: Length 31 cm ($12\frac{1}{4}$ inches); side seam 21 cm ($8\frac{1}{4}$ inches); sleeve seam 2.5 cm (1 inch). Christening robe: Length 60 cm ($23\frac{1}{2}$ inches); side seam 50.5 cm ($19\frac{3}{4}$ inches); sleeve seam 15 cm (6 inches). Bonnet: Depth 15 cm (6 inches); all round face edge 36.5 cm ($13\frac{3}{4}$ inches). Helmet: Depth 15.5 cm ($6\frac{1}{2}$ inches); all round widest part 40.5 cm (16 inches). Vest: Length 23.5 cm ($9\frac{1}{4}$ inches); side seam 16.5 cm ($6\frac{1}{2}$ inches); sleeve seam 4.5 cm ($1\frac{3}{4}$ inches). Cardigan: Length 23 cm (9 inches); side seam 12.5 cm (5 inches); sleeve seam 15 cm (6 inches). Leggings: All round at widest part 63.5 cm (25 inches); back waist to crotch 20 cm (8 inches); inside leg seam 19 cm ($7\frac{1}{2}$ inches). Bootees: Foot length 9.5 cm ($3\frac{1}{4}$ inches). Shawl: 114.5 cm (45 inches) square, including edging.*

ABBREVIATIONS: To be read before working: *K., knit plain; st., stitch; p., purl; tog., together; sl., slip; s.s., stocking st. (k. on right side and p. on wrong side); y.fwd., yarn forward to make a st.; p.s.s.o., pass sl.st. over; s.k.p.o., (sl. 1, k, 1, p.s.s.o.); y.r.n., yarn round needle to make a st.; inc., increase (by working twice into same st.); dec., decrease (by taking 2 sts. tog.); g.st., garter st. (k. plain on every row).*

THE ANGEL TOP

Illustrated on pages 22–3

TO MAKE: (Worked in one piece to underarms): With No. 10 ($3\frac{1}{4}$ mm) needles and 4-ply cast on 193 sts. and k. 4 rows, then p. 1 row.

1st pattern row (right side): K. 6, * k. 2 tog., y.fwd., k. 1, y.fwd., s.k.p.o., k. 11; repeat from * ending last repeat with k. 6 instead of k. 11.

2nd and every alternate row: P. to end.

3rd row: K. 5, * k. 2 tog., y.fwd., k. 3, y.fwd., s.k.p.o., k. 9; repeat from * ending last repeat with k. 5.

5th row: K. 4, * k. 2 tog., y.fwd., k. 5, y.fwd., s.k.p.o., k. 7; repeat from * ending last repeat with k. 4.

7th row: K. 3, * k. 2 tog., y.fwd., k. 7, y.fwd., s.k.p.o., k. 5; repeat from * ending last repeat with k. 3.

9th row: K. 2, * k. 2 tog., y.fwd., k.9, y.fwd., s.k.p.o., k. 3; repeat from * ending last repeat with k. 2.

11th row: K. 1, * k. 2 tog., y.fwd., k. 11, y.fwd., s.k.p.o., k. 1; repeat from * to end.

13th row: K. 3, * y.fwd., s.k.p.o., k. 7, k. 2 tog., y.fwd., k. 5; repeat from * ending last repeat with k. 3.

15th row: K. 4, * y.fwd., s.k.p.o., k. 5, k. 2 tog., y.fwd., k. 7; repeat from * ending last repeat with k. 4.

17th row: K. 5, * y.fwd., s.k.p.o., k. 3, k. 2 tog., y.fwd., k. 9; repeat from * ending last repeat with k. 5.

19th row: K. 6, * y.fwd., s.k.p.o., k. 1, k. 2 tog., y.fwd., k. 11; repeat from * ending last repeat with k. 6.

21st row: K. 7, * y.fwd., sl. 1, k. 2 tog., p.s.s.o., y.fwd., k. 13; repeat from * ending last repeat with k. 7.

22nd row: P. to end.

23rd to 30th rows: As 1st to 8th rows.

31st to 36th rows: As 17th to 22nd rows.

37th to 40th rows: As 1st to 4th rows.

41st and 42nd rows: As 21st and 22nd rows.

Repeat the 37th to 42nd rows, twice more, then 37th row again.

To divide for backs and front: Next row: P. 46 and leave for right half back, cast off 4 sts., p. a further 92 and leave these 93 sts. for front, cast off 4 sts., p. to end and work on these last 46 sts. for left half back.

The left half back: Keeping continuity of the pattern dec. 1 st. at armhole edge on next row and the 4 following alternate rows—41 sts.

Dec. row: P. 2 tog., * p. 1, p. 2 tog.; repeat from * to end—27 sts.

Break yarn and leave these sts. on a spare needle.

The front: With right side facing, rejoin yarn to inner end of 93 sts. and keeping continuity of the pattern, dec. 1 st. each end of next row and the 4 following alternate rows—83 sts.

Dec. row: P. 1, * p. 2 tog., p. 1; repeat from * until 1 st. remains, p. 1 more—56 sts.

Break yarn and leave with sts. on a spare needle.

The right half back: With right side facing, rejoing yarn to inner end of 46 sts. and work as left half back.

THE SLEEVES (2 alike): With No. 10 ($3\frac{1}{4}$ mm) needles and 4-ply cast on 39 sts. and k. 5 rows.

Inc. row: K. 1, * inc., k. 3: repeat from * until 2 sts. remain, inc., k. 1—49 sts.

P. 1 row.

1st pattern row: K. 2, * k. 2 tog., y.fwd., k. 1, y.fwd., s.k.p.o., k. 3; repeat from * ending last repeat with k. 2 instead of k. 3.

2nd and alternate row: P. to end.

3rd row: K. 1, * k. 2 tog., y.fwd., k. 3, y.fwd., s.k.p.o., k. 1; repeat from * to end.

5th row: K. 3, * y.fwd., sl. 1, k. 2 tog., p.s.s.o., y.fwd., k.5; repeat from * ending last repeat with k. 3.

6th row: P. to end.

Repeat last 6 rows, twice, then keeping continuity of pattern, inc. 1 st. each end of next row and the following 12th row—53 sts.

Pattern 17 rows.

To shape sleeve top: Cast off 3 sts. at beginning of next

2 rows, then dec. 1 st. each end of next row and the 4 following alternate rows—37 sts.

Dec row: P. 7, * p. 2 tog., p. 8; repeat from * to end—34 sts.

Break yarn and leave.

THE YOKE: With No. 10 (3¼ mm) needles and 4-ply, k. across all sts. with right side facing thus: left half back, one sleeve, front, second sleeve, then right half back—178 sts.

K. 3 rows.

1st dec. row: K 1, k. 2 tog., * k. 4, k. 2 tog.; repeat from * until 1 st. remains, k. 1—148 sts.

K. 1 row.

Buttonhole row: K. 2, y.fwd., k. 2 tog. for buttonhole, k. to end.

K. 5 rows.

2nd dec. row: K. 5, * k. 2 tog., k. 3; repeat from * until 3 sts. remain, k. 3—120 sts.

K. 5 rows, then repeat the buttonhole row.

K. 1 row.

3rd dec. row: K. 5, * k. 2 tog., k. 2; repeat from * until 3 sts. remain, k. 3—92 sts.

K. 3 rows.

4th dec. row: K. 4, * k. 2 tog., k. 1; repeat from * until 4 sts. remain, k. 4—64 sts.

K. 3 rows.

5th dec. row: K. 3, * k. 2 tog., k. 6; repeat from * until 5 sts. remain, k. 2 tog., k. 3—56 sts.

K. 1 row, then repeat the buttonhole row.

K. 2 rows., then cast off k. wise.

THE BUTTON BAND: With No. 10 (3¼ mm) needles and 4-ply cast on 4 sts. and k. 33 rows.

Cast off k. wise.

TO MAKE UP THE ANGEL TOP: Press avoiding the g.st. using a warm iron over a dry cloth. Join back seam as far as yoke. Sew buttonband to right back edge, catching cast on edge to wrong side. Join sleeve seams then join tiny underarm seams. Add buttons. Using yellow straight sts. and green stem sts., embroider a daffodil in centre of each large diamond round lower edge.

THE MATINEE JACKET
Not illustrated

Work main part, sleeves and yoke as given for angel top, but omitting buttonholes.

THE BUTTON BAND: With No. 10 (3¼ mm) needles and 4-ply, cast on 4 sts. and work in g.st. until band fits up edge from cast on edge to cast off edge. Cast off.

THE BUTTONHOLE BAND: Work as given for button band, until band fits up edge to beginning of yoke.

K. a further 6 rows.

Buttonhole row: K. 2, y.fwd., k. 2 tog.

K. 11 rows.

Repeat last 12 rows, once, then the buttonhole row again.

K. 2 rows, then cast off.

TO MAKE UP THE MATINEE JACKET: Press as for angel top. Reverse knitting so that opening is in front. Sew

buttonhole band to right front edge and button band to left front edge. Join sleeve seams then tiny underarm seams. Add buttons. Embroider lower edge as on angel top.

THE DRESS
Illustrated on page 22

Work main part as given for angel top, but working 37th and 42nd rows, 5 times instead of twice, then 37th row again.

THE SLEEVES (2 alike): With No. 10 (3¼ mm) needles and 4-ply cast on 41 sts. and k. 3 rows.

Inc. row: K. 1, * inc., k. 1, inc., k. 2; repeat from * to end—57 sts.

P. 1 row.

Work the 6-row pattern of angel top sleeves, once.

To shape sleeve top: Keeping continuity of pattern cast off 3 sts. at beginning of next 2 rows, then dec. 1 st. each end of next row and the 4 following alternate rows—41 sts.

Dec. row: P. 4, * p. 2 tog., p. 3; repeat from * until 2 sts. remain, p. 2 more—34 sts.

Break yarn and leave.

Work yoke and complete as given for angel top.

THE CHRISTENING ROBE
Illustrated on page 19

TO MAKE: With No. 10 (3¼ mm) needles and 4-ply cast on 353 sts. and k. 4 rows then p. 1 row.

Work the 1st and 22nd pattern rows of angel top, twice, then 23rd to 42nd rows.

Repeat the 37th and 42nd rows 19 times, then 37th row again.

To divide for backs and front: Next row: P. 86 and leave for right half back, cast off 4 sts., p. a further 172 and leave these 173 sts. for front, cast off 4 sts., p. to end and work on these last 86 sts. for left half back.

The left half back: Keeping continuity of the pattern, dec. 1 st. at armhole edge on next row and the 4 following alternate rows—81 sts.

Dec. row: * P. 3 tog.; repeat from * to end—27 sts.

Break yarn and leave these sts. on a spare needle.

The front: With right side facing, rejoin yarn to 173 sts. and keeping continuity of pattern, dec. 1 st. each end of next row and the 4 following alternate rows—163 sts.

Dec. row: P. 1, * p. 3 tog.; repeat from * 52 times, p. 2 tog., p. 1—56 sts.

Break yarn and leave these sts. on a spare needle.

The right half back: With right side facing, rejoin yarn to inner end of 86 sts. and work as left half back.

Work sleeves, yoke and complete as given for angel top. Embroider daffodils in centre of each diamond round the 2 rows of large diamonds at lower edge.

Continued on page 18

BONNET
Not illustrated

With No. 10 (3¼ mm) needles and 4-ply cast on 97 sts. for face edge and k. 6 rows, then p. 1 row.

Work for 1st to 22nd pattern rows given for angel top.

S.s 10 rows—mark each end of last row.

To shape crown: 1st row: K. 1, * k. 2 tog., k. 10; repeat from * to end—89 sts.

2nd and every alternate row: P. to end.

3rd row: K. 1, * k. 2 tog., k. 9; repeat from * to end.

Repeat 2nd and 3rd rows, 8 times more, working 1 st. less between decreases on each repeat of the 3rd row—17 sts.

Break yarn leaving an end, run end through remaining sts., draw up and fasten off securely, then join crown seam as far as markers.

The neck edging: With right side facing rejoin yarn and using No. 10 (3¼ mm) needles and 4-ply, pick up and k. 48 sts. from row ends of neck edge and k. 2 rows. Cast off k. wise.

Press as for angel top: Attach ribbon to each corner of face edge. Embroider flowers in each diamond as given for angel top.

HELMET
Not illustrated

THE BUTTONHOLE FLAP: With No. 10 (3¼ mm) needles and 4-ply cast on 3 sts. and k. 2 rows.

Continue in g.st. and inc. 1 st. each end of next row and the following alternate row—7 sts.

K. 3 rows.

Buttonhole row: K. 3, y.fwd., k. 2 tog., k. 2.

K. 25 rows, then inc. 1 st. each end of next row and the 6 following 4th rows—21 sts.

K. 3 rows.

Break yarn and leave.

THE BUTTON FLAP: Work as buttonhole flap, omitting buttonhole.

THE MAIN PART: With No. 10 (3¼ mm) needles and 4-ply cast on 9 sts., using same needle k. across 21 sts. of button flap, turn and cast on 45 sts., turn and k. across 21 sts. of buttonhole flap, then turn and cast on 9 sts.—105 sts.

K. 8 rows, then p. 1 row.

Work the 6 pattern rows of angel top sleeves, 5 times.

To shape crown: 1st row: K. 1, * k. 3 tog., k. 10: repeat from * to end—89 sts.

2nd and alternate row: P. to end.

3rd row: K. 1, * k. 2 tog., k. 9; repeat from * to end.

Repeat 2nd and 3rd rows, 7 times more, working 1 st. less between the decreases of each repeat of the 3rd row—25 sts.

Next row: P. to end.

Next row: K. 1, * k. 3 tog.; repeat from * to end.

Break yarn leaving an end, run end through remaining 9 sts., draw up tightly and fasten off then join centre back seam. Add button to button flap.

THE BOOTEES
Illustrated on page 22

TO MAKE (both alike): With No. 10 (3¼ mm) needles and 4-ply cast on 41 sts. and k. 4 rows, then p. 1 row.

Work the 6 pattern rows of angel top sleeves, 3 times.

Dec. row: K. 1, * k. 2 tog., k. 3; repeat from * to end—33 sts.

P. 1 row.

Slot row: K. 1, * k. 2 tog., y.fwd., k. 2; repeat from * to end.

P. 1 row.

To divide for instep: Next row: K. 22, turn leaving 11 sts. on a safety pin.

Next row: P. 11, turn leaving remaining 11 sts. on a safety pin.

On centre 11 sts., s.s. 12 rows for instep. Break yarn and leave.

Next row: With right side facing, slip 11 sts. at right side of instep onto a No. 10 (3¼ mm) needle with point to inner end, rejoin yarn and using same needle, pick up and k. 10 sts. from row ends of instep, k. across 11 instep sts., pick up and k. 10 sts. from row ends at other side of instep, then k. 11 sts. from safety pin—53 sts.

Beginning with a p. row, s.s. 7 rows.

To shape foot: 1st dec. row: K. 2, k. 2 tog., k. 16., s.k.p.o., k. 9, k. 2 tog., k. 16., s.k.p.o., k. 2—49 sts.

Next row: P. to end.

2nd dec. row: K. 1, k. 3 tog., k. 14, k. 3 tog., k. 7, k. 3 tog., k. 14, k. 3 tog., k. 1—41 sts.

Next row: P. to end.

3rd dec. row: K. 3, tog., k. 12, k. 3 tog., k. 5, k. 3 tog., k. 12, k. 3 tog.—33 sts.

P. 1 row then cast off.

TO MAKE UP THE BOOTEES: Press as for angel top. Join back and under foot seam. Thread ribbon through slot row to tie at front.

THE CARDIGAN
Illustrated on page 22

THE MAIN PART (worked in one piece to underarms): With No. 10 (3¼ mm) needles and 4-ply cast on 121 sts. and beginning odd-numbered rows with k. 1 and even-numbered rows with p. 1, work 9 rows in single rib, then p. 1 row.

Work the 6 pattern rows of angel top sleeves, once.

Beginning with a k. row, s.s. 31 rows.

To divide for fronts and back: Next row: P. 26 and leave on a spare needle for left half front, cast off 6 sts., p. 56 and leave these 57 sts. on a spare needle for back, cast off 6 sts., p. to end and work on these last 26 sts. for right half front.

Continued on page 20

Opposite Christening Robe (page 17) and Shawl (page 21)

The right half front: Dec. 1 st. each end of next row and the 3 following alternate rows—18 sts.

Work 1 row, then dec. 1 st. at front edge on next row and the 4 following 4th rows—13 sts.

S.s. 4 rows—s.s. 3 rows here when working left half front.

To slope shoulder: Cast off 6 sts. at beginning of next row.

Work 1 row, then cast off remaining 7 sts.

THE BACK: With right side facing rejoin yarn to 57 sts. on spare needle, and dec. 1 st. each end of next row and the 3 following alternate rows—49 sts.

S.s. 21 rows.

To slope shoulders: Cast off 6 sts. at beginning of next 2 rows and 7 sts. on the following 2 rows—23 sts.

S.s. 4 rows for back neck extension.

Cast off.

The left half front: With right side facing, rejoin yarn to 26 sts. on spare needle and work as given for right half front, noting variation.

THE SLEEVES (2 alike): With No. 10 (3¼ mm) needles and 4-ply cast on 41 sts. and work 9 rows in single rib as given on fronts and back.

Inc. row: P. 5, * inc., p. 5; repeat from * to end—47 sts.

1st pattern row: K. 21, k. 2 tog., y.fwd., k. 1, y.fwd., s.k.p.o., k. 21.

2nd and alternate rows: P. to end.

3rd row: K. 20, k. 2 tog., y.fwd., k. 3, y.fwd., s.k.p.o., k. 20.

5th row: K. 22, y.fwd., sl. 1. k. 2 tog., p.s.s.o., y.fwd., k. 22.

6th row: P. to end.

These 6 rows form the sleeve pattern.

Keeping continuity of the pattern and working extra sts. in s.s. as they occur, inc. 1 st. each end of next row and the 3 following 8th rows—55 sts.

Pattern 17 rows.

To shape sleeve top: Cast off 3 sts. at beginning of next 2 rows, then dec. 1 st. each end of next row and the 3 following alternate rows—41 sts.

Work 1 row, then cast off 16 sts. at beginning of next 2 rows—9 sts.

Pattern a further 18 rows for shoulder extensions. Cast off.

THE FRONT BAND: First join row ends of shoulder extensions at top of sleeves to shoulder cast off groups on back and front, setting the 4 rows ends of back neck extension half way across cast off group at top of shoulder extensions.

With No. 10 (3¼ mm) needles and 4-ply cast on 7 sts. and work 4 rows in single rib as given on back and fronts.

Buttonhole row: Rib 3, y.fwd., k. 2 tog., rib to end. Rib 9 rows.

Repeat last 10 rows, twice more, then buttonhole row again.

Continue in rib until band fits up right front, round neck and down left front, casting off when correct length is assured.

TO MAKE UP THE CARDIGAN: Press as for angel top. Join sleeve seams, then sew in sleeves setting shaped row ends together. Sew front band into place, setting top buttonhole level with first front dec. Add buttons.

THE VEST
Not illustrated

THE BACK: With No. 10 (3¼ mm) needles and 4-ply cast on 62 sts. and k. 6 rows.

Beginning with a k. row, s.s. 52 rows—mark each end of last row to denote end of side seams.

S.s. 23 rows.

To divide for back neck: Next row: P. 18 and leave for left shoulder flap, p. 26 and leave on a st. holder, p. to end and work on these last 18 sts. for right shoulder flap.

The right shoulder flap: S.s. 4 rows, then dec. 1 st. at neck edge on next row and following alternate row, work 1 row—mark straight edge of last row to denote front neck line.

Dec. 1 st. at neck edge on next row and the following alternate row.

Work 1 row, then dec. 1 st. at neck edge on each of the next 12 rows.

Take remaining 2 sts. tog. and fasten off.

The left shoulder flap: With right side facing, rejoin yarn to 18 sts. and work as right shoulder flap.

THE FRONT: Work as back to armhole markers. S.s. 21 rows.

K. 2 rows, then cast off loosely k. wise.

THE SLEEVES (2 alike): With No. 10 (3¼ mm) needles and 4-ply cast on 38 sts. and single rib 4 rows.

Continue in s.s., inc. 1 st. each end of 3rd row and following 4th row—42 sts.

S.s. 5 rows.

To shape sleeve top: Cast off 8 sts. at beginning of next 4 rows.

Cast off remaining 10 sts.

THE BACK NECK EDGING: With right side facing, rejoin 4-ply and using No. 10 (3¼ mm) needles pick up and k. 24 sts. up shaped row ends of right shoulder flap, k. across 26 sts. at back neck, and finally pick up and k. 24 sts. from shaped row ends of left shoulder flap—74 sts.

K. 2 rows, increasing 1 st. each end of each row, then cast off k. wise.

TO MAKE UP THE VEST: Press as for angel top. Lap shoulder flaps over fronts placing markers level with cast off group of front neck, and lightly catch double row ends together. Set cast off groups at top of sleeves between armhole markers on back and front. Join side and sleeve seams.

THE LEGGINGS
Illustrated on pages 22-3

THE RIGHT LEG: With No. 10 (3¼ mm) needles and 4-ply cast on 68 sts. and single rib 10 rows.

1st and 2nd (turning) rows: K. 10 turn for 1st row, sl. 1, p. to end for 2nd row.

3rd and 4th (turning) rows: K. 20 turn for 3rd row, sl. 1, p. to end for 4th row.

Continue in this way, for a further 6 rows, working 10 sts. more on each alternate row.

Beginning with a k. row, s.s. 2 rows across all sts., then

inc. 1 st. each end of next row and the 8 following 6th rows—86 sts.

S.s. 3 rows and mark each end of last row to denote beginning of leg seam.

To shape leg: Dec. 1 st. each end of the next 9 rows then the 15 following alternate rows—38 sts.

S.s. 29 rows—read 30 rows here when working right leg—decreasing 1 st. at end of last row—37 sts. **

To divide for instep: Next row: K. 30, turn leaving remaining 7 sts. on a safety pin.

Next row: P. 13 turn, leaving remaining 17 sts. on a st. holder.

S.s. 14 rows. Break yarn.

With right side facing, slip 17 sts. from st. holder onto No. 10 (3¼ mm) needle with point to inner end, rejoin yarn and pick up and k. 10 sts. from row ends of instep, work k. 2 tog., k. 9, k. 2 tog. across instep sts., pick up k. 10 sts. from other side of instep and finally k. 7 sts. from safety pin—55 sts.

S.s. 7 rows, then k. 2 rows.

*** **1st (dec.) row:** K. 3, k. 2 tog., s.k.p.o., k. 20, s.k.p.o., k. 7, k. 2 tog., k. 17—51 sts.

2nd and alternate rows: K. to end.

3rd (dec.) row: K. 2, k. 2 tog., s.k.p.o., k. 19, s.k.p.o., k. 5, k. 2 tog., k. 17—47 sts.

5th (dec.) row: K. 1, k. 2 tog., s.k.p.o., k. 18, s.k.p.o., k. 3, k. 2 tog., k. 17—43 sts.

7th (dec.) row: K. 2 tog., s.k.p.o., k. 17, s.k.p.o., k. 1, k. 2 tog., k. 17—39 sts.

K. 1 row—omit this row when working left leg. Cast off.

THE LEFT LEG: Work as right leg to ** but reading p. for k. and k. for p.

To divide for instep: Next row: K. 20, turn leaving remaining 17 sts. on a st. holder.

Next row: P. 13 turn, leaving remaining 7 sts. on a safety pin.

S.s. 14 rows. Break yarn.

With right side facing, slip 7 sts. from safety pin onto No. 10 (3¼ mm) needle with point to inner end, rejoin yarn and pick up and k. 10 sts. from row ends of instep, work k. 2 tog., k. 9, k. 2 tog. across instep sts., pick up and k. 10 sts. from other side of instep and finally k. 17 sts. from st. holder—55 sts.

S.s. 7 rows then k. 3 rows.

Work as right leg from *** to end.

TO MAKE UP THE LEGGINGS: Press as for angel top. Join back and front seams as far as markers, then join inside leg seams continuing down foot. Join underfoot seams. Run 3 rows of shirring elastic through wrong side of waist ribbing.

THE SHAWL

Illustrated on page 19

THE CENTRE: With No. 8 (4 mm) needles and 3-ply cast on 257 sts. and k. 2 rows.

Repeat the 1st to 22nd pattern rows given on angel top 18 times, but working k. instead of p. on every wrong side row.

K. 1 row then cast off loosely k. wise.

THE EDGING: With No. 8 (4 mm) needles and 3-ply cast on 11 sts. and k. 1 row.

1st row: K. 2, y.r.n., p. 2 tog., k. 2, (y.r.n.) twice, k. 2 tog., (y.r.n.) twice, k. 2 tog., k. 1.

2nd row: K. 3 (p. 1, k. 2) twice, y.r.n., p. 2 tog., k. 2—13 sts.

3rd row: K. 2 y.r.n., p. 2 tog., k. 4, (y.r.n.) twice, k. 2 tog., (y.r.n.) twice, k. 2 tog., k. 1.—15 sts.

4th row: K. 3, p. 1, k. 2, p. 1, k. 4, y.r.n., p. 2 tog., k. 2—15 sts.

5th row: K. 2, y.r.n., p. 2 tog., k. 6, (y.r.n.) twice, k. 2 tog., (y.r.n.) twice, k. 2 tog., k. 1—17 sts.

6th row: K. 3, p. 1, k. 2, p. 1, k. 6, y.r.n., p. 2 tog., k. 2—17 sts.

7th row: K. 2, y.r.n., p. 2 tog., k. 13—17 sts.

8th row: K. 13, y.r.n., p. 2 tog., k. 2—17 sts.

9th row: K. 2, y.r.n., p. 2 tog., k. 11, k. 2 tog.—16 sts.

10th row: Cast off 5 sts., k. 6, y.r.n., p. 2 tog., k. 2—11 sts. Repeat last 10 rows, 143 times more. Cast off. Sew edging round outer edges of shawl easing at corners. Join cast-on and cast-off edges. Pin out to size and press lightly Embroider daffodils in 6 diamonds of each corner.

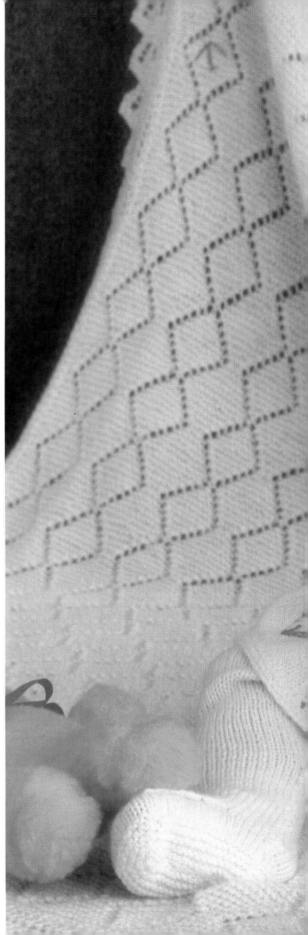

Top *Cardigan (page 18)* and *Leggings (page 20)*
Above *Dress (page 17)* and *Bootees (page 18)*
Right *Angel Top (page 16)*

Layette in Lacy Eyelet Pattern

Illustrated on pages 26 and 30

MATERIALS: *Allow the following quantities in 40 g balls of Robin Bambino Courtelle and Nylon in 3-ply and 4-ply: Shawl: 6 balls of 3-ply; a pair each of No. 6 (5 mm) and No. 8 (4 mm) knitting needles. Matinee Jacket, Dress and Angel Top: 2 balls of 4-ply for each garment; a pair of No. 10 (3¼ mm) knitting needles; a No. 10 (3¼ mm) circular needle; 3 buttons; 1 metre of narrow lace. Bootees: 1 ball of 4-ply; a pair of No. 10 (3¼ mm) knitting needles; ¾ metre of narrow ribbon. The Bonnet: 1 ball of 4-ply; a pair each of No. 10 (3¼ mm) and No. 11 (3 mm) knitting needles; 1 metre of 2.5 cm (1 inch) wide ribbon. The Vest: 1 ball of 3-ply; a pair of No. 10 (3¼ mm) knitting needles; 1 metre of narrow ribbon. The Leggings: 2 balls of 4-ply; a pair of No. 10 (3¼ mm) knitting needles; 41 cm (16 inches) of narrow ribbon; a waist length of elastic. The Helmet: 1 ball of 4-ply; a pair of No. 10 (3¼ mm) knitting needles; 1 button.*

TENSION AND MEASUREMENTS: *Worked at a tension of 28 stitches and 34 rows to measure 10 × 10 cm over the stocking stitch, using No. 10 (3¼ mm) needles and 4-ply, and 30 stitches and 38 rows to measure 10 × 10 cm over the stocking stitch, using No. 10 (3¼ mm) needles and 3-ply and 24 stitches and 30 rows to measure 10 × 10 cm, over the pattern, using No. 10 (3¼ mm) needles and 4-ply, the layette will be suitable for a 46 cm (18 inch) chest size. Shawl: 106 cm (41¾ inches) × 106 cm (41¾ inches). Matinee Jacket: Side seam, 15 cm (6 inches); length, 25 cm (9¾ inches); sleeve seam, 16 cm (6¼ inches). Dress: Side seam, 19.5 cm (7¾ inches); length, 29.5 cm (11½ inches); sleeve seam, 3 cm (1¼ inches). Angel Top: Side seam, 15 cm (6 inches); length, 25 cm (10 inches); sleeve seam, 16 cm (6¼ inches). Bootees: Foot length, 8.5 cm (3¼ inches). Bonnet: All round face edge, 34 cm (13½ inches); depth, 13 cm (5 inches). Vest: Side seam, 16 cm (16¼ inches), length, 26 cm (10¼ inches); sleeve seam, 4 cm (1½ inches). Leggings: All round at widest part, 66 cm (26 inches). Helmet: All round face edge, 37 cm (14½ inches).*

ABBREVIATIONS: To be read before working: *K., knit plain; p. purl; st., stitch; tog., together; inc., increase (by working twice into next st.); dec., decrease (by taking 2 sts. tog.); s.s., stocking st. (k. on the right side and p. on the wrong side); single rib is k. 1 and p. 1 alternately; g.st., garter st. (k. plain on every row); y.r.n., yarn round needle to make a st.; y.o.n., yarn over needle to make a st.; sl., slip; p.s.s.o., pass sl. st. over; s.k.p.o., sl. 1, k. 1, p.s.s.o.; y.fwd., yarn forward to make a st.; m.st., moss st.*

NOTE: *Instructions in brackets are worked the number of times stated after the last bracket.*

THE SHAWL

Not illustrated

TO MAKE THE CENTRE: With No. 8 (4 mm) needles and 3-ply yarn cast on 217 sts. and work in pattern as follows:

1st row: P. 1, * k. 3, p. 1; repeat from *.

2nd row: K. 1, * p. 3, k. 1; repeat from * to end.

3rd row: P. 1, * y.o.n., sl. 1, k. 2 tog., p.s.s.o., y.r.n., p. 1; repeat from * to end.

4th row: As 2nd row.

5th row: K. 2, * p. 1, k. 3; repeat from * ending last repeat with k. 2.

6th row: P. 2, * k. 1, p. 3; repeat from * ending last repeat with p. 2.

7th row: K. 2 tog., y.r.n., * p. 1, y.o.n., s. 1, k. 2 tog., p.s.s.o., y.r.n.; repeat from * until 3 sts. remain, p. 1, y.o.n., s.k.p.o.

8th row: As 6th row.

Repeat the last 8 rows, 35 times more.

Cast off.

THE BORDER (4 pieces alike): With long No. 6 (5 mm) needles cast on 227 sts.

1st row: K. 1, p. until 1 st. remains, k. 1.

Change to No. 8 (4 mm) needles.

1st row: K. 2, * y.fwd., k. 6, sl. 1, k. 2 tog., p.s.s.o., k. 6, y.fwd., k. 1; repeat from * until 1 st. remains, k. 1.

2nd and every alternate row: K. 2 tog., p. until 2 sts. remain, k. 2 tog.

3rd row: K. 2, * y.fwd., k. 5, sl. 1, k. 2 tog., p.s.s.o., k. 5, y.fwd., k. 1, y.fwd., k. 2 tog.; repeat from * ending last repeat with K. 2 instead of k. 1, y.fwd., k. 2 tog.

5th row: K. 2, * y.fwd., k. 4 sl. 1, k. 2 tog., p.s.s.o., k. 4, y.fwd., k. 1, (y.fwd., k. 2 tog.) twice; repeat from * until 13 sts. remain, y.fwd., k. 4, sl. 1, k. 2 tog., p.s.s.o., k. 4, y.fwd., k. 2.

7th row: K. 2, * y.fwd., k. 3, sl. 1, k. 2 tog., p.s.s.o., k. 3, y.fwd., k. 1, (y.fwd., k. 2 tog.) 3 times; repeat from * until 11 sts. remain, y.fwd., k. 3, sl. 1, k. 2 tog., p.s.s.o., k. 3, y.fwd., k.2.

9th row: K. 2, * y.fwd., k. 2, sl. 1, k. 2 tog., p.s.s.o., k. 2, y.fwd., k. 1, (y.fwd., k. 2 tog.) 4 times; repeat from * until 9 sts. remain, y.fwd., k. 2, sl. 1, k. 2 tog., p.s.s.o., k. 2, y.fwd., k. 2.

11th row: K. 2, * y.fwd., k. 1, sl. 1, k. 2 tog., p.s.s.o., k. 1, y.fwd., k. 1, (y.fwd., k. 2 tog.) 5 times; repeat from * until 7 sts. remain, y.fwd., k. 1, sl. 1, k. 2 tog., p.s.s.o., k. 1, y.fwd., k. 2.

13th row: K. 2, * yfwd., sl 1, k. 2 tog., p.s.s.o., y.fwd., k. 1, (y.fwd., k. 2 tog.) 6 times; repeat from * until 5 sts. remain, y.fwd., sl. 1, k. 2 tog., p.s.s.o., y.fwd., k. 2.

15th row: K. 2, * y.fwd., k. 2 tog.; repeat from * until 5 sts. remain, y.fwd., sl. 1, k. 2 tog., p.ss.o., y.fwd., k. 2.

16th rows: As 2nd row.

17th to 20th rows: Repeat 15th and 16th rows, twice—207 sts. Cast off.

TO MAKE UP THE SHAWL: Press work very lightly on the wrong side, using a cool iron over a dry cloth. Join cast off edges of borders to sides of centre piece, then join corner seams.

THE MATINEE JACKET

Illustrated on page 26

THE BACK: With No. 10 (3¼ mm) needles and 4-ply yarn cast on 97 sts.

M.st. row: K. 1, * p. 1, k. 1; repeat from * to end. M.st. 3 more rows.

Repeat the 8 pattern rows given for shawl centre, 7 times.

To shape the armholes: Cast off 3 sts. at the beginning of each of the next 2 rows, then dec. 1 st. at each end of the following 5 right side rows—81 sts.**

Next (dec.) row: * P. 2 tog., p. 1; repeat from * to end— 54 sts.

Break off yarn and leave sts. on a spare needle for yoke.

THE LEFT FRONT: With No. 10 (3¼ mm) needles cast on 54 sts.

1st. m.st. row: * K. 1, p. 1; repeat from * to end. **2nd row:** * P. 1, k. 1; repeat from * to end. M.st. 1 more row.

Next row: M.st. 5 and leave on a safety pin for front border, m.st. to end—49 sts.

*** Work 56 rows in pattern as given for shawl centre— work 57 rows here when working right front.

To shape the armhole: Cast off 3 sts. at the beginning of the next row, then 1 st. at the same edge on the 5 following right side rows—41 sts.

Next (dec.) row: P. 2 tog., * p. 1, p. 2 tog.; repeat from * to end—27 sts. Break off yarn and leave sts. on a spare needle.

THE RIGHT FRONT: With No. 10 (3¼ mm) needles cast on 54 sts.

Beginning with a 2nd row, m.st. 3 rows as given on left front.

Next row: M.st. until 5 sts. remain, turn and leave these sts. on a safety pin for front border—49 sts.

Work as given for left front from *** to end, noting variation.

THE SLEEVES (both alike): With No. 10 (3¼ mm) needles cast on 37 sts. and work 6 rows in m.st. as given for back.

Next (inc.) row: * K. 3, inc.; repeat from * until 5 sts. remain, k. to end—45 sts.

Beginning with the second pattern row as given for shawl, pattern 15 rows.

Maintaining continuity of the pattern and taking extra sts. into the pattern as they occur, inc. 1 st. at each end of the next row and the 3 following 8th rows—53 sts.

Pattern 15 rows.

To shape the sleeve top: Work as given for armhole shaping on back to ** when 37 sts. will remain.

Next (dec.) row: P. 7, * p. 2 tog., p. 8; repeat from * to end—34 sts. Break off yarn and leave sts. on a spare needle.

THE YOKE: With right side of work facing, sl. the 27 sts. of left front, 34 sts. of left sleeve, 54 sts. of back, 34 sts. of right sleeve, then the 27 sts. of right front on to a No. 10 (3¼ mm) circular needle—176 sts.

Working backwards and forwards in rows, beginning with a k. row, s.s. 2 rows.

1st (dec.) row: K. 8, * s.k.p.o., k. 2 tog., k. 8; repeat from * to end.

Beginning with a p. row, s.s. 5 rows.

2nd (dec.) row: K. 7, * s.k.p.o., k. 2 tog., k. 6; repeat from * until 1 st. remains, k. 1.

S.s. 5 rows.

3rd (dec.) row: K. 6, * s.k.p.o., k. 2 tog., k. 4; repeat from * until 2 sts. remain, k. 2.

S.s. 5 rows.

4th (dec.) row: K. 5, * s.k.p.o., k. 2 tog., k. 2: repeat from * until 3 sts. remain, k. 3.

S.s. 3 rows.

5th (dec.) row: Sl. 1, k. 2 tog., p.s.s.o., * k. 2, s.k.p.o.; repeat from * until 1 st. remains, k. 1—47 sts.

Break off yarn and leave sts. on a spare needle.

THE RIGHT FRONT BORDER: With wrong side of work facing, sl. the 5 sts. on safety pin at right front on to a No. 10 (3¼ mm) needle and work 71 rows in m.st.

Next (buttonhole) row: P. 1, k. 1, y.fwd., k. 2 tog., p. 1.

M.st. 13 rows, then repeat the buttonhole row.

M.st. 12 rows. Break off yarn and leave sts. on a safety pin.

Sew on border.

THE LEFT FRONT BORDER: With right side of work facing, sl. the 5 sts. on safety pin at left front on to a No. 10 (3¼ mm) needle and work 97 rows in m.st.

Do not break off yarn.

Sew on border.

THE NECK BORDER: With wrong side of work facing, m.st. across 5 sts. of left front border, the 47 sts. of yoke and the 5 sts. of right front border—57 sts.

Next (buttonhole) row: P. 1, k. 1, y.fwd., k. 2 tog., m.st. to end.

M.st. a further 2 rows. Cast off.

TO MAKE UP THE MATINEE JACKET: Press work lightly on the wrong side, using a cool iron over a dry cloth. Join tiny underarm seams, then join sleeve and side seams. Sew on buttons. Sew lace trimming to bottom of yoke.

THE DRESS
Illustrated on page 30

THE BACK: With No. 10 (3¼ mm) needles cast on 93 sts. M.st. 4 rows, and work 72 rows in pattern as shawl centre—work 56 rows here when working angel top.

To shape the armhole and divide for back opening: Next row: Cast off 3, pattern to end. **Next row:** Cast off 3, pattern a further 41 sts. and leave these 42 sts. on a spare needle for left half back, p. 3 and leave these sts. on a safety pin for border, pattern to end and work on these 42 sts. for right half back.

The right half back: Dec. 1 st. at armhole edge on the next row and the 4 following right side rows—37 sts.

Dec. row: P. 2, * p. 2 tog., p. 1, p. 2 tog., p. 2; repeat from * to end—27 sts.

Break off yarn and leave sts. on a spare needle for yoke.

The left half back: With right side of work facing, rejoin yarn to inner end of sts. on spare needle and work as given for right half back to end.

THE FRONT: With No. 10 (3¼ mm) needles cast on 93 sts.

Work as back until armhole shaping is reached.

To shape the armholes: Cast off 3 sts. at the beginning of each of the next 2 rows, then dec. 1 st. at each end of the next row and the 4 following right side rows—77 sts.

Continued on page 27

Next (dec.) row: * P. 2 tog., p. 1, p. 2 tog., p. 2; repeat from * ending last repeat with p. 2 tog. instead of p. 2—54 sts.

THE SLEEVES (both alike): With No. 10 (3¼ mm) needles cast on 41 sts. and work 4 rows in m.st. as given for back of matinee jacket.

Next (inc.) row: K. 3, * inc., k. 2; repeat from * until 2 sts. remain, k. 2—53 sts.

Beginning with the 2nd pattern row as given for shawl, pattern 7 rows.

To shape the sleeve top: Work as given for armhole shaping on back of matinee jacket, when 37 sts. will remain.

Next (dec.) row: P. 7, * p. 2 tog., p. 8; repeat from * to end—34 sts.

Break off yarn and leave sts. on a spare needle for yoke.

THE YOKE: With right side of work facing, sl. the 27 sts. of right half back, 34 sts. of right sleeve, 54 sts. from front, 34 sts. from left sleeve and 27 sts. of left half back on to a No. 10 (3¼ mm) circular needle—176 sts.

Work as given for yoke on matinee jacket to end. Break off yarn and leave sts. on a spare needle.

THE LEFT BACK BORDER: With No. 10 (3¼ mm) needles cast on 4 sts. and repeat the m.st. row given for the right front on matinee jacket, 39 times.

Break off yarn and leave sts. on a safety pin. Sew on border.

THE RIGHT BACK BORDER: With right side of work facing, sl. the 3 sts. on safety pin on to a No. 10 (3¼ mm) needle.

1st row: inc., k. 1, p. 1—4 sts.

M.st. 11 rows.

Next (buttonhole) row: k. 1, y.fwd., k. 2 tog., p. 1.

M.st. 13 rows.

Repeat the buttonhole row again.

M.st. a further 12 rows.

Do not break off yarn. Sew on border.

THE NECK BORDER: With right side of work facing, and using No. 10 (3¼ mm) needles, m.st. across 4 sts. of right back border, 47 sts. of yoke and 4 sts. of left back border—55 sts.

Next (buttonhole) row: K. 1, y.fwd., k. 2 tog., m.st. to end. M.st. 2 rows. Cast off.

TO MAKE UP THE DRESS: Press as for matinee jacket. Join tiny underarm seams, then join sleeve and side seams. Catch down cast on edge of left back border, behind right border. Sew on buttons. Sew lace trimming to bottom of yoke.

THE ANGEL TOP
Not illustrated

TO MAKE: Work back, front and yoke as given for dress, noting variations, then work sleeves as given for matinee jacket. Press and make up as given for dress.

Opposite *Matinée Jacket (page 24) and Bootees (this page)*

THE BOOTEES
Illustrated opposite

TO MAKE (both alike): With No. 10 (3¼ mm) needles and 4-ply, cast on 37 sts. and work 2 rows in m.st. as given for back of matinee jacket.

Work 16 rows in pattern as given for shawl centre.

Next (dec.) row: * K. 1, (p. 1, k. 1) 3 times, p. 2 tog.; repeat from * 3 times, K. 1—33 sts.

Next row: P. 1, * k. 1, p. 1; repeat from * to end. **Next (slot) row:** K. 1, * y.fwd., k. 2 tog.; repeat from * to end.

Rib 2 rows, then p. 1 row.

To divide for instep: Next row: K. 22, turn, leaving 11 sts. on a safety pin.

Next row: P. 11, turn, leaving remaining 11 sts. on a safety pin.

The instep: On centre 11 sts., s.s. 12 rows. Break off yarn.

With right side of work facing, sl. 11 sts. at right side on to a No. 10 (3¼ mm) needle with point to inner end, pick up and K. 10 sts. from row ends of instep, across instep sts., k. 2 tog., k. 7, k. 2 tog., pick up and k. 10 sts. down other side of instep and finally, k. 11 sts. from safety pin—51 sts.

S.s. 7 rows.

To shape for foot: 1st. (dec.) row: K. 1, s.k.p.o., k. 18, s.k.p.o. k. 5, k. 2 tog., k. 18 k. 2 tog., k. 1.

K. 1 row.

2nd (dec.) row: K. 1, s.k.p.o., k. 17, s.k.p.o., k. 3, k. 2 tog., k. 17, k. 2 tog., k. 1.

K. 1 row.

3rd (dec.) row: K. 1, s.k.p.o., k. 16, s.k.p.o., k. 1, k. 2 tog., k. 16, k. 2 tog., k. 1.

K. 1 row.

4th (dec.) row: K. 1, s.k.p.o., k. 15, sl. 1, k. 2 tog., p.s.s.o., k. 15, k. 2 tog., k. 1—35 sts. Cast off k. wise.

TO MAKE UP THE BOOTEES: Press as given for matinee jacket. Join back and underfoot seam. Thread ribbon through slot row to tie at front.

THE BONNET
Not illustrated

TO MAKE: With No. 10 (3¼ mm) needles and 4-ply, cast on 93 sts. and work 2 rows in m.st. as for back of matinee jacket.

Work 19 rows in pattern as given for shawl centre.

Dec. row: * P. 14, p. 2 tog.; repeat from * until 13 sts. remain, p. to end—88 sts.

Change to No. 11 (3 mm) needles and work 5 rows in single rib.

Change back to No. 10 (3¼ mm) needles and, beginning with a k. row to reverse brim, s.s. 24 rows.

To shape the crown: 1st row: * K. 9, k. 2 tog.; repeat from * to end.

2nd and every alternate row: All p.

3rd row: * K. 8, k. 2 tog.; repeat from * to end—72 sts.

Continue in this way, decreasing 8 sts. on every alternate row working 1 st. less between the decreases on each successive repeat of the dec. row for a further 7 dec. rows—16 sts.

Continued on page 28

P. 1 row.

Next row: * K. 2 tog.; repeat from * to end—8 sts.

Break off yarn leaving a long end, thread this through remaining sts., draw up tightly and fasten off securely. Join back seam for 5 cm (2 inches). Fold back brim.

THE EDGING: With right side of work facing and using No. 10 (3¼ mm) needles, pick up and k. 50 sts. around back neck edge, working through both thicknesses of brim. Cast off p. wise.

TO COMPLETE THE BONNET: Press as for matinee jacket. Sew a length of ribbon on each side of brim.

THE VEST
Not illustrated

THE BACK: With No. 10 (3¼ mm) needles and 3-ply cast on 68 sts. and k. 5 rows.

Beginning with a k. row, s.s. 58 rows.

To shape the armholes: Cast off 3 sts. at the beginning of each of the next 2 rows, then dec. 1 st. at each end of the next row and the 4 following right side rows—52 sts.

S.s. 19 rows.

To slope the shoulders: Cast off 7 sts. at the beginning of each of the next 4 rows—24 sts. Cast off.

THE LEFT FRONT: With No. 10 (3¼ mm) needles cast on 48 sts. and k. 4 rows.

Next row (wrong side): K. 4 and leave these sts. on a safety pin for border, k. to end—44 sts.

Beginning with a k. row, s.s. 50 rows.

To slope the front edge: Dec. 1 st. at front edge on each of the next 2 rows.

Work 1 row.

Repeat the last 3 rows, once more, then the first 2 rows again—38 sts.

To shape the armhole and continue sloping front edge: 1st row: Cast off 3 sts., k. to end. **2nd row:** Dec., p. to end.

3rd row: Dec., k. until 2 sts. remain, dec.

4th row: P. to end

5th row: As 3rd row.

6th row: As 2nd row.

7th row: Dec., k. to end.

8th row: As 2nd row.

9th row: As 3rd row.

10th row: As 4th row.

11th row: As 3rd row.

12th row: As 2nd row.

13th row: K. to end.

Dec. 1 st. at front edge on each of the next 2 rows.

Work 1 row.

Repeat the last 3 rows, twice more, then the 1st 2 rows again—14 sts.

**** S.s. 6 rows—s.s. 7 rows here when working right front.

To slope the shoulder: Cast off 7 sts. at the beginning of the next row—7 sts.

Work 1 row, then cast off.

THE RIGHT FRONT: With No. 10 (3¼ mm) needles cast on 48 sts. and k. 4 rows.

Next row (wrong side): K. until 4 sts. remain, turn, leaving these 4 sts. on a safety pin for border—44 sts.

Beginning with a k. row, s.s. 50 rows.

To slope the front edge: Dec. 1 st. at front edge on each of the next 2 rows.

Work 1 row.

Repeat the last 3 rows, twice—38 sts.

To shape the armhole and continue sloping front edge: 1st row: Cast off 3, p. until 2 sts. remain, dec. **2nd row:** Dec., k. until 2 sts. remain, dec.

3rd row: All p.

4th row: As 2nd row.

5th row: P. until 2 sts. remain, dec.

6th row: K. until 2 sts. remain, dec.

7th row: As 5th row.

8th row: As 2nd row.

9th row: As 3rd row.

10th row: As 2nd row.

11th row: As 5th row.

12th row: All k.

Dec. 1 st. at front edge on each of the next 2 rows.

Work 1 row.

Repeat the last 3 rows, twice, then the 1st 2 rows again—14 sts.

Work as given for left front from **** to end, noting variation.

THE SLEEVES (both alike): With No. 10 (3¼ mm) needles cast on 42 sts. and k. 5 rows. Beginning with a k. row, s.s. 2 rows.

Continuing in s.s., inc. 1 st. at each end of next row and following 4th row—46 sts.

S.s. 5 rows.

To shape the sleeve top: Cast off 3 sts. at the beginning of each of the next 2 rows, then dec. 1 st. at each end of the next 12 rows—16 sts. Cast off.

THE LEFT FRONT BORDER: First join shoulder seams. With right side of work facing and using No. 10 (3¼ mm) needles, work in g.st. until border is long enough when slightly stretched, to fit up left front to centre back neck, casting off when correct length is assured. Sew on border.

THE RIGHT FRONT BORDER: With wrong side of work facing and using No. 10 (3¼ mm) needles, work as given for left front border. Sew on border, joining cast-off edges together at centre back neck.

TO MAKE UP THE VEST: Press as for matinee jacket. Set in sleeves, then join sleeve and side seams, leaving a small opening in right seam, 2.5 cm (1 inch) below armhole. Sew narrow ribbon to each front border just below 1st front dec.

THE LEGGINGS
Illustrated on page 30

THE RIGHT LEG: With No. 10 (3¼ mm) needles and 4-ply cast on 74 sts. for waist and work 4 rows in single rib.

Next (slot) row: K. 1, * y.fwd., k. 2 tog., p. 1, k. 1; repeat from * until 1 st. remains, p. 1.

Rib 7 rows.

K. 1 row here when working left leg.

Work in s.s., shape for extra length on back as follows:
1st row: K. 10, turn, **2nd and every alternate row:** Sl. 1, p. to end. **3rd row:** K. 20, turn.

Continue in this way, working 10 sts. more on each alternate row until 10 turning rows have been completed.

S.s. 2 rows—s.s. 1 row here when working left leg.

Continuing in s.s., inc. 1 st. at each end of the next row and the 8 following 6th rows—92 sts.

S.s. 3 rows.

To shape the leg: Dec. 1 st. at each end of the next 9 rows and then on each end of the following 16 right side rows—42 sts.

S.s. 21 rows, decreasing 1 st. at end of the last row—41 sts.

Next (slot) row: K. 1, * y.fwd., k. 2 tog.; repeat from * to end.

S.s. 3 rows. *****

To divide for instep: Next row: K. 33, turn, leaving remaining 8 sts. on a safety pin.

Next row: P. 13, turn, leaving remaining 20 sts. on a safety pin.

On these 13 sts., s.s. 14 rows. Break off yarn.

With right side of work facing, sl. the 20 sts. at right side on to a No. 10 (3¼ mm) needle, with point to inner end, pick up and k. 10 sts. from row ends of instep, across instep sts., k. 2 tog., k. 9, k. 2 tog., pick up and k. 10 sts. from other side of instep and, finally, k. 8 sts. from safety pin—59 sts.

S.s. 7 rows.

To shape for foot: 1st dec. row: K. 4, k. 2 tog., s.k.p.o., k. 22, s.k.p.o., k. 7, k. 2 tog., k. to end.

Next and every alternate row: All k.

2nd dec. row: K. 3, k. 2 tog., s.k.p.o., k. 21, s.k.p.o., k. 5, k. 2 tog., k. to end.

3rd dec. row: K. 2, k. 2 tog., s.k.p.o., k. 20, s.k.p.o., k. 3, k. 2 tog., k. to end.

4th dec. row: K. 1, k. 2 tog., s.k.p.o., k. 19, s.k.p.o., k. 1, k. 2 tog., k. to end.

5th dec. row: K. 2 tog., s.k.p.o., k. 18, sl. 1, k. 2 tog., p.s.s.o., k. to end—39 sts.

Cast off k.wise.

THE LEFT LEG: Work as given for right leg to *****, noting the extra row to be worked after the waist ribbing, thus reversing the shaping for extra length on back, by reading p. for k. and k. for p.

To divide for instep: K. 21, turn, leaving remaining 20 sts. on a safety pin.

Next row: P. 13, turn, leaving remaining 8 sts. on a safety pin.

On these 13 sts., s.s. 14 rows. Break off yarn.

With right side of work facing, sl. the 8 sts. at right side on to a No. 10 (3¼ mm) needle with point to inner end, pick up and k. 10 sts. from row ends of instep, across instep sts., k. 2 tog., k. 9, k. 2 tog., pick up and k. 10 sts. from other side of instep and, finally, k. 20 sts. from safety pin—59 sts.

S.s. 7 rows.

To shape for foot: 1st dec. row: K. 18, s.k.p.o., k. 7, k. 2 tog., k. 22, k. 2 tog., s.k.p.o., k. 4.

Next and every alternate row: All k.

2nd dec. row: K. 18, s.k.p.o., k. 5, k. 2 tog., k. 21, k. 2 tog., s.k.p.o., k. 3.

Continue decreasing in this way on every alternate row until the 5th dec. row has been completed—39 sts. Cast off k. wise.

TO MAKE UP THE LEGGINGS: Press as for matinee jacket. Join front and back seams. Join under-foot seams,

then join leg seams. Thread length of narrow ribbon through slot row at ankles. Thread a length of elastic through slot row at waist and sew ends tog.

THE HELMET
Not illustrated

THE BUTTONHOLE FLAP: With No. 10 (3¼ mm) needles and 4-ply cast on 3 sts.

1st row: P. 1, k. 1, p. 1.

2nd row: Inc., inc., p. 1.

3rd row: (P. 1, k. 1) twice, p. 1.

4th row: Inc., k. 1, p. 1, inc., k. 1—7 sts. **5th and 6th rows:** K. 1, * p. 1, k. 1; repeat from * to end.

Buttonhole row: M.st. 3, y.fwd., k. 2 tog., p. 1, k. 1.

M.st. 21 rows.

Inc. 1 st. at each end of the next row.

M.st. 3 rows.

Repeat the last 4 rows, 5 times more—19 sts.

M.st. 4 rows. Break off yarn and leave sts. on a spare needle.

THE BUTTON FLAP: Work as for buttonhole flap, omitting buttonhole.

THE MAIN PART: With No. 10 (3¼ mm) needles cast on 8 sts., then on to this needle and with wrong side of work facing, m.st. across 19 sts. of button flap, turn, cast on 43 sts., turn and with wrong side of work facing, m.st. across 19 sts. of buttonhole flap, turn, cast on 8 sts.—97 sts.

M.st. 6 rows.

Work 32 rows of pattern as given for shawl centre.

To shape the crown: 1st dec. row: P. 1, * sl. 1, k. 2 tog., p.s.s.o., p. 1, (k. 1, p. 1) 4 times; repeat from * to end.

M.st. 3 rows. **2nd dec. row:** P. 1, * sl. 1, k. 2 tog., p.s.s.o., p. 1, (k. 1, p. 1) 3 times; repeat from * to end.

M.st. 3 rows. **3rd dec. row:** P. 1, * sl. 1, k. 2 tog., p.s.s.o., p. 1, (k. 1, p. 1) twice; repeat from * to end.

M.st. 3 rows. **4th dec. row:** P. 1, * sl. 1, k. 2 tog., p.s.s.o., p. 1, k. 1, p. 1; repeat from * to end.

M.st. 3 rows.

5th dec. row: P. 1, * sl. 1, k. 2 tog., p.s.s.o., p. 1; repeat from * to end—17 sts.

M.st. 1 row.

6th dec. row: As 5th dec. row—9 sts.

Break off yarn, leaving a long end, thread this through remaining sts., draw up tightly and fasten off securely.

TO MAKE UP THE HELMET: Press. Join back seam. Sew on button to correspond with buttonhole.

Above *Dress (page 25) and Leggings (page 29)*   Opposite *Matinée Jacket (page 32) and Blanket (page 33)*

Crochet Matinée Jacket and Blanket

Illustrated on page 31

MATERIALS: *Allow the following quantities in 40 g balls of Sirdar Snuggly Lustre Quick Knit: Matinee Jacket: 3 white and 1 each in blue, green, pink and yellow; a size 3.50 crochet hook; 4 buttons. Blanket: 4 white, 3 green, 2 pink and 2 each in blue and yellow; sizes 3.50 and 4.00 crochet hooks.*

TENSION AND MEASUREMENTS: *Worked at such a tension that 1 motif worked on size 4.00 hook measures 15 cm square, and 21 treble to measure 10 cm in width, using size 3.50 hook, the matinee jacket will measure: side seam, 17 cm (6¾ inches); length, 24.5 cm (9¾ inches); sleeve seam, 16 cm (6¼ inches) and will fit a 46 to 51 cm (18 to 20 inch) chest size. The blanket will measure 76 cm (30 inches) × 91 cm (36 inches).*

ABBREVIATIONS: To be read before working: *St., stitch; ch., chain; d.c., double crochet; h.tr., half treble; tr., treble; lp., loop; sp., space; M.B., make a bobble thus: work 5 tr. all into next st., withdraw hook, insert hook into top of first of these 5 tr. and draw loose loop through; w., white; bl., blue; pk., pink; g., green; y., yellow; y.o.h., yarn over hook; 2 tr. tog., (* y.o.h., insert hook into next tr., y.o.h. and draw loop through, y.o.h. and draw through 2 loops; repeat from * once, y.o.h. and draw through 3 loops).*

THE MATINEE JACKET

TO MAKE: With size 3.50 hook and w. make 67 ch. for neck edge.

1st row: 1 tr. in 4th ch. from hook, 1 tr. in each of next 2 ch., * 2 tr. in next ch., 1 tr. in each of next 7 ch.; repeat from * 6 times, 2 tr. in next ch., 1 tr. in each of remaining 4 ch., turn—73 tr.

Joining and breaking colours when required, continue as follows: 2nd row: With bl., 3 ch. for tr., 1 tr. in each of next 3 tr., * 2 tr. in next tr., 1 tr. in each of next 8 tr.; repeat from * ending last repeat with 5 tr. instead of 8 tr., turn—81 tr.

3rd row: With w., 3 ch. for tr., 1 tr. in each of next 4 tr., * 2 tr. in next tr., 1 tr. in each of next 9 tr.; repeat from * ending last repeat with 5 tr. instead of 9 tr., turn—89 tr.

4th row: With pk., 3 ch. for tr., 1 tr. in each of next 4 tr., * 2 tr. in next tr., 1 tr. in each of next 10 tr.; repeat from * ending last repeat with 6 tr., turn—97 tr.

5th row: With w., 3 ch. for tr., 1 tr. in each of next 5 tr., * 2 tr. in next tr., 1 tr. in each of next 11 tr.; repeat from * ending last repeat with 6 tr., turn—105 tr.

6th row: With g., 3 ch. for tr., 1 tr. in each of next 5 tr., * 2 tr. in next tr., 1 tr. in each of next 12 tr.; repeat from * ending last repeat with 7 tr., turn—113 tr.

7th row: With w., 3 ch. for tr., 1 tr. in each of next 6 tr., * 2 tr. in next tr., 1 tr. in each of next 13 tr.; repeat from * ending last repeat with 7 tr., turn—121 tr.

8th row: With y., 3 ch. for tr., 1 tr. in each of next 6 tr., * 2 tr. in next tr., 1 tr. in each of next 14 tr.; repeat from * ending last repeat with 8 tr., turn—129 tr. Continue with w. only.

9th row: 4 ch. for tr. and 1 ch.sp., 1 tr. in next tr., * 1 ch., 1 tr. in next tr.; repeat from * to end, turn—128 ch.sps.

To divide for back, fronts and sleeves: 10th row: 4 ch. for tr. and 1 ch.sp., 1 tr. in next tr., * 1 ch., 1 tr. in next tr. *; repeat from * to * 16 times, make 11 ch. for underarm, miss 28 ch.sps. for sleeve and work 1 tr. in next tr., repeat from * to * 36 times, make 11 ch. for underarm, miss 28 ch.sps. for sleeve and work 1 tr. in next tr.; repeat from * to * 18 times, turn.

11th row: 3 ch. for tr., * 1 tr. in next ch.sp., 1 tr. in next tr. *; repeat from * to * 17 times, 1 tr. in each of next 11 ch., 1 tr. in next tr., repeat from * to * 36 times, 1 tr. in each of next 11 ch., 1 tr. in next tr.; repeat from * to * 18 times, turn—169 tr.

12th row: 3 ch. for tr., 1 tr. in each tr. to end, turn.

13th to 17th rows: Repeat 12th row, 5 times.

18th row: With pk., repeat 12th row.

19th row: With g., 3 ch. for tr., * M.B., 1 tr. in each of next 2 tr.; repeat from * to end, turn.

20th row: With pk., 3 ch. for tr., 1 tr. in next tr., 1 tr. in next bobble, * 1 tr. in each of next 2 tr., 1 tr. in next bobble; repeat from * until 1 tr. remains, 1 tr. in tr. at end, turn.

21st and 22nd rows: With w., repeat 12th row, twice.

23rd row: With y., repeat 19th row.

24th row: With w., repeat 20th row.

25th row: With w., repeat 12th row.

26th and 27th rows: With bl., repeat 12th row, twice. Fasten off.

THE SLEEVES (both alike): With right side facing, rejoin w. to centre ch. of 11 ch. at underarm, 3 ch. for tr., 1 tr. in each of next 5 ch., 2 tr. into side of end tr. on dividing row, 1 tr. in base of end tr., 1 tr. in each of missed ch.sp. on dividing row, 1 tr. into base of end tr. on dividing row, 2 tr. into side of end tr., 1 tr. in each of remaining 5 ch. at underarm, turn—45 tr.

1st row: 3 ch. for tr., 1 tr. in each tr. to end, turn. Repeat last row, 12 times.

Next row: 3 ch. for tr., * 2 tr. tog.; repeat from * to end, turn—23 sts.

Break off w., join in bl.

Next row: 3 ch. for tr., 1 tr. in top of each 2 tr. tog. to end, turn.

Next row: 3 ch. for tr., 1 tr. in each tr. to end. Fasten off.

THE MAIN EDGING: Rejoin bl. to lower edge of right front, and using size 3.50 hook, work a row of d.c. evenly up right front edge, round neck and down left front edge to corner, then work along lower edge as follows: 1 d.c. into each of first 2 tr., * 3 ch., sl.st. into d.c. at base of 3 ch., 1 d.c. in each of next 3 tr.; repeat from * ending last repeat with 1 d.c. in each of next 2 tr. instead of 3.

Fasten off.

THE CUFF EDGINGS (both alike): With right side facing, rejoin bl. to lower edge of sleeve; with size 3.50 hook, work 2 ch. for d.c. in each of next 2 d.c., * 3 ch., sl.st. into d.c. at base of 3 ch., 1 d.c. in each of next 3 tr.; repeat from * ending last repeat with 1 d.c. in each of next 2 tr. Fasten off. Join sleeve seams.

THE BUTTONHOLES: With right side facing, rejoin bl. to d.c. at right front end of y. stripe on yoke, work 3 ch., work 2 d.c. into sts. at end of g. stripe, 3 ch., work 2 d.c. into sts. at end of pk. stripe, 3 ch., work 2 d.c. into sts. at end of bl. stripe, work 2 ch. and work 1 d.c. into corner d.c. at neck. Fasten off.

Press with a warm iron and a dry cloth. Add buttons.

THE BLANKET

THE MOTIF: With size 4.00 hook and w. make 6 ch. and join into a ring with a sl.st.

1st round: 2 ch. for d.c., 15 d.c. into ring, join with a sl.st. to top of first d.c.—16 d.c.

2nd round: 6 ch. for tr. and 3 ch.sp., miss 1 d.c., * 1 tr. in next d.c., 3 ch., miss 1 d.c.; repeat from * to end, join with a sl.st. to 3rd of 6 ch. at beginning. Fasten off.

3rd (flower) round: With g. join to any 3 ch.sp., 2 ch. for d.c., then 1 h.tr., 3 tr., 1 h.tr., 1 d.c. all into same 3 ch.sp., * 1 d.c.; 1 h.tr., 3 tr., 1 h.tr., 1 d.c. all into next 3 ch.sp.; repeat from * to end, join with a sl.st. to top of first d.c.

4th round: With g., keeping hook to back of petals, sl.st. round w. tr. on 2nd round, below join, * 5 ch., 1 d.c. round next w. tr. on 2nd round; repeat from * 6 times, 5 ch., join with a sl.st. at beginning and fasten off.

5th round: Rejoin w. yarn to any 5 ch.lp. of previous round, make 3 ch. for tr., 3 tr. into same lp., * 3 ch., 4 tr. in next 5 ch.lp., 4 tr. into following 5 ch.lp.; repeat from * twice, 3 ch., 4 tr. in next 5 ch.lp., join.

6th round: With w., 3 ch. for tr., 1 tr. in each of next 3 tr., * 2 tr., 2 ch., 2 tr. all into corner ch.lp., 1 tr. in each of next 8 tr.; repeat from * twice, 2 tr., 2 ch., 2 tr. all into corner ch.lp., 1 tr. in each of remaining 4 tr., join with y.

7th round: With y., 3 ch. for tr., 1 tr. in each tr. to next corner ch.lp., * 2 tr., 2 ch., 2 tr. all into corner ch.lp., 1 tr. in each tr. to next corner ch.lp.; repeat from * twice, 2 tr., 2 ch., 2 tr. all into corner ch.lp., 1 tr. in each of remaining tr., join with bl.

Repeat 7th round once with bl., once with pk. and once with g., joining at end of each round with colour of following round. Fasten off.

Make a further 5 motifs as set, then 7 more using bl. instead of g. on 3rd and 4th rounds, 6 more using pk. instead of g. on 3rd and 4th rounds, then a further 5 using y. instead of g. on 3rd and 4th rounds.

To join motifs: Place 2 motifs together with right sides facing, then rejoin g. and using size 4.00 hook, insert hook into first st. of front motif and first st. of back motif and work a d.c. in the usual way, work along one side of motif to corner in this manner.

Fasten off.

Join 6 motifs together, joining in 2 lines of 3 motifs each to form centre.

THE INNER BORDER: 1st round: With right side of centre facing, rejoin w. to middle of one long edge and using size 4.00 hook, work a tr. into top of each tr. and each ch.lp. at corner of motifs, to corner of centre piece, * 2 tr., 2 ch., 2 tr. all into corner ch.lp., 1 tr. into each tr. and ch.lp. along side to corner; repeat from * twice, 2 tr., 2 ch., 2 tr. all into corner ch.lp., 1 tr. in each tr. and ch.lp. to end, join.

2nd round: 3 ch. for tr., 1 tr. in each tr. to corner, * 2 tr., 2 ch., 2 tr. all into corner ch.lp., 1 tr. in each tr. to next corner; repeat from * twice, 2 tr., 2 ch., 2 tr. all into corner ch.lp., 1 tr. in each tr. to end, join.

Repeat 2nd round, 6 times. Fasten off.

Join on remaining motifs as before, placing 4 motifs down each long edge and 3 motifs along each short edge with 1 motif in each corner, alternating colours.

THE OUTER BORDER: With right side facing, rejoin g. to any point round outer edge, and using size 3.50 hook, work 2 ch. for d.c., 1 d.c. in each of next 2 sts., * 3 ch., sl.st. into d.c. at base of 3 ch., 1 d.c. in each of next 3 sts.; repeat from * to end, working 2 d.c. into corner ch.lps., join and fasten off.

Press with warm iron over a dry cloth.

Matinée Jacket, Bonnet, Bootees and Mitts

Illustrated on page 34

MATERIALS: *For the whole set allow 3 40 g balls of Robin Bambino 4-ply; a pair each of No. 10 (3¼ mm) and No. 11 (3 mm) knitting needles; 3 buttons for matinee jacket; 1 metre of 1.5 cm wide ribbon for bonnet; ¾ metre of narrow ribbon for bootees and ¾ metre of narrow ribbon for mittens.*

TENSION AND MEASUREMENTS: *Work at a tension of 28 stitches and 34 rows to measure 10 × 10 cm, over the pattern, using No. 10 (3¼ mm) needles, to obtain the following measurements: Matinee Jacket: Length, 24 cm (9½ inches); length from underarm, 14 cm (5½ inches); sleeve seam, 14 cm (5½ inches). Bonnet: All round at face edge, 33 cm (13 inches). Bootees: Foot length 9.5 cm (3¾ inches). Mittens: All round hand, 12 cm (4¾ inches).*

ABBREVIATIONS: To be read before working: *K., knit plain; p. purl; st. stitch; tog., together; inc., increase (by working twice into same st.); dec., decrease (by working 2 sts. tog.); k. 2 tog.b., k. 2 tog. through back of sts.; s.s., stocking st. (k. on the right side and p. on the wrong side); g.st., garter st. (k. plain on every row); y.fwd., yarn forward to make a st.; sl., slip; p.2 s.s.o., pass 2 sl. sts. over.*

NOTE: *Directions in brackets are worked as stated after the closing bracket.*

Continued on page 34

MATINEE JACKET

Above *Matinée Jacket (this page), Bonnet and Bootees (page 35); Mitts (page 36)*

THE BACK AND FRONTS (worked in one piece to armholes): With No. 11 (3 mm) needles cast on 211 sts. and g.st. 4 rows.

Next row: K. 5, and leave these sts. on a safety pin, k. until 5 sts. remain, turn and leave these 5 sts. on a safety pin—201 sts.

Change to No. 10 (3¼ mm) needles and continue to work the 16-row pattern as follows:

1st row: K. 4, (y.fwd., k. 2 tog.b., k. 6) until 5 sts. remain, y.fwd., k. 2 tog.b., k. 3.

2nd and alternate rows: All p.

3rd row: K. 2, (k. 2 tog., y.fwd., k. 1, y.fwd., k. 2 tog.b., k. 3) until 7 sts. remain, k. 2 tog., y.fwd., k. 1, y.fwd., k. 2 tog.b., k. 2.

5th row: K. 1, (k. 2 tog., y.fwd., k. 3, y.fwd., k. 2 tog.b., k. 1) to end.

7th row: K. 3 (y.fwd., sl. 2 k. wise, k. 1, p. 2 s.s.o., y.fwd., k 5) until 6 sts. remain, y.fwd., sl.2 k.wise, k. 1, p. 2 s.s.o., y.fwd., k. 3.

9th row: K. 8, (y.fwd., k. 2 tog.b., k. 6) until 1 st. remains, k. 1 more.

11th row: K. 1 (y.fwd., k. 2 tog.b., k. 3, k. 2 tog., y.fwd., k. 1) to end.

13th row: K. 2, (y.fwd., k. 2 tog.b., k. 1, k. 2 tog., y.fwd., k. 3) until 7 sts. remain, y.fwd., k. 2 tog.b., k. 1, k. 2 tog., y.fwd., k. 2.

15th row: K. 2 tog., y.fwd., k. 5, (y.fwd., sl. 2 k. wise, k. 1, p. 2 s.s.s.o., y.fwd., k. 5) until 2 sts. remain, y.fwd., k. 2 tog.b.

16th row: All p. Pattern 31 rows.

To divide for back and fronts: Next row: P. 47 and leave these sts. on a spare needle for left front, cast off 6, p. a further 94 and leave these 95 sts. on a spare needle for back, cast off 6, p. to end and work on these 47 sts. for right front.

The right front: Keeping continuity of pattern, dec. 1 st. at armhole edge on next 7 rows—40 sts.

Next (dec.) row: P. 1, (p. 2 tog., p. 1) to end—27 sts. Break yarn and leave these sts.

The back: With right side of work facing, rejoin yarn to 95 sts. on spare needle, then dec. 1 st. each end of next 7 rows—81 sts.

Next (dec.) row: (P. 2 tog., p. 1) to end—54 sts. Break yarn and leave these sts.

The left front: With right side of work facing, rejoin yarn to 47 sts. on spare needle and work as right front.

THE SLEEVES (both alike): With No. 11 (3 mm) needles cast on 37 sts. and g.st. 4 rows.

Inc. row: (K. 2, inc.) until 1 st. remains, k. 1—49 sts.

Change to No. 10 (3¼ mm) needles and work 16 rows in pattern as given for back.

Taking extra sts. into pattern as they occur, inc. 1 st. each end of next row, then on the 3 following 8th rows—57 sts. Pattern 5 rows.

To shape the sleeve top: Cast off 3 sts. at beginning of next 2 rows, then dec. 1 st. each end of following 7 rows—37 sts.

Next (dec.) row: P. 7, (p. 2 tog., p. 8) to end—34 sts. Leave sts. on a spare needle.

THE YOKE: With wrong side of work facing, sl. the 27 sts. of left front, 34 sts. of left sleeve, 54 sts. of back, 34 sts. of right sleeve and 27 sts. of right front on to a No. 10 (3¼ mm) needle—176 sts.

With right side of work facing and using No. 10 (3¼ mm) needles, rejoin yarn and g.st. 4 rows.

1st (dec.) row: K. 8, (k. 2 tog.b., k. 2 tog., k. 8) to end—148 sts.

Beginning with a p. row, s.s. 5 rows.

2nd (dec.) row: K. 7, (k. 2 tog.b., k. 2 tog., k. 6) until 1 st. remains, k. 1 more—120 sts.

S.s. 5 rows.

3rd (dec.) row: K. 6, (k. 2 tog.b., k. 2 tog., k. 4) until 2 sts. remain, k. 2 more—92 sts.

S.s. 5 rows.

4th (dec.) row: K. 5, (k. 2 tog.b., k. 2 tog., k. 2) until 3 sts. remain, k. 3 more—64 sts.

S.s. 3 rows.

5th (dec.) row: K. 1, (k. 2 tog.b., k. 2) until 3 sts. remain, k. 2 tog.b., k. 1—48 sts.

P. 1 row, then break yarn and leave sts.

The left front border: With right side of work facing using No. 11 (3 mm) needles, rejoin yarn to sts. on safety pin, g.st. 96 rows.

Break yarn and leave sts. on a safety pin.

The right front border: With wrong side of work facing and using No. 11 (3 mm) needles, rejoin yarn to sts. on safety pin and g.st. 67 rows.

Next (buttonhole) row: K. 2, y.fwd., k. 2 tog., k. 1. G.st. 15 rows, then repeat the buttonhole row again. G.st. 13 rows. Do not break yarn.

Leave sts. on a safety pin.

THE NECK BORDER: With right side of work facing and using No. 11 (3 mm) needles, k. across 5 sts. of right front border, 48 sts. from yoke, then 5 sts. of left front border—58 sts.

K. 1 row.

Next row: K. to end, making a buttonhole as before. G.st. 3 rows, then cast off.

TO MAKE UP THE JACKET: Press on the wrong side, using a cool iron over a dry cloth. Sew front bands into position. Join sleeve seams, then join tiny underarm seams. Add buttons.

BONNET

TO MAKE: With No. 11 (3 mm) needles cast on 89 sts. and g.st. 5 rows.

Change to No. 10 (3¼ mm) needles and work 32 rows in pattern as given for matinee jacket, decreasing 1 st. at the end of the last of these rows—88 sts.

G.st. 4 rows.

1st (dec.) row: (K. 9, k. 2 tog.) to end—80 sts.

2nd and alternate rows: All p.

3rd (dec.) row: (K. 8, k. 2 tog.) to end—72 sts.

Continue in this way, working 1 st. less between decreases on each successive repeat of the dec. row for a further 7 dec. rows—16 sts.

P. 1 row.

Next (dec.) row: (K. 2 tog.) to end—8 sts.

Break yarn leaving a long end. Thread this through remaining sts., draw up tightly and fasten off. Join back seam for 5 cm (2 inches).

THE EDGING: With right side of work facing and using No. 10 (3¼ mm) needles, rejoin yarn and pick up and k. 48 sts. evenly round neck edge.

Cast off p. wise.

TO COMPLETE THE BONNET: Press as for jacket. Sew a length of ribbon to either side at face edge, forming a small bow where ribbon is sewn to work.

BOOTEES

TO MAKE (both alike): With No. 11 (3 mm) needles cast on 41 sts. and g.st. 3 rows.

Change to No. 10 (3¼ mm) needles and work the 16 pattern rows as given for jacket, once.

Next (dec.) row: (K. 3, k. 2 tog.) until 1 st. remains, k. 1—33 sts.

K. 1 row.

Next (slot) row: K. 1, (y.fwd., k. 2 tog.) to end.

K. 1 row. **

Beginning with a k. row, s.s 2 rows.

To divide for instep: Next row: K. 22, turn and leave remaining 11 sts. on a safety pin.

Next row: P. 11, turn and leave remaining 11 sts. on a safety pin—11 sts.

S.s. 16 rows.

Break yarn.

Continued on page 36

With right side of work facing, sl. 11 sts. at right hand side on to a No. 10 (3¼ mm) needle with point to inner end, rejoin yarn and pick up and k. 12 sts. from row ends of instep, across instep sts. k. 2 tog., k. 7, k. 2 tog., pick up and k. 12 sts. from other side of instep, then k. 11 sts. from safety pin—55 sts.

S.s. 7 rows.

To shape for foot: 1st (dec.) row: K. 1, k. 2 tog.b., k. 19, k. 2 tog.b., k. 7, k. 2 tog., k. 19, k. 2 tog., k. 1.

K. 1 row.

2nd (dec.) row: K. 1, k. 2 tog.b., k. 18, k. 2 tog.b., k. 5, k. 2 tog., k. 18, k. 2 tog., k. 1.

K. 1 row.

3rd (dec.) row: K. 1, k. 2 tog.b., k. 17, k. 2 tog.b., k. 3, k. 2 tog., k. 17, k. 2 tog., k. 1.

K. 1 row.

4th (dec.) row: K. 1, k. 2 tog.b., k. 16, k. 2 tog.b., k. 1, k. 2 tog., k. 16, k. 2 tog., k. 1.

Cast off remaining 39 sts. k. wise.

TO MAKE UP THE BOOTEES: Press as given for jacket. Join back and underfoot seam. Thread ribbon through slot row to tie in a bow at front.

MITTS

TO MAKE (both alike): Work as bootees to ★★.

Beginning with a k. row, s.s. 16 rows, decreasing 1 st. at the end of the last of these rows—32 sts.

To shape the top: 1st (dec.) row: K. 1, k. 2 tog.b., k. 10, k. 2 tog., k. 2, k. 2 tog.b., k. 10, k. 2 tog., k. 1—28 sts.

P. 1 row.

2nd (dec.) row: K. 1, k. 2 tog.b., k. 8, k. 2 tog., k. 2, k. 2 tog.b., k. 8, k. 2 tog., k. 1—24 sts.

P. 1 row.

3rd (dec.) row: K. 1, k. 2 tog.b., k. 6, k. 2 tog., k. 2, k. 2 tog.b., k. 6, k. 2 tog., k. 1—20 sts.

P. 1 row.

4th (dec.) row: K. 1, k. 2 tog.b., k. 4, k. 2 tog., k. 2, k. 2 tog.b., k. 4, k. 2 tog., k. 1—16 sts.

Cast off p. wise.

TO MAKE UP THE MITTS: Press as for jacket. Join top and side seam.

Thread ribbon through slot row to tie in a bow at back.

Sweater and Romper

Illustrated on page 38

MEASUREMENTS				
To fit chest sizes	41	(16)	46	(18)
JUMPER				
All round at underarms	41.5	(16¼)	46.5	(18¼)
Side seam	13.5	(5¼)	14.5	(5¾)
Length	23	(9)	25.5	(10)
Sleeve seam	13	(5)	14	(5½)
ROMPER				
Leg seam from base of rib at top of foot to crotch	15	(6)	16.5	(6½)

MATERIALS: *Allow the following quantities in 20 g balls of Patons Fairytale 4-ply: Jumper: 3 cream for the 41 cm size; 4 cream for the 46 cm size. For either size: A pair each of No. 10 (3¼ mm) and No. 12 (2¾ mm) knitting needles; 2 buttons. Romper: 5 blue for the 41 cm size; 6 blue for the 46 cm size. For either size: A pair of No. 10 (3¼ mm) knitting needles; 2 buttons.*

TENSION: *Work at a tension of 28 stitches and 38 rows to measure 10 × 10 cm over the stocking stitch, using No. 10 (3¼ mm) knitting needles, to obtain the measurements given.*

ABBREVIATIONS: To be read before working: *K., knit plain; p., purl; st., stitch; tog., together; sl., slip; inc., increase (by working twice into same st.); k. or p. tog. through back of sts.; s.k.p.o. (sl. 1, k. 1, pass slipped st. over); up 1, pick up loop lying between needles and k. or p. into the back of it; y.r.n., yarn round needle to make a st.; y.fwd.,*
yarn forward to make a st.; s.s., stocking st. (k. on the right side and p. on the wrong side); dec., decrease (by working 2 sts. tog.); single rib is k. 1 and p. 1 alternately; c., cream; b., blue.

NOTE: *The instructions are given for the 41 cm (16 inch) size. Where they vary, work the figures within the brackets for the 46 cm (18 inch) size.*

THE JUMPER

THE BACK: With No. 12 (2¾ mm) needles and c. cast on 57 (65) sts. and beginning odd-numbered rows with k. 1 and even-numbered rows with p. 1, work 12 rows in single rib, increasing 1 st. at the end of the last of these rows on the first size only—58 (65) sts.

Change to No. 10 (3¼ mm) needles and beginning with a k. row, s.s. 42 (46) rows.

Mark each end of last row to denote end of side seams.

S.s. a further 24 (28) rows, decreasing 1 st. at the centre of the last of these rows on the first size only—57 (65) sts.

Work the 5-row pattern as follows:

1st row: P. 1, * k. 3, p. 1; repeat from * to end.

2nd row: P. 1, k. 1, * p. 5, k. 1, p. 1, k. 1; then repeat from * until 7 sts. remain, p. 5, k. 1, p. 1.

3rd row: K. 2, * p. 1, k. 3; repeat from * until 3 sts. remain, p. 1, k. 2.

4th row: P. 3, * k. 1, p. 1, k. 1, p. 5; then repeat from * until 6 sts. remain, k. 1, p. 1, k. 1, p. 3.

5th row: As 1st row.

Beginning with a p. row, s.s. 3 rows.

Then work 6 rows in single rib as given on welt. ★★

Next row: Cast off 42 (48) sts. in rib for shoulder and neck, rib to end and work on these 15 (17) sts. for button extension.

The button extension: Rib 4 rows.

Cast off in rib.

THE FRONT: Work as given for back to ★★.

Next row: Rib 15 (17) sts. for buttonhole extension, cast off the next 42 (48) sts. in rib for shoulder and neck.

The buttonhole extension: With wrong side of work facing, rejoin yarn to the 15 (17) sts. and rib 1 row.

Next buttonhole row: Rib 3, y.fwd., k. 2 tog., rib 4 (6), y.fwd., k. 2 tog., rib 4.

Rib a further 2 rows. Cast off in rib.

THE SLEEVES (both alike): With No. 12 (2¾ mm) needles and c. cast on 33 (37) sts. and work 9 rows in single rib as given on back.

Next (increase) row: Rib 1, * up 1, rib 4 (9); repeat from * to end—41 sts.

Change to No. 10 (3¼ mm) needles and work the 5-row pattern as given on back, once.

Continuing in s.s. only, beginning with a p. row, work 1 row.

Inc. 1 st. at each end of the next row and the 5 (7) following 3rd rows—53 (57) sts.

S.s. a further 20 (18) rows.

Cast off loosely.

TO MAKE UP THE JUMPER: Do not press. Join the first 15 (17) sts. at cast off edge for right shoulder. Overlap buttonhole extension over button extension and catch row ends at side edge tog. through both thicknesses. Set in sleeves between markers on back and front. Join side and sleeve seams. Sew on buttons to correspond with buttonholes.

THE ROMPER

THE LEFT LEG: With No. 10 (3¼ mm) needles and b. cast on 43 (47) sts. and p. 1 row, then shape foot as follows:

1st row: K. 6 (7), up 1, k. 1, up 1, k. 21 (23), up 1, k. 1, up 1, k. 14 (15).

2nd row: All p.

3rd row: K. 7 (8), up 1, k. 1, up 1, k. 23 (25), up 1, k. 1, up 1, k. 15 (16).

4th row: All p.

5th row: K. 8 (9), up 1, k. 1, up 1, k. 25 (27), up 1, k. 1, up 1, k. 16 (17).

6th row: All p.

7th row: K. 9 (10), up 1, k. 1, up 1, k. 27 (29), up 1, k. 1, up 1, k. 17 (18)—59 (63) sts.

Beginning with a p. row, s.s. 9 rows.

To shape the instep: 1st row: K. 38 (41), k. 2 tog.b., k. 1, k. 2 tog., k. 16 (17).

2nd row: P. 15 (16), p. 2 tog., p. 1, p. 2 tog.b., p. 37 (40).

3rd row: K. 36 (39), k. 2 tog.b., k. 1, k. 2 tog., k. 14 (15).

4th row: P. 13 (14), p. 2 tog., p. 1, p. 2 tog.b., p. 35 (38).

5th row: K. 34 (37), k. 2 tog.b., k. 1, k. 2 tog., k. 12 (13).

6th row: P. 11 (12), p. 2 tog., p. 1, p. 2 tog.b., p. 33 (36).

7th row: K. 32 (35), k. 2 tog.b., k. 1, k. 2 tog., k. 10 (11).

8th row: P. 9 (10), p. 2 tog., p. 1, p. 2 tog.b., p. 31 (34)—43 (47) sts.

Beginning with a k. row s.s. 4 rows.

Next row: K. 1, * p. 1, k. 1; repeat from * to end.

Next row: P. 1, * k. 1, p. 1; repeat from * to end.

Repeat the last 2 rows, 3 times more.

Beginning with a k. row, s.s. 2 rows.

Inc. 1 st. at each end of the next row and the 8 (9) following 4th rows.

Work 1 row, then inc. 1 st. at each end of the next row and the 5 following alternate rows—73 (79) sts.

S.s. a further 3 (5) rows, increasing 1 st. at the centre of the last of these rows—74 (80) sts. Leave these sts. on a spare needle.

THE RIGHT LEG: Work as given for left leg reversing all shaping rows by reading from right to left, so that first row of foot shaping will read: K. 14 (15), up 1, k. 1, up 1, k. 21 (23), up 1, k. 1, up 1, k. 6 (7), and 1st row of instep shaping will read K. 16 (17), k. 2 tog.b., k. 1, k. 2 tog., k. 38 (41).

Break yarn; leave these sts. on spare needle.

Next joining and dividing row: With right side of left leg facing, slip the first 37 (40) sts. of left leg on to a spare needle with point to outer edge, rejoin yarn and k. across the remaining 37 (40) sts., turn, cast on 13 (15) sts., turn, then with right side of right leg facing, k. across the first 37 (40) sts., turn and leave remaining 37 (40) sts. of right leg on a spare needle with point to inner edge, and work on the 87 (95) sts. as follows, for front of body.

THE FRONT BODY: P. 1 row.

★★ To shape the crotch: 1st row: K. 37 (40), s.k.p.o., k. 9 (11), k. 2 tog., k. 37 (41).

2nd and alternate rows: All p.

3rd row: K. 37 (40), s.k.p.o., k. 7 (9), k. 2 tog., k. 37 (40).

5th row: K. 37 (40), s.k.p.o., k. 5 (7), k. 2 tog., k. 37 (40).

7th row: K. 37 (40), s.k.p.o., k. 3 (5), k. 2 tog., k. 37 (40).

9th row: K. 37 (40), s.k.p.o., k. 1 (3), k. 2 tog., k. 37 (40).

10th row: All p.

For the second size only: Next row: K. 40, s.k.p.o., k. 1, k. 2 tog., k. 40.

Next row: All p.

For both sizes: Next row: K. 37 (40), sl. 1, k. 2 tog., p.s.s.o., k. 37 (40)—75 (81) sts.

Beginning with a p. row, s.s. 45 (49) rows—increasing 2 sts. evenly across the last of these rows on the second size only—75 (83) sts. ★★.

★★★ Work 10 rows in single rib as given at top of foot.

Next row: Cast off 4 sts. in rib, rib a further 8 sts., k. until 13 sts. remain, rib to end.

Continued on page 40

Opposite *Jumper (page 36) and Romper (page 37)*

Next row: Cast off 4 sts., rib a further 8 sts., p. until 9 sts. remain, rib 9—67 (75) sts.

Work the 4-row pattern for bib as follows:

1st row: Rib 9 for border, p. 1, * k. 3, p. 1; repeat from * until 9 sts. remain, rib 9 for border.

2nd row: Rib 9, p. 1, k. 1, * p. 5, k. 1, p. 1, k. 1; repeat from * until 16 sts. remain, p. 5, k. 1, p. 1, rib 9.

3rd row: Rib 9, k. 2, * p. 1, k. 3; repeat from * until 12 sts. remain, p. 1, k. 2, rib 9.

4th row: Rib 9, p. 3, * k. 1, p. 1, k. 1, p. 5; repeat from * until 15 sts. remain, k. 1, p. 1, k. 1, p. 3, rib 9.

Keeping continuity of pattern and borders as set, pattern 2 rows.

Next (dec.) row: Rib 9, s.k.p.o., pattern until 11 sts. remain, k. 2 tog., rib 9.

Pattern 3 rows.

Repeat the last 4 rows, 6 (7) times more, then the 1st of these rows again—51 (57) sts. Work 2 rows.

Next row: Rib 9, p. until 9 sts. remain, then rib 9.

Work 8 rows in rib as given at top of foot.

Next row: Rib 9 and leave these sts. on a safety pin for 2nd strap, cast off the next 33 (39) sts., rib to end and work on these 9 sts. for 1st strap.

1st strap: Rib 17 (21) rows.

Next (buttonhole) row: Rib 3, k. 2 tog., y.r.n., rib 4.

Rib 1 row.

Next row: S.k.p.o., rib 5, k. 2 tog.—7 sts.

Next row: P. 2, k. 1, p. 1, k. 1, p. 2.

Cast off in rib.

2nd strap: With wrong side of work facing, rejoin yarn to the 9 sts. on safety pin and work as given for 1st strap.

THE BACK BODY: With right side of work facing, rejoin yarn to the 37 (40) sts. of right leg left on spare needle and k. across these sts., turn, cast on 13 (15) sts., turn, then k. across 37 (40) sts. of left leg—87 (95) sts.

P. 1 row, then work as given for front body from ** to **.

1st turning row: K. 65 (71), turn.

2nd turning row: P. 55 (59), turn.

3rd turning row: K. 45 (47), turn.

4th turning row: P. 35 (35), turn.

5th turning row: K. 25 (23), turn.

6th row: P. 15 (11), turn, then k. to end of row.

P. 1 row across all sts.

Work as given for front body from *** to end, omitting buttonholes on straps.

TO MAKE UP THE ROMPER: Do not press. Join side seams. Join inside leg seams and crotch. Join under foot seam. Add buttons.

Cabled V-neck Sweater

Illustrated on page 39

MEASUREMENTS	*in centimetres (and inches, in brackets)*			
To fit chest sizes	46	(18)	51	(20)
All round at underarms,				
slightly stretched	49	($19\frac{1}{4}$)	52.5	($20\frac{3}{4}$)
Side seam	16	($6\frac{1}{4}$)	16.5	($6\frac{1}{2}$)
Length	28.5	($11\frac{1}{4}$)	30	($11\frac{3}{4}$)
Sleeve seam	19.5	($7\frac{3}{4}$)	20	(8)

MATERIALS: *For either size: Allow one 100 g ball of Patons Fairytale Magic Value Big Ball D K; a pair each of No. 8 (4 mm) and No. 10 ($3\frac{1}{4}$ mm) knitting needles.*

TENSION: *Work at a tension of 22 stitches and 28 rows to measure 10 × 10 cm in width over the stocking stitch, and each 17 stitch twist stitch panel to measure 7 cm in width, using No. 8 (4 mm) needles, to obtain the measurements given above.*

ABBREVIATIONS: To be read before working: *K., knit plain; p., purl; st., stitch; tog., together; inc., increase (by working twice into same st.); dec., decrease (by working 2 sts. tog.); up 1, pick up loop lying between needles and k. into back of it; single rib is k. 1 and p. 1 alternately; s.s., stocking st. (k. on the right side and p. on the wrong side); k. 2 tog.b., k. 2 tog. through back of sts.; sl., slip.*

NOTE: *The instructions are given for the 46 cm (18 inch) chest size. Where they vary, work figures within the brackets for the 51 cm (20 inch) chest size.*

THE BACK: With No. 10 ($3\frac{1}{4}$ mm) needles cast on 51 (55) sts. and beginning odd-numbered rows with k. 1 and even-numbered rows with p. 1, work 11 rows in single rib.

Next (increase) row: Rib 3 (5), * up 1, rib 9; repeat from * until 3 (5) sts. remain, up 1, rib 3 (5)—57 (61) sts.

Change to No. 8 (4 mm) needles and work the 6-row pattern as follows:

1st row: K. 5 (6), * p. 2, k. 1, p. 1, k. 1; repeat from * twice, p. 2, k. 13 (15), ** p. 2, k. 1, p. 1, k. 1; repeat from ** twice, p. 2, k. 5 (6).

2nd row: P. 5 (6), * k. 2, p. 1, k. 1, p. 1; repeat from * twice, k. 2, p. 13 (15), ** k. 2, p. 1, k. 1, p. 1; repeat from ** twice, k. 2, p. 5 (6).

3rd and 4th rows: As 1st and 2nd rows.

5th row: K. 5 (6), * p. 2, k. into 3rd st. on left-hand needle at front of work, k. into 2nd st., k. into 1st st., then sl. all 3 sts. off needle tog.; repeat from * twice, p. 2, k. 13 (15), ** p. 2, k. into 3rd st. on left-hand needle at front of work, p. into 2nd st., k. into 1st st., then sl. all 3 sts. off needle tog.; repeat from ** twice, p. 2, k. 5 (6).

6th row: As 2nd row.

These 6 rows form the pattern. ***

Pattern a further 30 (32) rows. Mark each end of the last row, to denote end of side seams.

Pattern 30 (32) rows.

To slope the shoulders: Cast off 6 (7) sts. at the beginning of each of the next 2 rows and 7 sts. at the beginning of each of the next 4 rows.

Leave remaining 17 (19) sts. on a spare needle.

THE FRONT: Work as given for back to ***.

Pattern a further 27 (29) rows.

Divide sts. for "V" neck: Next row: Pattern 28 (30) and leave these sts. on a spare needle for right half front, p. next st. and leave on a safety pin, pattern to end and work on these 28 (30) sts. for left half front.

The left half front: To shape the neck: Dec. 1 st. at neck edge on the next row. Work 3 rows, marking the end—read beginning here when working right half front—of the 1st of these 3 rows.

Dec. 1 st. at neck edge on the next row and the 6 (7) following 4th rows—20 (21) sts.

Pattern 3 (1) row(s)—pattern 4 (2) rows here when working right half front.

To slope the shoulder: Cast off 6 (7) sts. at the beginning of the next row, then 7 sts. at the beginning of the following alternate row—7 sts.

Work 1 row, then cast off.

The right half front: With right side of work facing, rejoin yarn to inner end of sts. on spare needle and work as given for left half front, noting variations.

THE SLEEVES (both alike): With No. 10 (3¼ mm) needles cast on 31 (33) sts. and work 11 rows in rib as given for back.

Next (increase) row: Rib 3 (4), * up 1, rib 8; repeat from * until 4 (5) sts. remain, up 1, rib 4 (5)—35 (37) sts.

Change to No. 8 (4 mm) needles and s.s. 4 rows.

Continuing in s.s., inc. 1 st. at each end of the next row and the 6 following 6th rows—49 (51) sts.

S.s. 5 (7) rows. Cast off.

THE NECKBAND: First join right shoulder seam. With right side of work facing and using No. 10 (3¼ mm) needles, pick up and k. 37 (39) sts. down left front neck edge, k. the st. from safety pin at centre front, pick up and k. 37 (39) sts. up right front neck edge, then work across back neck sts. as follows: k. 4 (5), * up 1, k. 3: repeat from * twice, up 1, k. 4 (5)—96 (102) sts.

1st row: * K. 1, p. 1; repeat from * to within 2 sts. of centre front st., k. 2 tog., p. 1, k. 2 tog.b., ** p. 1, k. 1; repeat from ** until 1 st. remains, p. 1.

2nd row: K. 1, p. 1; repeat from * to within 2 sts. of centre front st., k. 2 tog.b., k. 1, k. 2 tog., rib to end.

Rib a further 5 rows, decreasing 1 st. at each side of centre front st. as before on each row.

Cast off in rib, decreasing 1 st. at each side of centre front st. as before.

TO MAKE UP THE SWEATER: Press work lightly on the wrong side, using a warm iron over a dry cloth. Join left shoulder seam, continuing seam across neckband. Set in sleeves between markers, then join sleeve and side seams.

Blue/White Sweater

Illustrated on page 43

MEASUREMENTS	*in centimetres (and inches, in brackets)*					
To fit chest sizes	46	(18)	51	(20)	56	(22)
All round at underarms	47	(18½)	52	(20½)	57.5	(22¾)
Side seam	14.5	(5¾)	16.5	(6½)	19	(7½)
Length	24.5	(9½)	27.5	(10¾)	31	(12¼)
Sleeve seam	16	(6¼)	18	(7)	20.5	(8)

MATERIALS: *Allow the following quantities in 40 g balls of Robin Bambino 4-ply: 2 main colour and 1 contrast for the 46 cm size; 2 main colour and 1 contrast for the 51 cm size; 3 main colour and 1 contrast for the 56 cm size. For any one size: A pair each of No. 10 (3¼ mm) and No. 12 (2¾ mm) knitting needles; 4 buttons.*

TENSION: *Work at a tension of 31 stitches and 33 rows to measure 10 × 10 cm over the pattern, using No. 10 (3¼ mm) needles, to obtain the measurements given above.*

ABBREVIATIONS: To be read before working: *K., knit plain; p., purl; st., stitch; tog., together; dec., decrease (by working 2 sts. tog.); inc., increase (by working twice into same st.); y.fwd., yarn forward to make a st.; s.s., stocking st.*

(k. on the right side and p. on the wrong side); nil, meaning nothing is worked here for this size; m., main colour; c., contrast colour; single rib is k. 1 and p. 1 alternately.

NOTE: *The instructions are given for the 46 cm (18 inch) chest size. Where they vary, work the figures within the first brackets for the 51 cm (20 inch) chest size; work the figures within the second brackets for the 56 cm (22 inch) chest size.*

THE BACK: With No. 12 (2¾ mm) needles and m. cast on 73 (81) (89) sts. and, beginning odd-numbered rows with k. 1 and even-numbered rows with p. 1, work 12 rows in single rib.

Continued on page 42

Change to No. 10 (3¼ mm) needles and continue to work in pattern as follows, which is worked entirely in s.s. beginning with a k. row, so only the colour details are given. Join in and break off colours as required and twist yarns when changing colours to avoid a hole.

1st and 2nd rows: All m.

3rd row: 2 m., * 1 c., 3 m.; repeat from * ending last repeat with 2 m. instead of 3 m.

4th row: 1 m., * 3 c., 1 m.; repeat from * to end.

5th row: As 3rd row.

6th and 7th rows: All m.

8th row: 1 c., * 3 m., 1 c.; repeat from * to end.

9th row: 3 m., * 1 c., 1 m., 1 c., 5 m.; repeat from * ending last repeat with 3 m. instead of 5 m.

10th row: As 3rd row.

11th row: 1 m., * 1 c., 2 m., 1 c., 2 m., 1 c., 1 m.; repeat from * to end.

12th row: As 3rd row.

13th row: As 9th row.

14th row: As 8th row.

These 14 rows form the pattern. Pattern a further 26 (32) (40) rows.

To shape the armholes: Keeping continuity of pattern, cast off 4 (5) (6) sts. at the beginning of each of the next 2 rows, then dec. 1 st. at each end of the next row and the 4 (5) (6) following alternate rows—55 (59) (63) sts. **

Pattern a further 17 (19) (21) rows.

To slope the shoulders: Cast off 8 (8) (9) sts. at the beginning of each of the next 2 rows, then 8 (9) (9) sts. at the beginning of the following 2 rows—23 (25) (27) sts.

Change to No. 12 (2¾ mm) needles and, using m. only, work 14 rows in single rib as given on welt for back neckband.

Cast off loosely in rib.

THE FRONT: Work as given for back to **.

Pattern a further 6 (8) (10) rows.

To divide for neck: Next row: Pattern 22 (23) (24) and leave these sts. on a spare needle for right half neck, pattern 11 (13) (15) and leave these sts. on a safety pin for neckband, pattern to end and work on these 22 (23) (24) sts. for left half neck.

The left half neck: Dec. 1 st. at neck edge on each of the next 6 rows—16 (17) (18) sts.

Pattern 4 rows—pattern 5 rows here when working right half neck.

To slope the shoulder: Cast off 8 (8) (9) sts. at the beginning of the next row—8 (9) (9) sts.

Work 1 row.

Cast off.

The right half neck: With right side of work facing, rejoin yarn to inner edge of the 22 (23) (24) sts. left on spare needle and work as given for left half neck, noting variation.

THE SLEEVES (both alike): With No. 12 (2¾ mm) needles and m. cast on 36 (38) (40) sts. and work 15 rows in single rib.

Next (inc.) row: Rib 5 (8) (3), * inc., rib 5 (9) (3); repeat from * until 7 (nil) (5) sts. remain, inc., rib 6 (nil) (inc., rib 4)—41 (41) (49) sts.

Change to No. 10 (3¼ mm) needles and work 12 (6) (12) rows in pattern as given on back.

Maintaining continuity of the pattern and taking extra sts. into pattern as they occur, inc. 1 st. at each end of the next row and the 4 (7) (6) following 6th (5th) (6th) rows—51 (57) (63) sts.

Pattern a further 3 (4) (5) rows.

To shape sleeve top: Cast off 4 (5) (6) sts. at the beginning of each of the next 2 rows.

Dec. 1 st. at the beginning of each of the next 8 rows—35 (39) (43) sts.

Cast off 2 sts. at the beginning of the following 8 (10) (12) rows—19 sts.

Cast off.

THE FRONT NECKBAND: With right side of work facing, rejoin m. and using No. 12 (2¾ mm) needles, pick up and k. 15 sts. down left side of neck, k. across the 11 (13) (15) sts. at centre front, and finally, pick up and k. 15 sts. up right side of neck—41 (43) (45) sts.

Work 14 rows in single rib as given at beginning of back.

Cast off loosely in rib.

THE BACK SHOULDER EDGINGS (both alike): First fold neckband in half to wrong side and sl.st. into place, then join shoulder seams for 2.5 (2.5) (3) cm—1 (1) (1¼) inches. With right side of work facing, using No. 12 (2¾ mm) needles and m., pick up and k. 16 (17) (17) sts. evenly along shoulder and row ends of neckband. K. 2 rows. Cast off.

THE RIGHT FRONT SHOULDER EDGINGS: With right side of work facing, using No. 12 (2¾ mm) needles and m., pick up and k. 16 (17) (17) sts. evenly along row ends of neckband and along shoulder and k. 1 row.

Next (buttonhole) row: K. 1, k. 2 tog., y.fwd., k. 6 (7) (7), k. 2 tog., y.fwd., k. 5.

K. 1 row, then cast off.

THE LEFT FRONT SHOULDER: With right side of work facing, using No. 12 (2¾ mm) needles and m., pick up and k. 16 (17) (17) sts. evenly along shoulder and row ends of neckband.

K. 1 row.

Next (buttonhole) row: K. 5, y.fwd., k. 2 tog., k. 6 (7) (7), y.fwd., k. 2 tog., k. 1.

K. 1 row.

Cast off.

TO MAKE UP THE JERSEY: Press on the wrong side with a cool iron over a dry cloth. Set in sleeves. Join side and sleeve seams. Catch down front shoulder edgings over the back, then sew on buttons to correspond with buttonholes.

Opposite *Blue/White Sweater (page 41)*

Sweater, Pilch and Top with Bunny Motif

Illustrated on page 46

MEASUREMENTS	in centimetres (and inches, in brackets)	
To fit chest sizes	46–48(18–19)	51–53(20–21)
THE JUMPER		
All round at underarms,	53.5 (21)	58.5 (23)
Side seam	13 (5)	15 (6)
Length	24 (9½)	26.5 (10½)
THE TOP		
Side seam	7 (2¾)	8 (3¼)
Length to shoulder	21 (8¼)	23 (9)
THE PILCH		
Length from crotch	23 (9)	24 (9½)

MATERIALS: *Allow the following quantities in 20 g balls of Patons Fairytale Quickerknit: The jumper: 3 balls white and 1 ball blue for the 46–48 cm and 51–53 cm sizes. The top: 2 balls of blue and 1 ball white for the 46–48 cm and 51–53 cm sizes. The pilch: 3 balls of blue for the 46–48 cm and 51–53 cm sizes. For any one garment or size: a pair each of No. 9 (3¾ mm) and No. 11 (3 mm) knitting needles; 4 small buttons for the jumper and a length of elastic for the pilch.*

TENSION: *Work at a tension of 24 stitches and 34 rows to measure 10 × 10 cm, over the stocking stitch, using No. 9 (3¼ mm) needles, to obtain measurements given above.*

ABBREVIATIONS: To be read before working: *K., knit plain; p., purl; st., stitch; sl., slip; tog., together; dec., decrease (by working 2 sts. tog.); inc., increase (by working twice into same st.); y.fwd., yarn forward to make a st.; k. or p. 2 tog. b., k. or p. 2 tog. through back of sts.; up 1, pick up loop lying between needles and k. or p. into the back of it; s.s., stocking st. (k. on the right side and p. on the wrong side); single rib is k. 1 and p. 1 alternately; a., blue; b., white.*

NOTE: *The instructions are given for the 46–48 cm (18–19 inch) size. Where they vary, work the figures within the brackets for the 51–53 cm (20–21 inch) size.*

THE JUMPER

THE BACK: With No. 11 (3 mm) needles and a., cast on 58 (64) sts. and work 9 rows in single rib.

Next (inc.) row: Rib 4 (5), up 1, * rib 10 (11), up 1; repeat from * 4 times, rib 4—64 (70) sts. **

Break off a., join in b. and continue in b. only.

Change to No. 9 (3¾ mm) needles and, beginning with a k. row, s.s. 34 (38) rows.

To shape the armholes: Cast off 3 sts. at the beginning of each of the next 2 rows, then dec. 1 st. at each end of the next row and the 4 (5) following alternate rows—48 (52) sts.

S.s. 2 (nil) row(s).

To divide for back opening: Next row: P. 22 (24) and leave these sts. on a spare needle for left half back, p. 4 and leave these sts. on a safety pin for buttonhole border, p. to end and work on these 22 (24) sts. for right half back.

The right half back: S.s. 18 (22) rows—s.s. 19 (23) rows here when working left half back.

To slope the shoulder: Cast off 5 sts. at the beginning of the next row and the following alternate row, the 4 (5) sts. at the beginning of the next following alternate row—8 (9) sts.

Work 1 row.

Leave these sts. on a safety pin.

The left half back: With right side of work facing, rejoin yarn to the 22 (24) sts. left on spare needle and work as given for right half back, noting variation.

THE FRONT: Work as given for back to **.

Change to No. 9 (3¾ mm) needles, join in b. and work the 19-row motif as follows, which is worked entirely in s.s. beginning with a k. row, so only the colour details are given, twisting yarns when changing colours to avoid a hole.

1st row: 11 (14) b., 18 a., 6 b., 18 a., 11 (14) b.
2nd row: 11 (14) b., 19 a., 5 b., 19 a., 10 (13) b.
3rd row: 10 (13) b., 19 a., 5 b., 19 a., 11 (14) b.
4th row: 12 (15) b., 18 a., 6 b., 18 a., 10 (13) b.
5th row: 11 (14) b., 16 a., 8 b., 16 a., 13 (16) b.
6th row: 12 (15) b., 16 a., 8 b., 16 a., 12 (15) b.
7th row: 11 (14) b., 17 a., 7 b., 17 a., 12 (15) b.
8th row: 12 (15) b., 17 a., 7 b., 17 a., 11 (14) b.
9th row: 11 (14) b., 18 a., 6 b., 18 a., 11 (14) b.
10th row: 10 (13) b., 19 a., 5 b., 19 a., 11 (14) b.
11th row: 11 (14) b., 19 a., 5 b., 19 a., 10 (13) b.
12th row: 10 (13) b., 19 a., 5 b., 19 a., 11 (14) b.
13th row: 12 (15) b., 10 a., 1 b., 7 a., 6 b., 10 a., 1 b., 7 a., 10 (13) b.
14th row: 11 (14) b., 6 a., 2 b., 8 a., 8 b., 6 a., 2 b., 8 a., 13 (16) b.
15th row: 15 (18) b., 4 a., 3 b., 6 a., 11 b., 4 a., 3 b., 6 a., 12 (15) b.
16th row: 14 (17) b., 5 a., 19 b., 5 a., 21 (24) b.
17th row: 20 (23) b., 5 a., 19 b., 5 a., 15 (18) b.
18th row: 16 (19) b., 4 a., 20 b., 4 a., 20 (23) b.
19th row: 20 (23) b., 3 a., 21 b., 3 a., 17 (20) b.

Break off a., continuing in b. only and beginning with a p. row, s.s. 19 rows.

To shape the armholes: Cast off 3 sts. at the beginning of each of the next 2 rows, then dec. 1 st. at each end of the next row and the 4 (5) following alternate rows—48 (52) sts.

S.s. 10 rows.

To divide for neck: Next row: P. 19 (21) and leave these sts. on a spare needle for right half neck, p. 10 and leave these sts. on a safety pin for neckband, p. to end and work on these 19 (21) sts. for left half neck.

The left half neck: Dec. 1 st. at neck edge on the next 5 (6) rows—14 (15) sts.

S.s. 5 (6) rows—s.s. 6 (7) rows here when working right half neck.

To slope shoulder: Cast off 5 sts. at the beginning of the next row and the following alternate row—4 (5) sts.

Work 1 row.

Cast off.

The right half neck: With right side of work facing, rejoin yarn to the 19 (21) sts. left on spare needle and work as given for left half neck, noting variation.

THE SLEEVES (both alike): With No. 11 (3 mm) needles and a., cast on 34 (38) sts. and work 10 rows in single rib increasing 1 st. at each end of the last of these rows—36 (40) sts.

Break off a., join in b. and continue in b. only.

Change to No. 9 (3¾ mm) needles and, beginning with a k. row, s.s. 2 rows.

Inc. 1 st. at each end of the next row and the 5 following 6th rows—48 (52) sts.

S.s. 7 (11) rows.

To shape the sleeve top: Cast off 3 sts. at the beginning of each of the next 2 rows, dec. 1 st. at each end of the next row and the 7 (9) following alternate rows, then dec. 1 st. at each end of the next 8 rows—10 sts.

Work 1 row.

Cast off.

THE NECKBAND: First join shoulder seams. With right side of work facing, using No. 11 (3 mm) needles and a., k. across the 8 (9) sts. of left half back, pick up and k. 14 (16) sts. down left side of front neck, k. across the 10 sts. at centre front, pick up and k. 14 (16) sts. up right side of front neck and finally k. across the 8 (9) sts. from right half back—54 (60) sts.

Work 7 rows in single rib.

Cast off loosely in rib.

THE BUTTONHOLE BORDER: With right side of work facing using No. 11 (3 mm) needles and a., rejoin yarn to the 4 sts. left on safety pin at centre back and k. 1 row increasing 1 st. at the beginning of row—5 sts.

K. 3 (5) rows.

Next (buttonhole) row: K. 1, k. 2 tog., y.fwd., k. 2.

K. 15 rows.

Repeat the last 16 rows twice, then the buttonhole row again.

K. 4 (6) rows.

Cast off k. wise.

THE BUTTON BORDER: With No. 11 (3 mm) needles and a., cast on 5 sts. and work as given for buttonhole border omitting buttonholes.

TO MAKE UP THE JUMPER: Press with a warm iron over a dry cloth. Set in sleeves. Join side and sleeve seams. Sew on borders catching down cast on edge of button border behind buttonhole border at base of back opening. Sew on buttons. Embroider eyes as in photograph on page 46.

THE TOP

BACK AND FRONT ALIKE: With No. 11 (3 mm) needles and a., cast on 58 (64) sts. and work 23 (27) rows in single rib.

Next (inc.) row: Rib 4 (5), up 1, * rib 10 (11), up 1; repeat from * 4 times, rib 4—64 (70) sts.

Change to No. 9 (3¾ mm) needles, join in b. and work the 1st pattern row as follows, twisting yarn when changing colours to avoid a hole.

1st row: With a., cast off 10 (13) sts. in rib, k. 8 a. and leave these 9 sts. on a safety pin for first border, k. 4 b., k. 18 a., k. 4 b., k. 9 a. and leave these 9 sts. on a safety pin for second border, with a. cast off the remaining 10 (13) sts. in rib.

With wrong side of work facing, rejoin a. to the remaining 26 sts. and continue to work the motif which is worked entirely in s.s. beginning with a p. row so only the colour details are given.

2nd row: 4 b., 19 a., 3 b.
3rd row: 3 b., 19 a., 4 b.
4th row: 5 b., 18 a., 3 b.
5th row: 4 b., 16 a., 6 b.
6th row: 5 b., 16 a., 5 b.
7th row: 4 b., 17 a., 5 b.
8th row: 5 b., 17 a., 4 b.
9th row: 4 b., 18 a., 4 b.
10th row: 3 b., 19 a., 4 b.
11th row: 4 b., 19 a., 3 b.
12th row: 3 b., 19 a., 4 b.
13th row: 5 b., 10 a., 1 b., 7 a., 3 b.
14th row: 4 b., 6 a., 2 b., 8 a., 6 b.
15th row: 8 b., 4 a., 3 b., 6 a., 5 b.
16th row: 7 b., 5 a., 14 b.
17th row: 13 b., 5 a., 8 b.
18th row: 9 b., 4 a., 13 b.
19th row: 13 b., 3 a., 10 b.

Break off a. and continue in b. only, and beginning with a p. row, s.s. 5 rows.

Leave these 26 sts. on a spare needle.

THE BORDERS (both alike): With wrong side of work facing using No. 9 (3¾ mm) needles, rejoin a. to the 9 sts. left on safety pin and k. 23 rows, leave second border on a safety pin.

Next row: With right side of work facing, using No. 9 (3¾ mm) needles and continuing in a. only, k. 9 across first border, k. across the 26 sts. left on spare needle, then k. across the 9 sts. left on safety pin—44 sts.

K. 12 rows.

Next row: K. 9 and leave these sts. on a safety pin for second border, cast off the next 26 sts., k. 8 and work on these 9 sts. for first border.

The first border: K. 35 (39) rows.

Cast off.

The second border: With right side of work facing, rejoin a. to inner end of sts. left on safety pin and work as given for first border.

TO MAKE UP THE TOP: Press as given for jumper. Join side seams. Join row ends of borders to the row ends of motif section. Join straps at shoulder.

Continued on page 46

THE PILCH

THE BACK: With No. 11 (3 mm) needles and a., commencing at waist, cast on 67 (73) sts.

Beginning odd-numbered rows with k. 1 and even-numbered rows with p. 1, work 20 rows in single rib. **★★**

Change to No. 9 (3¾ mm) needles and, beginning with a k. row, s.s. 2 rows.

    To shape the back: 1st turning row: K. 38 (41), turn.

    2nd turning row: P. 9, turn.

    3rd turning row: K. 17, turn.

    4th turning row: P. 25, turn.

    5th to 8th turning rows: Continue in this way, working 8 sts. more on every row until the row, p. 57 turn has been worked.

    Next row: K. to end of row.

Beginning with a p. row, s.s. 43 rows over all sts.

    ★★★To shape the legs: Cast off 5 sts. at the beginning of each of the next 2 rows—57 (63) sts.

    Next row: K. 2, k. 2 tog.b., k. until 4 sts. remain, k. 2 tog., k. 2.

Above *Jumper (page 44) and Pilch (this page)*; *Top (page 45)*

Opposite *Crossover Cardigan with Dot Pattern (page 48)*

    Next row: K. 2, p. 2 tog., p. until 4 sts. remain, p. 2 tog.b., k. 2.

Repeat these 2 rows, 9 (10) times more—17 (19) sts. Cast off.

THE FRONT: Work as for back to **★★**.

Change to No. 9 (3¾ mm) needles and, beginning with a k. row, s.s. 46 rows.

Work as given for back, from **★★★** to end.

TO MAKE UP THE PILCH: Press as given for jumper. Join side seams. Join cast off edges to form crotch. Fold ribbing in half to wrong side and leaving an opening to thread elastic, sl. st. into position. Insert elastic and close opening.

Crossover Cardigan with Dot Pattern

Illustrated on page 47

MEASUREMENTS	*in centimetres (and inches, in brackets)*					
To fit chest sizes	46	(18)	51	(20)	56	(22)
Side seam	12	($4\frac{3}{4}$)	13	($5\frac{1}{4}$)	14	($5\frac{1}{2}$)
Length	23.5	($9\frac{1}{4}$)	25	($9\frac{3}{4}$)	27	($10\frac{1}{2}$)
Sleeve seam	14	($5\frac{1}{2}$)	16	($6\frac{1}{4}$)	18	(7)

MATERIALS: *Allow the following quantities in 40 g balls of Robin Bambino 4-ply: 2 main (shade 3701) for the 46 cm size; 2 main for the 51 cm size; 3 main for the 56 cm size.*

For any one size: A ball each of the same yarn in a. (1st contrast colour-shade 3761), b. (2nd contrast colour-shade 3721), c. (3rd contrast colour-shade 3741); a pair each of No. 10 ($3\frac{1}{4}$ mm) and No. 12 ($2\frac{3}{4}$ mm) knitting needles; 4 buttons.

TENSION: *Work at a tension of 29 stitches and 35 rows to measure 10 × 10 cm over the pattern, using No. 10 ($3\frac{1}{4}$ mm) needles, to obtain the measurements given above.*

ABBREVIATIONS: To be read before working: *K., knit plain; p., purl; st., stitch; tog., together; dec., decrease (by working 2 sts. tog.); s.s., stocking st. (k. on the right side and p. on the wrong side); single rib is k. 1 and p. 1 alternately; nil, meaning nothing is worked here for this size; m., main colour; a., 1st contrast colour; b., 2nd contrast colour; c., 3rd contrast colour.*

NOTE: *The instructions are given for the 46 cm (18 inch) size. Where they vary, work the figures within first brackets for the 51 cm (20 inch) size; work the figures within the second brackets for the 56 cm (22 inch) size.*

THE BACK: With No. 12 ($2\frac{3}{4}$ mm) needles and m. cast on 70 (78) (86) sts. and work 18 rows in single rib.

Change to No. 10 ($3\frac{1}{4}$ mm) needles and work in pattern as follows, which is worked entirely in s.s. beginning with a k. row, so only the colour details are given, joining in and breaking off colours as required and twisting yarns when changing colours to avoid a hole.

1st and 2nd rows: All m.

3rd row: 2 m., * 2 a., 2 m.; repeat from * to end.

4th and 5th rows: All m.

6th row: As 3rd row, but using b. instead of a.

7th and 8th rows: All m.

9th row: As 3rd row, but using c. instead of a.

These 9 rows form the pattern. Pattern a further 19 (23) (27) rows.

To shape for sleeves: Keeping continuity of the pattern, cast on 6 (6) (8) sts. at the beginning of each of the next 8 (2) (6) rows, then 8 (8) (10) sts. at the beginning of the following 2 (8) (4) rows—134 (154) (174) sts.

Pattern a further 24 (26) (28) rows.

To shape the sleeves and slope the shoulders: Keeping continuity of pattern, cast off 32 (38) (44) sts. at the beginning of each of the next 2 rows for sleeves, then 12 (13) (15) sts. at the beginning of each of the following 2 rows and 12 (14) (15) sts. at the beginning of the next 2 rows for shoulders—22 (24) (26) sts.

Cast off.

THE LEFT FRONT: With No. 12 ($2\frac{3}{4}$ mm) needles and m. cast on 63 (71) (79) sts. and beginning odd-numbered rows with k. 1 and even-numbered rows with p. 1, work 17 rows in single rib.

Next row: Rib 5 and leave these sts. on a safety pin for border, rib to end—58 (66) (74) sts.

** Change to No. 10 ($3\frac{1}{4}$ mm) needles and work 3 rows in pattern as given on back.

Keeping continuity of the pattern to match back, dec. 1 st. at front edge on each of the next 16 (18) (20) rows, then on the 4 (5) (6) following alternate rows—38 (43) (48) sts.

Work 1 row—work 2 rows here when working right front, decreasing 1 st. at front edge on the 2nd of these rows.**

To shape for sleeves and continue shaping the front edge: Keeping continuity of the pattern, cast on 6 (6) (8) sts. at the beginning of the next row and the 3 (nil) (2) following alternate rows, then 8 (8) (10) sts. at the beginning of the 1 (4) (2) following alternate rows, *at the same time*, dec. 1 st. at front edge on the 1st of these rows and the 13 (15) (17) following alternate rows—56 (65) (74) sts.

*** Pattern a further 7 (5) (3) rows—pattern 8 (6) (4) rows here when working right front.

To shape the sleeve and slope the shoulder: Keeping continuity of the pattern, cast off 32 (38) (44) sts. at the beginning of the next row, then 12 (13) (15) sts. on the following alternate row—12 (14) (15) sts.

Work 1 row. Cast off.

THE RIGHT FRONT: With No. 12 ($2\frac{3}{4}$ mm) needles and m. cast on 63 (71) (79) sts. and work 2 rows in single rib as given on left front.

Next (buttonhole) row: Rib 3, cast off 2 sts., rib a further 45 (53) (61) sts., cast off 2 sts., rib to end.

Next (buttonhole) row: Rib to end, casting on 2 sts. over those cast off in previous row.

Rib a further 10 rows, then work the 2 buttonhole rows again.

Rib 1 row.

Next row: Rib until 5 sts. remain, turn and leave these sts. on a safety pin for border.

Work as given for left front from ** to **, noting variation.

To shape for sleeves and continue shaping front edge: Cast on 6 (6) (8) sts. at the beginning of the next row and the 3 (nil) (2) following alternate rows, then 8 (8) (10) sts. at the beginning of the 1 (4) (2) following alternate rows, *at the same time*, dec. 1 st. at front edge on the 2nd of these rows and the 12 (14) (16) following alternate rows—56 (65) (74) sts.

Work as given for left front from *** to end, noting variation.

THE SLEEVE RIBBING (both alike): First join top sleeve and shoulder seams. With right side of work facing, using No. 12 (2¾ mm) needles and m., pick up and k. 34 (36) (38) sts. evenly along row ends of sleeve and work 11 rows in single rib.

Cast off in rib.

THE LEFT FRONT BORDER: With right side of work facing and using No. 12 (2¾ mm) needles, rejoin m. to the 5 sts. left on safety pin and work in rib until border is long enough, when slightly stretched, to fit up left front to centre back neck.

Cast off.

THE RIGHT FRONT BORDER: With wrong side of work facing and using No. 12 (2¾ mm) needles, rejoin m. to the 5 sts. left on safety pin and work in rib until border is long enough, when slightly stretched, to fit up right front to centre back neck.

Cast off.

TO MAKE UP THE CARDIGAN: Press on the wrong side with a cool iron over a dry cloth. Join side and underarm seams. Sew on buttons to correspond with buttonholes. Sew on front borders, then join row ends of border tog. at centre back neck.

Crossover Cardigan with Contrasting Borders

Illustrated on page 50

MEASUREMENTS	*in centimetres (and inches, in brackets)*					
To fit chest sizes	46	(18)	51	(20)	56	(22)
Side seam	12.5	(4¾)	14	(5½)	15	(6)
Length	23.5	(9¼)	25.5	(10)	27	(10½)
Sleeve seam	14	(5½)	16.5	(6½)	19	(7½)

MATERIALS: *Allow the following quantities in 40 g balls of Argyll Babytime Double Knitting: 2 white and 1 blue for the 46 cm size; 2 white and 1 blue for the 51 cm size; 3 white and 1 blue for the 56 cm size. For any one size: a pair each of No. 9 (3¾ mm) and No. 11 (3 mm) knitting needles, 2 buttons.*

TENSION: *Work at a tension of 26 stitches and 33 rows to measure 10 × 10 cm over the stocking stitch, using No. 9 (3¾ mm) needles to obtain the measurements given above.*

ABBREVIATIONS: To be read before working: *K., knit plain; p., purl; st., stitch; tog., together; inc., increase (by working twice into the same stitch); dec., decrease (by working 2 sts. tog.); s.s., stocking stitch (k. on right side and p. on wrong side); single rib is k. 1 and p. 1 alternately; w., white; b., blue; nil meaning nothing is worked here for this size.*

NOTE: *The instructions are given for the 46 cm (18 inch) size. Where they vary, the figures within the first brackets for the 51 cm (20 inch) size; the figures within the second brackets for the 56 cm (22 inch) size.*

THE BACK: With No. 11 (3 mm) needles and b. cast on 63 (69) (75) sts. and, beginning odd numbered rows with k. 1 and even numbered rows with p. 1, work 10 rows in single rib.

Change to No. 9 (3¾ mm) needles and w. and beginning with a k. row, s.s. 32 (36) (40) rows.

Mark each end of last row to denote end of side seams. S.s. a further 30 (32) (34) rows.

To slope shoulders: Cast off 7 (8) (9) sts. at the beginning of each of the next 4 rows, then cast off 8 sts. at the beginning of the next 2 rows.

Cast off the remaining 19 (21) (23) sts.

THE LEFT FRONT: With No. 11 (3 mm) needles and b. cast on 43 (47) (51) sts. and work 9 rows in single rib as given for back.

Next row: Rib 6 and leave these sts. on a safety pin for front border, rib to end—37 (41) (45) sts.

****Change to No. 9 (3¾ mm) needles and w. and beginning with a k. row s.s. 2 rows.

To shape the front edge: Dec. 1 st. at front edge on the next row and the 7 (8) (9) following 4th rows—29 (32) (35) sts.

S.s. 1 row.

Mark *end* of last row to denote end of side seam—read *beginning* here when working right front.

S.s. 2 rows.

Dec. 1 st. at front edge on the next row and the 1 following 4th row—27 (30) (33) sts.

S.s. 3 rows.

Work the 11 row motif as follows, beginning with a k. row so only the colour details are given. Twist yarns when changing colours to avoid a hole.

1st row: 9 (11) (13) w., 2 b., 3 w., 2 b., 9 (10) (11) w., with w. work 2 tog.

2nd row: 10 (11) (12) w., 3 b., 1 w., 3 b., 9 (11) (13) w.

3rd row: 7 (9) (11) w., 2 b., 1 w., 2 b., 1 w., 2 b., 1 w., 2 b., 8 (9) (10) w.

4th row: 8 (9) (10) w., 3 b., 1 w., 1 b., 1 w., 1 b., 1 w., 3 b., 7 (9) (11) w.

5th row: 8 (10) (12) w., 3 b., 1 w., 1 b., 1 w., 3 b., 7 (8) (9) w., with w., work 2 tog.

6th row: 11 (12) (13) w., 3 b., 11 (13) (15) w.

7th row: 8 (10) (12) w., 3 b., 1 w., 1 b., 1 w., 3 b., 8 (9) (10) w.

Continued on page 50

8th row: 7 (8) (9) w., 3 b., 1 w., 1 b., 1 w., 1 b., 1 w., 3 b., 7 (9) (11) w.

9th row: 7 (9) (11) w., 2 b., 1 w., 2 b., 1 w., 2 b., 1 w., 2 b., 5 (6) (7) w., with w. work 2 tog.

10th row: 8 (9) (10) w., 3 b., 1 w., 3 b., 9 (11) (13) w.

11th row: 9 (11) (13) w., 2 b., 3 w., 2 b., 8 (9) (10) w.
Break off b. and continue in w. only, s.s. 1 row.

Dec. 1 st. at front edge on the next row and the 1 (2) (2) following 4th rows—22 (24) (27) sts.

S.s. 3 (1) (3) rows—s.s. 4 (2) (3) rows here when working front right.***

For the 46 cm and 51 cm sizes only: To slope the shoulders: Cast off 7 (8) sts. at the beginning of the next row and the following alternate—8 sts.

For 56 cm size only: To slope shoulder: Cast off 9 sts., work until 2 sts. remain, dec.
Cast off 9 sts. at the beginning of the following alternate row—8 sts.

For all sizes: Work 1 row. Cast off.

THE RIGHT FRONT: With No. 11 (3 mm) needles and b. cast on 43 (47) (51) sts. and work 4 rows in single rib.

1st buttonhole row: Rib 3, cast off 2 sts., rib the next 13 (15) (17) sts., cast off 2 sts., rib to end.

2nd buttonhole row: Rib across all sts. casting on 2 sts. over those cast off in previous row. Rib 3 rows.

Next row: Rib until 6 sts. remain, turn leaving these 6 sts. on a safety pin for front border—37 (41) (45) sts.

Work as given for left front from ** to *** noting variations, but during the 1st to 11th motif rows read each row backwards.

For the 56 cm size only: Dec., k. to end.

For all sizes: To slope the shoulder: Cast off 7 (8) (9) sts. at the beginning of the next row and the following alternate rows—8 sts.

Work 1 row. Cast off.

Continued on page 52

Opposite *Crossover Cardigan with Contrasting
Borders (page 49)*
Below *Cardigan, Trousers and Hat (page 52)*

THE SLEEVES (2 alike): With No. 11 (3 mm) needles and b. cast on 31 (33) (35) sts. and work 10 rows in single rib as given for back.

Change to No. 9 (3¾ mm) needles and w. and beginning with a k. row s.s. nil (2) (4) rows.

Continuing in s.s., inc. 1 st. at each end of the next row and the 5 (6) (7) following 6th rows—43 (47) (51) sts.

S.s. 3 rows.

Break off w. and continuing in b. only, k. 2 rows.

Next row: Inc., k. until 1 st. remains, inc.—45 (49) (53) sts.

K. 3 rows. Cast off loosely.

THE LEFT FRONT BORDER: With right side of work facing rejoin b. to the 6 sts. left on safety pin and using No.

11 (3 mm) needles, continue in single rib until border is long enough, when slightly stretched, to fit up left front to centre back neck. Cast off.

THE RIGHT FRONT BORDER: With wrong side of work facing, rejoin b. to the 6 sts. left on safety pin and using No. 11 (3 mm) needles work as given for left front border to fit up right front to centre back neck. Cast off.

TO MAKE UP THE CARDIGAN: Press on the wrong side with a cool iron over a dry cloth. Join shoulder seams. Sew cast off edges of sleeves to rows ends above markers on back and fronts. Join side and sleeve seams. Sew on front borders, then join row ends of borders tog. at centre back. Sew on buttons to correspond with buttonholes.

Cardigan, Trousers and Hat

Illustrated on page 51

MEASUREMENTS	in centimetres (and inches, in brackets)					
To fit chest sizes	46	(18)	51	(20)	56	(22)
CARDIGAN						
All round at underarms	49	(19¼)	53.5	(21)	58.5	(23)
Side seam	15.5	(6)	17.5	(7)	20	(8)
Length	26.5	(10½)	30	(12)	33.5	(13¼)
Sleeve seam	19.5	(7¾)	21.5	(8½)	23.5	(9¼)
TROUSERS						
Inside leg seam	22.5	(9)	22.5	(9)	26.5	(10½)
Length from crotch to						
waist	17.5	(7)	18.5	(7¼)	19	(7½)

MATERIALS: *Allow the following quantities in 20 g balls of Littlewoods Stores Baby Quicknit: 9 blue, 1 yellow and 1 white for the 46 cm size; 10 blue, 2 yellow and 1 white for the 51 cm size; 12 blue, 2 yellow and 1 white for the 56 cm size. For any one size or garment: A pair each of No. 8 (4 mm) and No. 10 (3¼ mm) knitting needles; 5 buttons for cardigan and a waist length of narrow elastic for trousers.*

TENSION: *Work at a tension of 26 stitches and 28 rows to measure 10 × 10 cm, over the stocking stitch, using No. 8 (4 mm) needles, to obtain the measurements given above.*

ABBREVIATIONS: To be read before working: *K., knit plain; p., purl; st., stitch; tog., together; dec., decrease (by working 2 sts tog.); inc., increase (by working twice into same st.); y.r.n., yarn round needle to make a st.; s.s., stocking st. (k. on the right side and p. on the wrong side); single rib is k. 1 and p. 1 alternately; bl., blue; y., yellow; w., white; sl., slip; nil, meaning nothing is worked here for this size.*

NOTE: *The instructions are given for the 46 cm (18 inch) size. Where they vary, work the figures within the first brackets for the 51 cm (20 inch) size, and so on.*

THE BACK AND FRONTS (worked in one piece to armholes): With No. 10 (3¼ mm) needles and bl. cast on

139 (151) (163) sts. and, beginning odd-numbered rows with k. 1 and even-numbered rows with p. 1, work 2 rows in single rib.

Next (buttonhole) row: Rib until 6 sts. remain, cast off 3 sts., rib to end.

Next (buttonhole) row: Rib 3, turn, cast on 3 sts., turn, rib to end.

Rib a further 7 rows.

Next row: Rib 9, and leave these sts. on a safety pin for buttonhole border, rib until 9 sts. remain, turn leaving these 9 sts. on a safety pin for button border—121 (133) (145) sts.

Change to No. 8 (4 mm) needles and work the 16-row pattern as follows, which is worked entirely in s.s. beginning with a k. row, so only the colour details are given, joining in and breaking off colours as required and twisting yarns when changing colours to avoid a hole.

1st and 2nd rows: All bl.

3rd row: 1 bl., * 2 y., 1 bl.; repeat from * to end.

4th and 5th rows: 1 y., * 2 bl., 1 y.; repeat from * to end.

6th row: As 3rd row.

7th and 8th rows: All bl.

9th row: 1 bl., * 2 w., 1 bl.; repeat from * to end.

10th row: 2 w., * 3 bl., 3 w.; repeat from * ending last repeat with 2 w.

11th row: As 4th row.

12th row: As 3rd row.

13th to 16th rows: Work the 12th row, back to 9th row in that reverse order.

Pattern a further 17 (23) (29) rows.

To divide for back and fronts: Next row: Pattern 26 (28) (30) and leave these sts. on a spare needle for left front, cast off 6 (8) (10) sts., pattern a further 56 (60) (64) and leave these 57 (61) (65) sts. on a spare needle for back, cast off 6 (8) (10) sts., pattern to end and work on these 26 (28) (30) sts. for right front.

The right front: Dec. 1 st. at armhole edge on the next row and the 3 following alternate rows—22 (24) (26) sts.

Pattern 11 (13) (15) rows—pattern 10 (12) (14) rows here when working left front.

To shape the neck. Next row: Cast off 3 (4) (5) sts., pattern to end. Dec. 1 st. at neck edge on each of next 4 rows—15 (16) (17) sts.

Pattern 4 (6) (8) rows.

To slope the shoulder: Cast off 8 (8) (9) sts. at the beginning of next row—7 (8) (8) sts.

Work 1 row. Cast off.

The back: With right side of work facing, rejoin yarn to the 57 (61) (65) sts. on spare needle and dec. 1 st. at each end of the next row and the 3 following alternate rows—49 (53) (57) sts.

Pattern a further 19 (23) (27) rows.

To slope the shoulders: Cast off 8 (8) (9) sts. at the beginning of each of the next 2 rows, then 7 (8) (8) sts. at the beginning of the following 2 rows—19 (21) (23) sts. Cast off.

The left front: With right side of work facing, rejoin yarn to the 26 (28) (30) sts. left on spare needle and work as given for right front, noting variation.

THE SLEEVES (both alike): With No. 10 (3¼ mm) needles and bl. cast on 32 (34) (36) sts. and work 12 rows in single rib, increasing nil (2) (4) sts. evenly across the last of these rows—32 (36) (40) sts.

Change to No. 8 (4 mm) needles and, beginning with a k. row, s.s. 4 rows.

Maintaining continuity of s.s., inc. 1 st. at each end of the next row and the 6 (7) (8) following 6th rows—46 (52) (58) sts.

S.s. a further 3 rows.

To shape the sleeve top: Cast off 3 (4) (5) sts. at the beginning of each of the next 2 rows, then dec. 1 st. at the beginning of the following 8 rows.

Cast off 2 sts. at the beginning of the next 8 (10) (12) rows—16 sts. Cast off.

THE BUTTONHOLE BORDER: With right side of work facing, using No. 10 (3¼ mm) needles and bl., rib across the 9 sts. left on left front safety pin.

Rib a further 7 (9) (11) rows.

Next (buttonhole) row: Rib 3, cast off 3 sts., rib to end.

Next (buttonhole) row: Rib 3, turn, cast on 3 sts., turn, rib to end.

Rib a further 16 (18) (20) rows.

Repeat the last 18 (20) (22) rows, once, then the 2 buttonhole rows again.

Rib a further 14 (16) (18) rows.

Break yarn and leave sts. on a safety pin.

THE BUTTON BORDER: With wrong side of work facing, using No. 10 (3¼ mm) needles and bl., rib across the

9 sts. left on right front safety pin. Rib 1 row, then work as given for buttonhole border, omitting buttonholes, but do not break yarn.

THE NECKBAND: First join shoulder seams. With right side of work facing, using No. 10 (3¼ mm) needles and bl., rib across the 9 sts. of button border, pick up and k. 15 (16) (17) sts. up right side of neck, 19 (21) (23) sts. across back neck, 15 (16) (17) sts. down left side of neck, and finally, rib across the 9 sts. of buttonhole border—67 (71) (75) sts.

Rib 1 row, then work the 2 buttonhole rows as given on welt.

Rib a further 2 rows. Cast off in rib.

TO MAKE UP THE CARDIGAN: Press with a cool iron over a dry cloth. Set in sleeves. Join side and sleeve seams. Sew on front borders. Add buttons.

TROUSERS

THE LEFT BACK LEG: With No. 10 (3¼ mm) needles and bl. cast on 20 sts. and work 12 rows in single rib.

Change to No. 8 (4 mm) needles.

Next (inc.) row: * K. 1, inc.; repeat from * to end—30 sts.—work * k. 2, inc.; repeat from * until 2 sts. remain, k. 2—26 sts. here when working *right front leg*.

Beginning with a p. row, s.s. 17 (9) (9) rows.

Maintaining continuity of s.s., inc. 1 st. at each end of the next row and the 3 (4) (5) following 8th rows—38 (40) (42) sts.—read 34 (36) (38) sts. here for *right front leg*.

S.s. a further 11 (11) (13) rows—s.s. 12 (12) (14) rows here when working *right back leg* and *left front leg*.★★

To shape the crutch: Cast off 3 sts. at the beginning of the next row and the following alternate row.

Work 1 row, then dec. 1 st. at this same shaped edge on the next two rows—30 (32) (34) sts. Leave these sts. on a spare needle.

THE RIGHT BACK LEG: Work as given for *left back leg*, noting variation, but do not break yarn. With needle holding *right back leg* sts., k. across the 30 (32) (34) sts. of *left back leg*—60 (64) (68) sts.

S.s. 35 (37) (39) rows.

To shape for extra back length: 1st (turning) row: K. until 6 sts. remain, turn.

2nd (turning) row: Sl. 1, p. until 6 sts. remain, turn.

Repeat the last 2 rows, 3 times more.

Next row: Sl. 1, k. to end.

Next row: All p.

★★★ Change to No. 10 (3¼ mm) needles and work 5 rows in single rib.

Next (slot) row: * Rib 2, y.r.n., p. 2 tog.; repeat from * to end.

Rib a further 3 rows. Cast off in rib.

THE RIGHT FRONT LEG: Work as given for left back leg to ★★, noting variations.

To shape the crutch: Cast off 2 sts. at the beginning of the next row, then dec. 1 st. at this same edge on the 2 following alternate rows—30 (32) (34) sts.

Work 1 row. Break yarn and leave these sts.

Continued on page 54

THE LEFT FRONT LEG: Work as given for right front leg, but do not break yarn. With needle holding *left front leg* sts. k. across the 30 (32) (34) sts. of *right front leg*—60 (64) (68) sts.

S.s. 36 (38) (40) rows.

Work as given for extra back length from *** to end.

TO MAKE UP THE TROUSERS: Press as given for cardigan. Join small crutch seams, then join side and inside leg seams. Thread elastic through slot row and fasten ends.

THE HAT

TO MAKE: With No. 10 (3¼ mm) needles and bl. cast on 96 (102) (108) sts. and work 8 rows in single rib, increasing 1 st. at the end of the last of these rows—97 (103) (109) sts.

Change to No. 8 (4 mm) needles and beginning with a k. row, s.s. nil (nil) (2) rows, then work 22 rows in pattern as given on back and fronts of cardigan.

Break off y. and w. and continue in bl. only.

S.s. 4 rows, decreasing 1 st. at the end of the last of these rows—96 (102) (108) sts.

For the 51 cm and 56 cm sizes only: Next row: * K. 15 (7), k. 2 tog.; repeat from * to end—96 sts.

S.s. 3 rows.

For all sizes: To shape the crown: 1st row: * K. 6, k. 2 tog.; repeat from * to end—84 sts.

2nd row: All p.

3rd row: * K. 5, k. 2 tog.; repeat from * to end—72 sts.

Repeat the 2nd and 3rd rows, 4 times more, working 1 st. less between decs. on each repeat of the 3rd row—24 sts. P. 1 row.

Next row: * K. 2 tog.; repeat from * to end—12 sts.

Next row: * P. 2 tog.; repeat from * to end—6 sts.

Break yarn, leaving a long end, thread this through remaining 6 sts., draw up and secure.

TO MAKE UP THE HAT: Press as given for cardigan. Join back seam. With bl. make a small pom-pon and attach to top of hat.

Cardigan with Contrasting Bands
Illustrated opposite

MEASUREMENTS	in centimetres (and inches, in brackets)					
To fit chest sizes	48	(18)	51	(20)	56	(22)
All round at widest part	50	(19¾)	55.5	(21¾)	60.5	(23¾)
Length from underarm	13.5	(5¼)	15	(6)	17	(6¾)
Length	24	(9½)	27	(10½)	29.5	(11½)
Sleeve seam	17	(6¾)	19.5	(7¾)	21.5	(8½)

MATERIALS: *Allow the following quantities in 40 g balls of Robin Bambino 4-ply: 2 white, 1 blue and 1 yellow for the 48 cm size; 2 white, 1 blue and 1 yellow for the 51 cm size; 3 white, 1 blue and 1 yellow for the 56 cm size. For any one size: A pair each of No. 10 (3¼ mm) and No. 12 (2¾ mm) knitting needles; 4 buttons.*

TENSION: *Work at a tension of 28 stitches and 36 rows to measure 10 × 10 cm, over the stocking stitch, using No. 10 (3¼ mm) needles, to obtain the measurements given above.*

ABBREVIATIONS: To be read before working: *K., knit plain; p., purl; st., stitch; tog., together; dec., decrease (by working 2 sts. tog.); inc., increase (by working twice into same st.); k. or p. 2 tog.b., k. or p. 2 tog. through back of sts.; s.s., stocking st. (k. on the right side and p. on the wrong side); single rib is k. 1 and p. 1 alternately; w., white; bl., blue; y., yellow.*

NOTE: *The instructions are given for the 48 cm (18 inch) chest size. Where they vary, work the figures within the first brackets for the 51 cm (20 inch) chest size; work the figures within the second brackets for the 56 cm (22 inch) chest size.*

THE BACK AND FRONTS (worked in one piece to armholes): With No. 12 (2¾ mm) needles and w. cast on 149 (165) (179) sts. and beginning odd-numbered rows with k. 1 and even-numbered rows with p. 1, work 2 rows in single rib.

1st (buttonhole) row: Rib 3, cast off 2 sts., rib to end.

2nd (buttonhole) row: Rib to end, casting on 2 sts. over those cast off in previous row.

Rib a further 7 rows.

Next row: Rib 7 and leave these sts. on a safety pin for button border, rib until 7 sts. remain, turn, leaving these sts. on a safety pin for buttonhole border—135 (151) (165) sts.

Continued on page 56

Opposite *Cardigan with Contrasting Bands*

Change to No. 10 (3¼ mm) needles and, beginning with a k. row, s.s. 2 rows increasing 1 st. in the centre of the last of these rows on the 48 cm and 56 cm sizes only—136 (151) (166) sts.

*** Work the 12-row border pattern as follows, which is worked entirely in s.s. beginning with a k. row, so only the colour details are given, joining in and breaking off colours as required, and twisting yarns when changing colours to avoid a hole.

1st row: 1 bl., * 4 w., 1 bl.; repeat from * to end.

2nd row: 2 bl., * 2 w., 3 bl.; repeat from * ending last repeat with 2 bl. instead of 3 bl.

3rd row: All bl.

4th row: 1 y., * 4 bl., 1 y.; repeat * to end.

5th row: 2 y., * 2 bl., 3 y.; repeat from * ending last repeat with 2 y. instead of 3 y.

6th and 7th rows: 1 bl., * 4 y., 1 bl.; repeat from * to end.

8th and 12th rows: Work the 5th row, back to 1st row, in that reverse order.

Break off bl. and y. and continue in w. only. ***

Beginning with a k. row, s.s. 20 (26) (32) rows.

To shape the front edges: Dec. 1 st. at each end of the next row, then s.s. 2 rows—134 (149) (164) sts.

To divide for back and fronts: Next row: P. 27 (30) (33) and leave these sts. on a spare needle for left front, cast off the next 8 (10) (12) sts., p. a further 63 (68) (73) and leave these 64 (69) (74) sts. on a spare needle for back, cast off 8 (10) (12) sts., p. to end and work on these 27 (30) (33) sts. for right front.

The right front: To shape the armhole and continue shaping front edge: Next row: K. until 3 sts. remain, k. 2 tog., k. 1.

Next row: K. 1, p. 2 tog., p. to end.

Repeat the last 2 rows, twice, then the 1st of these rows again, *at the same time*, dec. 1 st. at front edge on the 3rd of these rows.

Next row: K. 1, p. to end.

Next row: K. until 3 sts. remain, k. 2 tog., k. 1.

** Repeat the last 2 rows, 13 (15) (17) times, *at the same time*, dec. 1 st. at front edge on the 4th of these rows and the 2 (3) (3) following 8th rows—2 (2) (3) sts.

Work 1 row, then k. 2 (2) (3) tog. and fasten off.

The back: With right side of work facing, rejoin yarn to the 64 (69) (74) sts. left on spare needle and work as follows:

To shape the armholes: Next row: K. 1, k. 2 tog.b., k. until 3 sts. remain, k. 2 tog., k. 1.

Next row: K. 1, p. 2 tog., p. until 3 sts. remain, p. 2 tog.b., k. 1.

Repeat the last 2 rows twice, then the 1st of these rows again.

Next row: K. 1, p. until 1 st. remains, k. 1.

Next row: K. 1, k. 2 tog.b., k. until 3 sts remain, k. 2 tog., k. 1.

Repeat the last 2 rows, 13 (15) (17) times, then the 1st of these rows again—22 (23) (24) sts.

Cast off.

The left front: With right side of work facing, rejoin yarn to the 27 (30) (33) sts. left on spare needle and work as follows:

To shape the armhole and continue shaping front edge: Next row: K. 1, k. 2 tog.b., k. to end.

Next row: P. until 3 sts. remain, p. 2 tog.b., k. 1.

Repeat the last 2 rows, twice, then the 1st of these rows again, *at the same time*, dec. 1 st. at front edge on the 3rd of these rows.

Next row: P. until 1 st. remains, k. 1.

Next row: K. 1, k. 2 tog.b., k. to end.

Work as for right front from ** to end.

THE SLEEVES (both alike): With No. 12 (2¾ mm) needles and w. cast on 36 (38) (40) sts. and work 11 rows in single rib.

Next (inc.) row: Rib 1 (2) (4), * inc., rib 6 (11) (5); repeat from * to end—41 (41) (46) sts.

Change to No. 10 (3¼ mm) needles and beginning with a k. row, s.s. 2 rows.

Work as for back and fronts from *** to ***.

Inc. 1 st. at each end of the next row and the 4 (7) (7) following 6th rows—51 (57) (62) sts.

S.s. a further 9 (1) (7) row(s).

To shape the raglan sleeve top: Cast off 4 (5) (6) sts. at the beginning of each of the next 2 rows.

Next row: K. 1, k. 2 tog.b., k. until 3 sts. remain, k. 2 tog., k. 1.

Next row: K. 1, p. until 1 st. remains, k. 1.

Repeat the last 2 rows, 17 (19) (21) times—7 (7) (6) sts. Cast off.

THE BUTTONHOLE BORDER: First join raglan seams. With wrong side of work facing, and using No. 12 (2¾ mm) needles, rejoin w. to the 7 sts. left on right front safety pin and rib to end of row.

Rib a further 6 (8) (10) rows.

Next (buttonhole) row: Rib 3, cast off 2, rib to end.

Next (buttonhole) row: Rib to end, casting on 2 sts. over those cast off in previous row.

Rib a further 14 (16) (18) rows.

Repeat the last 16 (18) (20) rows, once, then the 2 buttonhole rows again.

Continue in rib until border is long enough, when slightly stretched, to fit up front, across sleeve top to centre back neck.

Cast off.

THE BUTTON BORDER: With right side of work facing, and using No. 12 (2¾ mm) needles, rejoin w. to the 7 sts. left on left front safety pin and work as given for buttonhole border, omitting buttonholes.

TO MAKE UP THE CARDIGAN: Press on the wrong side with a cool iron over a dry cloth. Join sleeve seams. Sew on front borders, then join cast off edges tog. at centre back. Sew on buttons.

Crossover Cardigan and Romper

Illustrated on pages 58 and 59

MEASUREMENTS	in centimetres (and inches, in brackets)					
To fit chest sizes	51	(20)	56	(22)	61	(24)
CARDIGAN						
Side seam	12.5	(5)	13.5	(5¼)	14.5	5¾
Length	24.5	(9¾)	26	(10¼)	28	(11)
Sleeve seam	17	(6¾)	18	(7)	19	(7½)
ROMPER						
All round at widest part	57	(22½)	61.5	(24¼)	65.5	(25¾)
Length, from waist to crotch	19.5	(7¾)	20	(8)	21.5	(8½)

MATERIALS: *Allow the following quantities in 100 g balls of Emu Baby 4-ply: For either garment in any one size, 1 white and 1 pink or for both garments in any one size, 2 white and 1 pink; a pair each of No. 10 (3¼ mm) and No. 12 (2¾ mm) knitting needles; a crochet hook for Romper; 4 buttons for cardigan.*

TENSION: *Work at a tension of 26 stitches and 36 rows, to measure 10 × 10 cm over the stocking stitch and 28 stitches and 43 rows, to measure 10 × 10 over the ridge pattern, using No. 10 (3¼ mm) needles, to obtain the measurements given above.*

ABBREVIATIONS: To be read before working: *K., knit plain; p., purl; st., stitch; tog., together; dec., decrease (by working 2 sts. tog.); inc., increase (by working twice into same st.); s.s., stocking st. (k. on the right side and p. on the wrong side); g. st., garter st. (k. plain on every row); y.fwd., yarn forward to make a st.; y.r.n., yarn round needle to make a st., nil, meaning nothing is worked here for this size; pk., pink; w., white; single rib is k. 1 and p. 1 alternately.*

NOTE: *Instructions are given for the 51 cm (20 inch) chest size. Where they vary, work figures within first brackets for the 56 cm (22 inch) size; work figures within second brackets for the 61 cm (24 inch) size.*

CARDIGAN

THE BACK: With No. 12 (2¾ mm) needles and pk. cast on 74 (80) (88) sts. and work 14 rows in single rib.

Change to No. 10 (3¼ mm) needles and w., then beginning with a k. row, s.s. 32 (36) (40) rows.

To shape the armholes: Cast off 6 sts. at the beginning of each of the next 2 rows, then dec. 1 st. at each end of the next row and the 5 (6) (7) following alternate rows—50 (54) (60) sts.

S.s. a further 27 rows.

To slope the shoulders: Cast off 7 (7) (8) sts. at the beginning of each of the next 2 rows and 6 (7) (8) sts. at the beginning of each of following 2 rows—24 (26) (28) sts. Cast off.

THE LEFT FRONT: With No. 12 (2¾ mm) needles and pk. cast on 69 (75) (83) sts. and beginning odd-numbered rows with k. 1 and even-numbered rows with p. 1, work 13 rows in single rib.

Next row: Rib 7 and leave these sts. on a safety pin for left front border, rib to end—62 (68) (76) sts.

** Change to No. 10 (3¼ mm) needles and w., then beginning with a k. row, s.s. 2 rows.

To shape the front edge: Continuing in s.s., dec. 1 st. at front edge on each of the next 5 (9) (13) rows and then on the 12 following alternate rows—45 (47) (51) sts. S.s. 1 row.**

To shape the armhole and continue shaping the front edge: Next row: Cast off 6 sts., k. until 2 sts. remain, dec.

S.s. 1 row.

*** Dec. 1 st. at each end of the next row and the 5 (6) (7) following alternate rows—26 (26) (28) sts.

Keeping armhole edge straight, s.s. 1 row, then dec. 1 st. at front edge on the next row and the 12 (11) (11) following alternate rows—13 (14) (16) sts.

S.s. 1 (3) (3) row(s)—s.s. 2 (4) (4) rows here when working right front.

To slope the shoulder: Cast off 7 (7) (8) sts. at the beginning of the next row—6 (7) (8) sts.

S.s. 1 row.

Cast off.

THE RIGHT FRONT: With No. 12 (2¾ mm) needles and pk. cast on 69 (75) (83) sts. and work 2 rows in rib as given on left front.

Next (buttonhole) row: Rib 3, y.fwd., k. 2 tog., rib until 10 sts. remain, y.fwd., k. 2 tog., rib to end.

Rib a further 7 rows, then work the buttonhole row again.

Rib 2 rows.

Next row: Rib until 7 sts. remain, turn and leave these sts. on a safety pin for right front border—62 (68) (76) sts.

Work as left front from ** to **.

Next row: Dec., k. to end.

To shape armhole and continue shaping the front edge: Next row: Cast off 6 sts., p. to end.

Work as left front from *** to end, noting variation.

THE SLEEVES (both alike): With No. 12 (2¾ mm) needles and pk. cast on 38 (38) (40) sts. and work 14 rows in single rib.

Continued on page 60

Opposite *Crossover Cardigan (page 57)*   Above *Romper (page 60)*

Change to No. 10 (3¼ mm) needles and w., then beginning with a k. row., s.s. 4 rows.

Continuing in s.s., inc. 1 st. at each end of the next row and the 6 (8) (9) following 6th (5th) (5th) rows—52 (56) (60) sts.

S.s. a further 7 (7) (6) rows.

To shape the sleeve top: Cast off 6 sts. at the beginning of each of the next 2 rows, then dec. 1 st. at each end of the next row and the 3 following 4th rows—32 (36) (40) sts.

S.s. 1 row, then dec. 1 st. at each end of the next row and the 4 (5) (5) following alternate rows.

S.s. 1 row, then dec. 1 st. at each end of the next 4 (4) (6) rows—14 (16) (16) sts.

Cast off.

THE LEFT FRONT BORDER: First join shoulder seams. With right side of work facing, using No. 12 (2¾ mm) needles and pk., rib across the 7 sts. on left front safety pin, then continue in rib until border is long enough, when slightly stretched, to fit up left front to centre back neck.

Cast off in rib.

THE RIGHT FRONT BORDER: With wrong side of work facing, using No. 12 (2¾ mm) needles and pk., rib across the 7 sts. on right front safety pin, then continue in rib until border is long enough when slightly stretched to fit up right front to centre back neck.

Cast off in rib.

TO MAKE UP THE CARDIGAN: Press on the wrong side with a cool iron over a dry cloth. Set in sleeves. Join side and sleeve seams. Sew on front borders, then join cast off edges of borders tog. at centre back neck. Sew on buttons to correspond with buttonholes.

ROMPER

TO MAKE: (Worked in one piece, commencing at waist of back): With No. 12 (2¾ mm) needles and w. cast on 72 (78) (84) sts. and work 6 rows in single rib.

Next (eyelet) row: Rib 2 (5) (2), * y.r.n. (y.fwd.) (y.r.n.), work 2 tog., rib 4; repeat from * until 4 (7) (4) sts. remain, y.r.n. (y.fwd.) (y.r.n.), work 2 tog., rib 2 (5) (2).

Rib a further 5 rows.

Change to No. 10 (3¼ mm) needles, join in pk. and work the 4-row ridge pattern as follows:

1st and 2nd rows: With w., all k.

3rd and 4th rows: With pk., beginning with a k. row, s.s. 2 rows.

To shape the sides: Maintaining continuity of pattern and taking extra sts. into pattern as they occur, inc. 1 st. at each end of the next row and the 3 following 6th rows—80 (86) (92) sts.

Pattern a further 25 (25) (29) rows.

To shape for legs: Cast off 4 sts. at the beginning of each of the next 16 rows, then 3 sts. at the beginning of each of the following nil (2) (4) rows—16 sts.

Pattern a further 14 rows for crotch.

To shape for legs: Cast on 3 sts. at the beginning of each of the next nil (2) (4) rows, then 4 sts. at the beginning of each of the following 16 rows—80 (86) (92) sts.

Pattern a further 24 (24) (28) rows.

To shape the sides: Dec. 1 st. at each end of the next row and the 3 following 6th rows—72 (78) (84) sts.

Pattern a further 5 rows.

Break off pk. and continue in w. only.

Change to No. 12 (2¾ mm) needles and work 5 rows in single rib.

Next row: Work eyelet row as given at beginning.

Work a further 6 rows in single rib.

Next row: Cast off 18 sts. in rib, k. until 18 sts. remain, cast off these 18 sts. in rib—36 (42) (48) sts.

The bib: With wrong side of work facing, slip the 1st 7 sts. onto a safety pin for right edging and strap, with No. 10 (3¼ mm) needles and w., k. until 7 sts. remain, turn and leave these 7 sts. on a safety pin for left edging and strap—22 (28) (34) sts.

Join in pk. and beginning with the 3rd pattern row, pattern a further 30 (34) (34) rows.

Break off pk. and continue in w. only.

Change to No. 12 (2¾ mm) needles and g.st. 6 rows. Cast off.

THE RIGHT AND LEFT EDGING AND STRAPS (both alike): With wrong side of work facing, using No. 12 (2¾ mm) needles and w., k. across the 7 sts. on safety pin, then work 13 (14) (15) inches—33 (36) (38) cm—in g.st.

Cast off.

THE LEG EDGINGS (both alike): With right side of work facing, using No. 12 (2¾ mm) needles and w., pick up and k. 74 (80) (86) sts. evenly all round leg edge, then work 7 rows in single rib.

Cast off in rib.

TO MAKE UP THE ROMPER: Press as given for cardigan. Join side seams, including leg edgings. Sew row ends of bib to row ends of straps. Overlap right strap over left at back and catch down straps at waist. Using 1 strand of pk. and 1 strand of w. tog. and a medium size crochet hook, make a crochet cord and thread through eyelet row at waist bringing ends out to tie at centre front. Make 2 tassels and attach to each end of cord.

Striped Jersey and Pilch

Illustrated on pages 62–3

MEASUREMENTS	*in centimetres (and inches, in brackets)*					
To fit chest sizes	46	(18)	48	(19)	51	(20)
JERSEY						
All round at underarms	50	(19¾)	52.5	(20¾)	55	(21¾)
Side seam	15	6)	16	(6¼)	17	(6¾)
Length	24.5	(9¾)	26	(10¼)	27.5	(10¾)
Sleeve seam	16.5	(6½)	18.5	(7¼)	20.5	(8)
PILCH						
All round at widest part	50	(19¾)	52.5	(20¾)	55	(21¾)
Depth at side seam,						
including ribbing	15	(6)	16	(6¼)	17	(6¾)

MATERIALS: *Allow the following quantities in 40 g balls of Robin Bambino 3-ply: 2 main for 46 cm size set; 3 main for 48 cm size set; 3 main for 51 cm size set. For any one size: 1 ball each in 2 contrast colours; a pair each of No. 11 (3 mm) and No. 13 (2¼ mm) knitting needles; 4 buttons for jersey; a waist length of narrow elastic for the pilch.*

TENSION: *Work at a tension of 32 stitches and 40 rows to measure 10 × 10 cm, over the stocking stitch, using No. 11 (3 mm) needles, to obtain the measurements given above.*

ABBREVIATIONS: To be read before working: *K., knit plain; p., purl; st., stitch; tog., together; inc., increase (by working twice into same st.); dec., decrease (by working 2 sts. tog.); s.s., stocking st. (k. on the right side and p. on the wrong side); y.fwd., yarn forward to make a st.; y.r.n., yarn round needle to front of work to make a st.; sl., slip; m., main; a., 1st contrast; b., 2nd contrast; single rib is k. 1 and p. 1 alternately.*

NOTE: *The instructions are given for the 46 cm (18 inch) chest size set. Where they vary, work figures within first brackets for the 48 cm (19 inch) chest size set; work figures within second brackets for the 51 cm (20 inch) chest size set.*

THE JERSEY

THE BACK: With No. 13 (2¼ mm) needles and m. cast on 80 (84) (88) sts. and work 16 rows in single rib.

Change to No. 11 (3 mm) needles and joining and breaking colours as necessary, work stripes as follows, which are worked in s.s. beginning with a k. row; 4 rows m., 2 rows a., 2 rows b., 2 rows a., 2 rows m., 2 rows a., 2 rows b., and 2 rows a.

Continue with m. only, s.s. 30 (34) (38) rows.

To shape armholes: Cast off 4 (5) (6) sts. at beginning of next 2 rows, then dec. 1 st. each end of next row and the 5 following alternate rows—60 (62) (64) sts. ★★

S.s. 21 (23) (25) rows.

To slope shoulders: Cast off 9 sts. at beginning of next 2 rows, then 9 (9) (10) sts. on the following 2 rows—24 (26) (26) sts.

Change to No. 13 (2¼ mm) needles and work 14 rows in single rib for back neck band.

Cast off in rib.

THE FRONT: Work exactly as given for back to ★★.

S.s. 8 (10) (12) rows.

To divide for neck: Next row: P. 24 (24) (25) and leave on a spare needle for right front neck, p. 12 (14) (14) and leave on a st. holder, p. to end and work on these last 24 (24) (25) sts. for left front neck.

The left front neck: Dec. 1 st. at neck edge on each of the next 6 rows—18 (18) (19) sts.

S.s. 6 rows—s.s. 7 rows here when working right front neck.

To slope shoulder: Cast off 9 sts. at beginning of next row.

Work 1 row, then cast off remaining 9 (9) (10) sts.

The right half neck: With right side facing, rejoin m. to inner end of sts. on spare needle and work as given for left half neck, noting variation.

THE SLEEVES (2 alike): With No. 13 (2¼ mm) needles and m. cast on 40 (42) (44) sts. and work 15 rows in single rib.

Inc. row: Rib 3 (4) (5), inc., ★ rib 10, inc.; repeat from ★ twice, rib 3 (4) (5)—44 (46) (48) sts.

Change to No. 11 (3 mm) needles and working in stripes then m. as given on back, inc. 1 st. each end of 11th row and the 5 (6) (7) following 8th rows—56 (60) (64) sts.

S.s. 3 rows.

To shape sleeve top: Cast off 4 (5) (6) sts. at beginning on next 2 rows, then 2 sts. on the following 14 (16) (18) rows.

Cast off remaining 20 (18) (16) sts.

THE FRONT NECKBAND: With right side facing, rejoin m. and using No. 13 (2¼ mm) needles, pick up and k. 16 sts. from row ends of left front neck, k. across 12 (14) (14) sts. at centre front and finally, pick up and k. 16 sts. from row ends of right front neck—44 (46) (46) sts.

Work 14 rows in single rib.

Cast off in rib.

Continued on page 62

THE BACK SHOULDER EDGINGS (2 alike): First join shoulder seams for 3 (3) (3.5) cm at sleeve end only, then fold back and front neck bands in half and catch to wrong side.

With right side facing, rejoin m. and using No. 13 (2¼ mm) needles, pick up and k. 18 sts. along edge of back shoulder opening working through both thicknesses across neck ribbing.

K. 2 rows, then cast off.

THE FRONT SHOULDER EDGINGS (2 alike): Pick up sts. as on back edgings and k. 1 row.

Buttonhole row: K. 5 for left opening or k. 2 for right opening, then y.fwd., k. 2 tog., k. 8, y.fwd., k. 2 tog., k. to end.

K. 1 row, then cast off.

TO MAKE UP THE JERSEY: Press lightly with a warm iron over a dry cloth. Set in sleeves, then join side and sleeve seams. Add buttons.

THE PILCH

TO MAKE: With No. 13 (2¼ mm) needles and m. cast on 80 (84) (88) sts. for front waist edge and work 4 rows in single rib.

Slot row: * Rib 2, y.r.n., p. 2 tog.; repeat from * to end.
Rib 5 rows.

Change to No. 11 (3 mm) needles and s.s. 46 (50) (54) rows.

To shape for front legs: Cast off 9 (10) (9) sts. at beginning of next 2 rows, then 3 sts. on the following 12 (12) (14) rows—26 (28) (28) sts.

S.s. 12 (14) (14) rows.

To shape for back legs: Cast on 3 (4) (3) sts. at beginning of next 2 rows, then 3 sts. on the following 16 (16) (18) rows—80 (84) (88) sts.

S.s. 44 (48) (52) rows.

To shape for extra length: 1st and 2nd turning rows: K. until 8 sts. remain, for 1st row, turn, sl. 1, p. until 8 sts. remain, turn for 2nd row.

3rd and 4th turning rows: Sl. 1, k. until 14 sts. remain, turn, sl. 1, p. until 14 sts. remain, turn.

5th and 6th turning rows: Sl. 1, k. until 20 sts. remain, turn, sl. l, p. until 20 sts. remain, turn.

7th and 8th turning rows: Sl. 1, k. until 26 sts. remain, turn, sl. 1, p. until 26 sts. remain, turn.

9th row: Sl. 1, k. to end of row.

Change to No. 13 (2¼ mm) needles and single rib 5 rows, then repeat slot row given at beginning.

Rib 4 rows, then cast off in rib for back waist edge.

THE LEG RIBBINGS (2 alike): With right side facing, rejoin m. and using No. 13 (2¼ mm) needles, pick up and k. 78 (82) (88) sts. all round leg edge and work 14 rows in single rib. Cast off.

TO MAKE UP THE PILCH: Press as for jersey. Join side seams, continuing across leg ribbings. Fold leg ribbing in half and catch to wrong side. Thread elastic through slot row at waist and join ends.

Right Striped Jersey (page 61) and Pilch (this page)

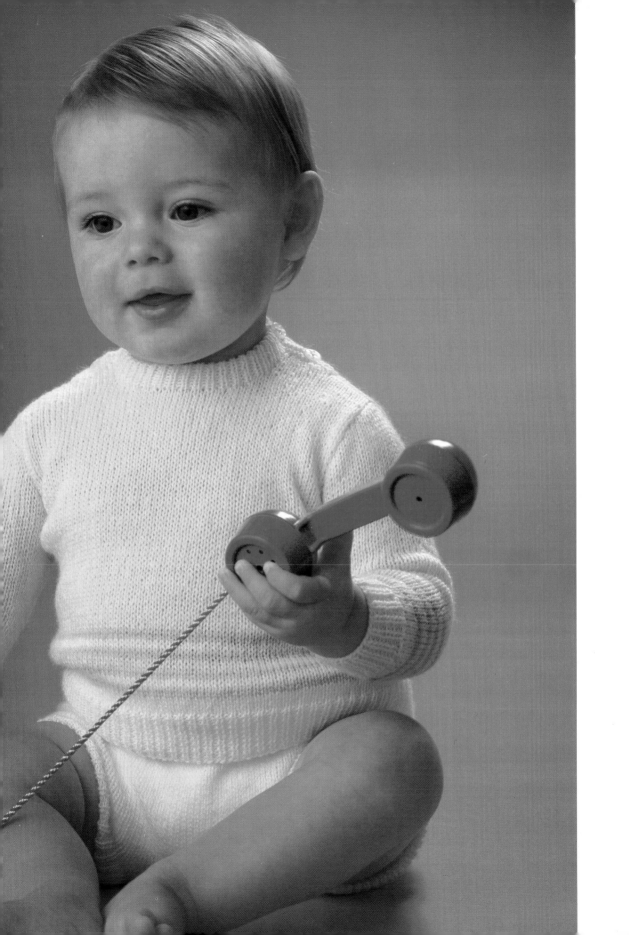

Toddlers

Tyrolean Cardigan

Illustrated opposite

MEASUREMENTS	*in centimetres (and inches, in brackets)*							
To fit sizes	46	(18)	51	(20)	56	(22)	61	(24)
All round fastened at underarms	49	(19¼)	54.5	(21½)	60	(23½)	65.5	(25¾)
Side seam	18.5	(7½)	19.5	(7¾)	20.5	(8)	21.5	(8½)
Length	27.5	(10¾)	29	(11½)	31	(12¼)	32.5	(12¾)
Sleeve seam	20.5	(8)	23	(9)	24	(9½)	25.5	(10)

MATERIALS: *Allow the following quantities in 40 g balls of Sirdar Wash 'n' Wear 4-ply: 3 balls for the 46 cm and 51 cm sizes; 3 balls for the 56 cm and 61 cm sizes. For any one size: a pair each of No. 10 (3¼ mm) and No. 11 (3 mm) knitting needles; 5 buttons; small amounts of blue and green yarn for embroidery.*

TENSION: *Work at a tension of 29 stitches and 39 rows to measure 10 × 10 cm over the stocking stitch, using No. 10 (3¼ mm) needles to obtain the measurements given above.*

ABBREVIATIONS: To be read before working: *K., knit; p., purl; st., stitch; tog., together; s.s., stocking st. (k. on the right side and p. on the wrong side); y.fwd., yarn forward to make a st.; dec., decrease (by taking 2 sts. tog.); single rib is k. 1, p. 1 alternately.*

NOTE: *The instructions are given for the 46 cm (18 inch) size. Where they vary, work figures within first brackets for 51 cm (20 inch) size; work figures within second brackets for 56 cm (22 inch) size, and so on.*

THE BACK: With No. 10 (3¼ mm) needles cast on 72 (80) (88) (96) sts. and k. 2 rows.

Beginning with a k. row, s.s. 24 (26) (28) (30) rows.

Change to No. 11 (3 mm) needles and work 6 rows in single rib.

Next (eyelet) row: Rib 3, * y.fwd., k. 2 tog.; repeat from * until 1 st. remains, p. 1.

Work a further 5 rows in single rib.

Change back to No. 10 (3¼ mm) needles, and s.s. 34 (36) (38) (40) rows.

To shape the armholes: Cast off 2 (3) (4) (5) sts. at the beginning of each of the next 2 rows, then dec. 1 st. at each end of the next row and the 3 (3) (4) (4) following alternate rows—60 (66) (70) (76) sts.

S.s. 23 (25) (27) (29) rows.

To slope the shoulders: Cast off 9 (10) (10) (11) sts. at the beginning of each of the next 2 rows and 9 (10) (11) (12) sts. at the beginning of each of the following 2 rows.

Cast off the 24 (26) (28) (30) sts.

THE LEFT FRONT: With No. 10 (3¼ mm) needles cast on 33 (37) (41) (45) sts. and k. 2 rows.

Beginning with a k. row, s.s. 24 (26) (28) (30) rows.

Change to No. 11 (3 mm) needles and beginning odd-numbered rows with k. 1 and even-numbered rows with p. 1, work 6 rows in single rib.

Next (eyelet) row: K. 1, * y.fwd., k. 2 tog.; repeat from * to end.

Work a further 5 rows in single rib.

Change back to No. 10 (3¼ mm) needles and work the 14-row pattern as follows:

1st row: K. 10 (12) (13) (15), y.fwd., k. 2 tog., k. 9 (9) (11) (11), y.fwd., k. 2 tog., k. 10 (12) (13) (15).

2nd row: All p.

3rd to 12th rows: Repeat 1st and 2nd rows, 5 times more.

13th row: K. 1, * y.fwd., k. 2 tog.; repeat from * to end.

14th row: All p.

Pattern a further 20 (22) (24) (26) rows. **

To shape the armhole and shape the neck: Keeping continuity of pattern, cast off 2 (3) (4) (5) sts. at the beginning of the next row, then dec. 1 st. at armhole edge at the beginning of the 4 (4) (5) (5) following alternate rows—*at the same time*, dec. 1 st. at front edge on the first of these rows then on the 8 (9) (10) (11) following 3rd rows—18 (20) (21) (23) sts.

*** Pattern 7 (6) (7) (6) rows—pattern 8 (7) (8) (7) rows here when working right front.

To slope the shoulder: Cast off 9 (10) (10) (11) sts. at the beginning of the next row, work 1 row.

Cast off remaining 9 (10) (11) (12) sts.

THE RIGHT FRONT: Work as given for left front to **.

To shape the armhole and shape the neck: Keeping continuity of pattern, dec. 1 st. at the beginning of the next row and at this same edge on the 8 (9) (10) (11) following 3rd rows—*at the same time*, cast off 2 (3) (4) (5) sts. at the beginning of the 2nd of those rows, then dec. 1 st. at the same edge on the 4 (4) (5) (5) following right side rows—18 (20) (21) (23) sts.

Work as left front from ***, noting variation.

THE SLEEVES (both alike): With No. 11 (3 mm) needles cast on 46 (48) (50) (52) sts. and work 16 rows in single rib.

Change to No. 10 (3¼ mm) needles and, beginning with a k. row, s.s. 4 rows.

Inc. 1 st. at each end of the next row, then inc. 1 st. at each end of the 5 (5) (6) (6) following 10th rows—58 (60) (64) (66) sts.

S.s. 9 (19) (13) (19) rows.

To shape the sleeve top: Cast off 2 (3) (4) (5) sts. at the beginning of each of the next 2 rows, then dec. 1 st. at each end of the next and the 2 (2) (3) (3) following alternate rows, work 1 row, then cast off 3 sts. at the beginning of the next 8 rows. Cast off.

THE BUTTONHOLE BAND: With No. 11 (3 mm) needles cast on 7 sts.

1st row: K. 2, p. 1, k. 1, p. 1, k. 2.

2nd row: K. 1, * p. 1, k. 1; repeat from * to end.

Repeat the last 2 rows, 3 times more, then the 1st row again.

Buttonhole row: K. 1, p. 1, k. 1, y.fwd., k. 2 tog., p. 1, k. 1.

Rib 15 (17) (19) (21) rows.

Repeat the last 16 (18) (20) (22) rows, 3 times more, then buttonhole row again.

Continue in rib until band is long enough when slightly stretched to fit up right front to centre back neck.

Cast off in rib.

THE BUTTON BAND: Work as for buttonhole band, omitting buttonholes.

TO MAKE UP THE CARDIGAN: Press work lightly on the wrong side using a warm iron over a dry cloth. Join shoulder seams, set in sleeves then join side and sleeve seams. Sew on bands, joining tog. at centre back neck, and placing last buttonhole level with first front dec. Add buttons. Embroider petals and leaves in lazy daisy stitch and the stems in stem stitch on fronts, as in photograph. Using 3 strands of yarn tog., make a twisted cord to measure 114 cm (45 inches) in length and thread through eyelet holes at waist.

Below *Tyrolean Cardigan*

Aran-style Cardigan

Illustrated on page 70

MEASUREMENTS	*in centimetres (and inches, in brackets)*					
To fit chest sizes	51	(20)	56	(22)	61	(24)
All round at underarms, fastened	56.5	(22¼)	59.5	(23½)	63	(24¾)
Side seam	18.5	(7¼)	20.5	(8)	22	(8¾)
Length	31.5	(12½)	34.5	(13½)	37.5	(14¾)
Sleeve seam	22	(8¾)	24	(9½)	25.5	(10)

MATERIALS: *Allow the following quantities in 20 g balls of Littlewoods Stores Baby Quicknit: 7 for 51 cm size; 8 for 56 cm size; 9 for 61 cm size. For any one size: A pair each of No. 9 (3¾ mm) and No. 10 (3¼ mm) knitting needles; a cable needle; 6 buttons.*

TENSION: *Work at a tension of 21 stitches (1 pattern panel) to measure 8 cm and 13 rice stitches to 5 cm in width and 34 rows to 10 cm in depth, using No. 9 (3¾ mm) needles, to obtain the measurements given above.*

ABBREVIATIONS: To be read before working: *K., knit plain; p., purl; st., stitch; tog., together; inc., increase (by working twice into same st.); dec., decrease (by working 2 sts. tog.); up 1, pick up loop lying between needles and k. into back of it; y.r.n., yarn round needle to make a st.; single rib is k. 1 and p. 1 alternately; r.st., rice st.; tw. 2 rt., twist 2 right (k. into front of 2nd st. on left-hand needle, then k. into front of 1st st. and slip both sts. off needle tog.); tw. 2 lt., twist 2 left (k. into back of 2nd st. on left-hand needle, then k. into front of 1st st. and slip both sts. off needle tog.); cr. 3 rt., cross 3 right (slip next st. on to cable needle and leave at back of work, k. 2, then p. 1 from cable needle); cr. 3 lt., cross 3 left (slip next 2 sts. on to cable needle and leave at front of work, p. 1, then k. 2 from cable needle).*

NOTE: *The instructions are given for the 51 cm (20 inch) size. Where they vary, work figures within first brackets for the 56 cm (22 inch) size; work figures within second brackets for the 61 cm (24 inch) size.*

THE BACK: With No. 10 (3¼ mm) needles cast on 71 (75) (79) sts. and beginning odd-numbered rows with k. 1 and even-numbered rows with p. 1, work 16 rows in single rib.

Change to No. 9 (3¾ mm) needles and work in pattern as follows:

1st row: * K. 1, p. 1; repeat from * 3 (4) (5) times, ** tw. 2 rt., tw. 2 lt., p. 3, cr. 3 rt., p. 1, cr. 3 lt., p. 3, tw. 2 rt., tw. 2 lt. ** then *** k. 1, p. 1; repeat from *** 5 times, k. 1; repeat from ** to ** once, * p. 1, k. 1; repeat from this * 3 (4) (5) times.

2nd row: K. 8 (10) (12), * p. 4, k. 3, p. 2, k. 3, p. 2, k. 3, p. 4 *, k. 13; repeat from * to * once, k. 8 (10) (12).

These 2 rows form the pattern for the r.st.

3rd row: R.st. 8 (10) (12), * k. 4, p. 2, cr. 3 rt., p. 3, cr. 3 lt., p. 2, k. 4 *, r.st. 13; repeat from * to * once, r.st. 8 (10) (12).

4th row: R.st. 8 (10) (12), * p. 4, k. 2, p. 2, k. 5, p. 2, k. 2, p. 4 *, r.st. 13; repeat from * to * once, r.st. 8 (10) (12).

5th row: R.st. 8 (10) (12), * tw. 2 rt. tw. 2 lt., p. 1, cr. 3 rt., p. 5, cr. 3 lt., p. 1, tw. 2 rt., tw. 2 lt. *, r.st. 13: repeat from * to * once, r.st. 8 (10) (12).

6th row: R.st. 8 (10) (12), * p. 4, k. 1, p. 2, k. 7, p. 2, k. 1, p. 4 *, r.st. 13; repeat from * to * once, r.st. 8 (10) (12).

7th row: R.st. 8 (10) (12), * k. 4, p. 1, cr. 3 lt., p. 5, cr. 3 rt., p. 1, k. 4 *, r.st. 13; repeat from * to * once, r.st. 8 (10) (12).

8th row: R.st. 8 (10) (12), * p. 4, k. 2, p. 2, k. 5, p. 2, k. 2, p. 4 *, r.st. 13; repeat from * to * once, r.st. 8 (10) (12).

9th row: R.st. 8 (10) (12), * tw. 2 rt., tw. 2 lt., p. 2, cr. 3 lt., p. 3, cr. 3 rt., p. 2, tw. 2 rt., tw. 2 lt *, r.st. 13; repeat from * to * once, r.st. 8 (10) (12).

10th row: R.st. 8 (10) (12), * p. 4, k. 3, p. 2, k. 3, p. 2, k. 3, p. 4 *, r.st. 13; repeat from * to * once, r.st. 8 (10) (12).

11th row: K. 4, p. 3, cr. 3 lt., p. 1, cr. 3 rt., p. 3, k. 4 *, r.st. 13; repeat from * to * once, r.st. 8 (10) (12).

12th row: R.st. 8 (10) (12), * p. 4, k. 4, p. 2, k. 1, p. 2, k. 4, p. 4 *, r.st. 13; repeat from * to * once, r.st. 8 (10) (12).

These 12 rows form the pattern.

Pattern a further 36 (42) (48) rows.

To shape the armholes: Keeping continuity of pattern, cast off 6 sts. at the beginning of each of the next 2 rows—59 (63) (67) sts.

Pattern a further 36 (40) (44) rows.

To slope the shoulders: Cast off 6 (7) (7) sts. at the beginning of each of the next 2 rows, 7 sts. at the beginning of each of the following 2 rows and 7 (7) (8) sts. at the beginning of each of the next 2 rows.

Leave remaining 19 (21) (23) sts. on a spare needle.

THE LEFT FRONT: With No. 10 (3¼ mm) needles cast on 43 (45) (47) sts.

1st row: * P. 1, k. 1; repeat from * until 1 st. remains, k. 1 more.

2nd row: * K. 1, p. 1; repeat from * until 1 st. remains, k. 1.

Repeat the last 2 rows 6 times, then the 1st row again.

Next row: Rib 7 and leave these sts. on a safety pin for button border, rib to end—36 (38) (40) sts.

Change to No. 9 (3¾ mm) needles.

1st row: * K. 1, p. 1; repeat from * 3 (4) (5) times, tw. 2 rt., tw. 2 lt., p. 3, cr. 3 rt., p. 1, cr. 3 lt., p. 3, tw. 2 rt., tw. 2 lt., ** p. 1, k. 1.; repeat from ** twice, p. 1.

2nd row: K. 7, p. 4, k. 3, p. 2, k. 3, p. 2, k. 3, p. 4, k. 8 (10) (12).

These 2 rows set the position of the pattern for the left front.

*** Keeping continuity of pattern to match back,

pattern a further 46 (52) (58) rows—pattern 47 (53) (59) rows here when working right front.

To shape the armhole: Cast off 6 sts. at the beginning of the next row—30 (32) (34) sts.

Pattern 28 (32) (36) rows.

To shape the neck: Cast off 3 (4) (5) sts. at the beginning of the next row, then dec. 1 st. at neck edge on each of the next 7 rows.

Pattern 1 row.

To slope the shoulder: Cast of 6 (7) (7) sts. at the beginning of the next row, 7 sts. at the beginning of the following alternate row—7 (7) (8) sts. Work 1 row. Cast off.

THE RIGHT FRONT: With No. 10 (3¼ mm) needles cast on 43 (45) (47) sts.

1st row: K. 2, * p. 1, k. 1; repeat from * until 1 st. remains, p. 1.

2nd row: * K. 1, p. 1; repeat from * until 1 st. remains, k. 1.

Buttonhole row: Rib 3, y.r.n., work 2 tog., rib to end. Rib a further 12 rows.

Next row: Rib until 7 sts. remain, turn and leave these 7 sts. on a safety pin for buttonhole border—36 (38) (40) sts. Change to No. 9 (3¾ mm) needles.

1st row: * P. 1, k. 1; repeat from * twice, p. 1, tw. 2 rt., tw. 2 lt., p. 3, cr. 3 rt., p. 1, cr. 3 lt., p. 3, tw. 2 rt., tw. 2 lt., ** p. 1, k. 1; repeat from ** 3 (4) (5) times.

2nd row: K. 8 (10) (12), p. 4, k. 3, p. 2, k. 3, p. 2, k. 3, p. 4, k. 7.

These 2 rows set the position of the pattern for the right front.

Work as given for left front from *** to end, noting variation.

THE SLEEVES (both alike): With No. 10 (3¼ mm) needles cast on 37 (39) (41) sts. and work 15 rows in rib as given on back.

Next (increase) row: Rib 6 (6) (2), * up 1, rib 5 (4) (4); repeat from * until 6 (5) (3) sts. remain, up 1, rib to end—43 (47) (51) sts.

Change to No. 9 (3¾ mm) needles.

1st row: * K. 1, p. 1; repeat from * 4 (5) (6) times, k. 1, tw. 2 rt., tw. 2 lt., p. 3, cr. 3 rt., p. 1, cr. 3 lt., p. 3, tw. 2 rt., tw. 2 lt., ** k. 1, p. 1; repeat from ** 4 (5) (6) times, k. 1.

2nd row: K. 11 (13) (15), p. 4, k. 3, p. 2, k. 3, p. 2, k. 3, p. 4, k. 11 (13) (15).

These 2 rows set the position of the pattern for the sleeves.

Pattern a further 4 rows.

Maintaining continuity of the pattern and taking extra sts. into r.st. as they occur, inc. 1 st. at each end of the next row and the 9 following 4th (6th) (6th) rows—63 (67) (71) sts.

Pattern 17 (5) (11) rows. Mark each end of the last row with a coloured thread.

Pattern a further 6 rows. Cast off.

THE BUTTONHOLE BORDER: With wrong side of work facing and using No. 10 (3¼ mm) needles, rejoin yarn to 7 sts. on safety pin at right front and rib 5 (7) (9) rows with sts. as set.

Next (buttonhole) row: Rib 3, y.r.n., work 2 tog., rib to end.

Repeat the last 18 (20) (22) rows twice, then the buttonhole row again.

Rib a further 15 (17) (19) rows. Leave sts. on a safety pin. Sew on border.

THE BUTTON BORDER: With right side of work facing and using No. 10 (3¼ mm) needles, rejoin yarn to the 7 sts. on safety pin at left front and work as given for buttonhole border omitting buttonholes. Sew on border.

THE NECKBAND: First join shoulder seams. With right side of work facing and using No. 10 (3¼ mm) needles, rib across the 7 sts. of buttonhole border, pick up and k. 15 (16) (17) sts. up right front neck edge, work across the 19 (21) (23) sts. at back neck as follows: K. 3 (3) (5), * up 1, k. 4 (3) (2); repeat from * 3 (5) (7) times, k. nil (nil) (2), pick up and k. 15 (16) (17) sts. down left front neck edge, then k. across the 7 sts. of button border—67 (73) (79) sts.

Rib 3 rows, then repeat buttonhole row.

Rib a further 3 rows. Cast off in rib.

TO MAKE UP THE CARDIGAN: Press work lightly on the wrong side, using a warm iron over a dry cloth. Set in sleeves, sewing the 6 row ends above the markers to the sts. cast off at underarms on back and fronts. Join sleeve and side seams. Add buttons.

Below *Aran-style Cardigan (page 68)*
Opposite *Crew-neck Sweater (page 72) and Skirt*
(page 73)

Girl's Crew-neck Sweater and Skirt

Illustrated on page 71

MEASUREMENTS	*in centimetres (and inches, in brackets)*					
To fit chest sizes	51	(20)	56	(22)	61	(24)
JERSEY						
All round at underarms	53.5	(21)	58.5	(23)	63	(24¾)
Side seam	13	(5)	15	(5¾)	17	(6¾)
Length	27	(10½)	30.5	(12)	33.5	(13¼)
Sleeve seam	14	(5½)	17	(6¾)	19	(7½)
SKIRT						
Length, including waistband	20	(8)	21.5	(8½)	24	(9½)

MATERIALS: *Allow the following quantities in 20 g balls of Hayfield Babykin D.K: Jersey: 6 yellow for 51 cm size; 7 yellow for 56 cm size; 8 yellow for 61 cm size. For any one size; a pair each of No. 10 (3¼ mm) and No. 8 (4 mm) knitting needles. Skirt: 5 green, 2 yellow for 51 cm size; 6 green, 2 yellow for 56 cm size; 7 green, 2 yellow for 61 cm size. For any one size: a No. 8 (4 mm) circular knitting needle; a pair of No. 10 (3¼ mm) knitting needles; one button; a waist length of elastic.*

TENSION: *Work at a tension of 25 stitches and 31 rows to measure 10 × 10 cm, over the stocking stitch using No. 8 (4 mm) needles, and 31 rows to measure 10 cm in depth over the skirt pattern, using No. 8 (4 mm) circular needle, to obtain measurements given above.*

ABBREVIATIONS: To be read before working: *K., knit plain; p., purl; st., stitch; tog., together; inc., increase (by working twice into same st.); dec., decrease (by working 2 sts. tog.); k. 2 tog.b., k. 2 tog. through back of sts.; y.o.n., yarn over needle to make a st.; s.s., stocking st. (k. on right side and p. on wrong side); single rib is k. 1 and p. 1 alternately; y., yellow; g., green; y.r.n., yarn round needle to make a st.*

NOTE: *The instructions are given for the 51 cm (20 inch) size. Where they vary, work figures within first brackets for 56 cm (22 inch) size, and so on.*

THE JERSEY

BACK: With No. 10 (3¼ mm) needles cast on 66 (72) (78) sts. and work 14 rows in single rib, increasing 1 st. at the end of the last of these rows—67 (73) (79) sts.
Change to No. 8 (4 mm) needles.**
Beginning with a k. row, s.s. 28 (34) (40) rows.
*** **To shape the raglan armholes: 1st and 2nd rows:** Dec., work to end.
3rd row: K. 2, k. 2 tog.b., work until 4 sts. remain, k. 2 tog., k. 2.
4th row: K. 2, work until 2 sts. remain, k. 2.***
Repeat 3rd and 4th rows, 20 (22) (24) times more—23 (25) (27) sts. Leave sts.

THE FRONT: Work as back to **.

1st pattern row: K. 29 (32) (35), p. 3, k. 3, p. 3, k. to end.
2nd row: P. 29 (32) (35), k. 3, p. 3, k. 3, p. to end.
3rd row: K. 29 (32) (35), p. 3, y.o.n., k. 3 tog., y.r.n., p. 3, k. to end.
4th row: As 2nd row.
These 4 rows form the pattern.
Pattern a further 24 (30) (36) rows.
Work as back from *** to ***.
Repeat 3rd and 4th rows, 11 (13) (15) times more, then the 3rd row again—39 (41) (43) sts.
To divide for neck: Next row: Work 14 and leave these sts. on a spare needle for right half neck, pattern 11 (13) (15) and leave on a st. holder, work to end and continue on these 14 sts. for left half neck.
The left half neck: To shape the neck and continue armhole shaping: Dec. 1 st. at armhole edge as before on next row, then on the 6 following alternate rows, *at the same time*, dec. 1 st. at neck edge on the first of these rows and then on the 3 following alternate rows—3 sts. ****
Next row: P. 1, k. 2.
Next row: K. 1, k. 2 tog.b.
Take remaining 2 sts. tog. and fasten off.
The right half neck: With right side of work facing, rejoin yarn to sts. on spare needle and work as left half neck to ****.
Next row: K. 2, p. 1.
Next row: K. 2, tog., k. 1.
Take remaining 2 sts. tog. and fasten off.

THE SLEEVES (both alike): With No. 10 (3¼ mm) needles cast on 40 (42) (44) sts. and work 8 rows in single rib.
Change to No. 8 (4 mm) needles.
Beginning with a k. row, s.s. 2 rows, then inc. 1 st. each end of next row, then on the 4 (5) (6) following 6th rows—50 (54) (58) sts.
S.s. 11 rows.
To shape the raglan sleeve top: Work as raglan armhole shaping on back, when 6 sts. will remain. Leave sts. on a safety pin.

THE NECK RIBBING: First join right raglan seams, then left sleeve to front only. With right side of work facing and using No. 10 (3¼ mm) needles, rejoin yarn and k. across 6 sts. of left sleeve, pick up and k. 18 sts. down left half neck, k. 11 (13) (15) sts. across front, pick up and k. 18 sts. up right half neck, k. 6 sts. across right sleeve, then k. 23

(25) (27) sts. across back neck—82 (86) (90) sts.

Work 12 rows in single rib. Cast off.

TO MAKE UP THE JERSEY: Press with a warm iron and a dry cloth. Join remaining raglan seam, continuing seam across neck ribbing. Join side and sleeve seams. Fold neck in half to wrong side and catch down.

SKIRT

TO MAKE: With No. 8 (4 mm) circular needle and g. cast on 270 (297) (297) sts.

1st row: K. 3, p. 3, * k. 6, p. 3; repeat from * until 3 sts. remain, k. 3.

2nd row: P. 3, k. 3 * p. 6, k. 3; repeat from * until 3 sts. remain, p. 3.

These 2 rows form the rib pattern.

Work a further 4 rows. Join in y.

Pattern 6 rows y., 4 rows g., 4 rows y., 2 rows g., 2 rows y. Break off y.

Work a further 26 (30) (38) rows.

Next row: Cast on 5 sts. for placket, pattern to end.

Work a further 3 rows.

Next (dec.) row: K. 8, * k. 3 tog., k. 1, k. 4 tog., k. 1: repeat from * until 6 sts. remain, k. 3 tog., k. 3—128 (140) (140) sts.

Change to No. 10 (3¼ mm) needles and beginning with a p. row, s.s. 5 rows.

1st buttonhole row: K. until 4 sts. remain, cast off 2, k. 1.

2nd buttonhole row: P. to end, casting on 2 sts. over those cast off in previous row.

K. 3 rows.

1st buttonhole row: P. 2, cast off 2, p. to end.

2nd buttonhole row: K. to end, casting on 2 sts. over those cast off in previous row.

S.s. 4 rows, then cast off.

TO MAKE UP THE SKIRT: Do not press. Join back seam as far as placket. Sew placket to inside. Fold waistband in half to wrong side and st. into place, neatening buttonhole. Add button. Thread elastic through waistband, join ends, then row ends of waistband.

Sweater with Duck Motifs

Illustrated on page 75

MEASUREMENTS	in centimetres (and inches, in brackets)					
To fit chest sizes	51	(20)	56	(22)	61	(24)
All round at underarms	54.5	(21½)	60	(23½)	65.5	(25¾)
Side seam	17.5	(7)	20.5	(8)	23	(9)
Length	30	(11¾)	34	(13¼)	38	(15)
Sleeve seam	17.5	(7)	20.5	(8)	23	(9)

MATERIALS: *Allow the following quantities in 50 g balls of Emu Supermatch Double Knitting: For any one size: 3 white and a small amount of the same yarn in yellow, red and black; a pair each of No. 8 (4 mm) and No. 10 (3¼ mm) knitting needles; 6 buttons.*

TENSION: *Work at a tension of 22 stitches and 29 rows to measure 10 × 10 cm, over the stocking stitch, using No. 8 (4 mm) needles, to obtain the measurements given above.*

ABBREVIATIONS: To be read before working: *K., knit plain; p., purl; st., stitch; tog., together; inc., increase (by working twice into same st.); dec., decrease (by taking 2 sts. tog.); s.s., stocking st. (k. on the right side and p. on the wrong side); single rib is k. 1 and p. 1 alternately; y.fwd., yarn forward to make a st.; w., white; r., red; y., yellow; bl., black.*

NOTE: *The instructions are given for the 51 cm (20 inch) size. Where they vary, work figures within first brackets for the 56 cm (22 inch) size; work figures within the second brackets for the 61 cm (24 inch) size.*

THE BACK: With No. 10 (3¼ mm) needles and w. cast on 60 (66) (72) sts. and work 10 rows in single rib. **★★**

Change to No. 8 (4 mm) needles and beginning with a k. row, s.s. 42 (50) (58) rows.

★★★ To shape the armholes: Cast off 3 sts. at the beginning of each of the next 2 rows, then dec. 1 st. at each end of the next row and the 3 (4) (4) following alternate rows—46 (50) (56) sts. **★★★**

S.s. a further 24 (26) (30) rows.

The shoulder edgings: Change to No. 10 (3¼ mm) needles and k. 5 rows.

Next row: Cast off 12 (13) (15) sts., k. 22 (24) (26), cast off 12 (13) (15) sts. Break off yarn.

With wrong side of work facing, rejoin yarn to the 22 (24) (26) sts. and k. 2 rows for back neckband. Cast off.

THE FRONT: Work as given for back to **★★**.

Change to No. 8 (4 mm) needles and beginning with a k. row, s.s. 10 rows.

Work the 16-row motif pattern, which is worked

Continued on page 74

entirely in s.s. beginning with a k. row, so only the colour details are given. Join in and break off colours as required and when changing from one colour to another, wind yarn round one just used to avoid a hole.

1st row: 3 (6) (9) w., 1 r., 7 w., 3 r., 3 w., 2 r., 4 w., 3 r., 8 w., 1 r., 3 w., 3 r., 7 w., 2 r., 3 w., 2 r., 5 (8) (11) w.

2nd row: 7 (10) (13) w., 1 r., 4 w., 1 r., 8 w., 1 r., 3 w., 1 r., 11 w., 1 r., 4 w., 1 r., 6 w., 1 r., 6 w., 1 r., 3 (6) (9) w.

3rd row: 3 (6) (9) w., 2 r., 1 w., 4 y., 8 w., 1 r., 1 w., 4 y., 10 w., 2 r., 4 y., 8 w., 1 r., 1 w., 3 y., 7 (10) (13) w.

4th row: 6 (9) (12) w., 5 y., 8 w., 6 y., 10 w., 6 y., 8 w., 6 y., 5 (8) (11) w.

5th row: 4 (7) (10) w., 8 y., 7 w., 2 y., 3 bl., 3 y., 8 w., 7 y., 1 w., 2 bl., 3 w., 7 y., 5 (8) (11) w.

6th row: 4 (7) (10) w., 1 bl., 4 y., 1 bl., 3 y., 3 w., 3 bl., 6 y., 7 w., 3 y., 3 bl., 3 y., 6 w., 9 y., 4 (7) (10) w.

7th row: 4 (7) (10) w., 1 y., 1 w., 2 y., 1 bl., 4 y., 5 w., 10 y., 7 w., 1 y., 1 w., 3 y., 3 bl., 6 w., 2 bl., 4 y., 2 bl., 3 (6) (9) w.

8th row: 6 (9) (12) w., 2 y., 2 w., 2 bl., 5 w., 5 y., 10 w., 6 y., 3 w., 1 y., 5 w., 4 y., 3 bl., 6 (9) (12) w.

9th row: 5 (8) (11) w., 3 bl., 1 w., 4 y., 4 y., 1 w., 1 r., 11 w., 3 y., 10 w., 4 y., 8 w., 3 y., 6 (9) (12) w.

10th row: 5 (8) (11) w., 5 y., 1 r., 7 w., 3 y., 7 w., 1 r., 1 w., 5 y., 10 w., 1 r., 3 y., 11 (14) (17) w.

11th row: 10 (13) (16) w., 5 y., 2 r., 8 w., 3 y., 1 bl., 1 y., 1 r., 8 w., 2 y., 9 w., 1 y., 1 bl., 3 y., 5 (8) (11) w.

12th row: 5 (8) (11) w., 5 y., 1 r., 8 w., 3 y., 6 w., 1 r., 1 w., 5 y., 10 w., 1 bl., 3 y., 10 (13) (16) w.

13th row: 10 (13) (16) w., 5 y., 11 w., 3 y., 8 w., 5 y., 1 w., 1 r., 5 w., 1 r., 1 w., 3 y., 6 (9) (12) w.

14th row: 17 (20) (23) w., 1 r., 1 y., 1 bl., 3 y., 23 w., 3 y., 11 (14) (17) w.

15th row: 37 (40) (43) w., 5 y., 1 w., 1 r., 16 (19) (22) w.

16th row: 19 (22) (25) w., 3 y., 38 (41) (44) w.

Break colours and continue with w. only.

Beginning with a k. row, s.s. 16 (24) (32) rows.

Work as given for back from ★★★ to ★★★.

S.s. 12 (12) (14) rows.

Divide sts. for front neck: Next row: P. 16 (18) (20) and leave these sts. on a spare needle for right front shoulder, p. 14 (14) (16) and leave these sts. on a st. holder for neckband, p. to end and work on these 16 (18) (20) sts. for left front shoulder.

The left front shoulder: To shape the neck: Dec. 1 st. at neck edge on each of the next 4 (5) (5) rows—12 (13) (15) sts.

S.s. 7 (8) (10) rows.

The shoulder edging: Change to No. 10 (3¼ mm) needles and k. 3 rows. ★★★

Buttonhole row: K. 4, (5) (5), ★ k. 2 tog., y.fwd., k. 2 (2) (3); repeat from ★ once.

K. 3 rows. Cast off.

The right front shoulder: With right side of work facing, rejoin yarn to inner end of sts. on spare needle and work as given for left front shoulder to ★★★.

Buttonhole row: ★ K. 2 (2) (3), y.fwd., k. 2 tog.; repeat from ★ once, k. 4 (5) (5).

K. 3 rows. Cast off.

THE FRONT NECKBAND: With right side of work facing and using No. 10 (3¼ mm) needles and w., pick up and k. 12 (14) (16) sts. down left front neck edge, k. across the 14 (14) (16) sts. at centre front, pick up and k. 12 (14) (16) sts. up right front neck edge—38 (42) (48) sts.

K. 1 row.

Buttonhole row: K. 2, y.fwd., k. 2 tog., k. until 4 sts. remain, k. 2 tog., y.fwd., k. 2.

K. 2 rows.
Cast off.

THE SLEEVES (both alike): With No. 10 (3¼ mm) needles and w. cast on 34 (36) (38) sts. and work 10 rows in single rib.

Change to No. 8 (4 mm) needles and, beginning with a k. row, s.s. 2 rows.

Continuing in s.s., inc. 1 st. at each end of the next row and the 4 (5) (5) following 8th rows—44 (48) (50) sts.

S.s. a further 11 (7) (15) rows.

To shape the sleeve top: Cast off 3 sts. at the beginning of the next 2 rows, then dec. 1 st. at each end of the next row and the 2 (2) (3) following 4th rows, and then at each end of the 6 (7) (5) following alternate rows. Dec. 1 st. at each end of the next 3 (3) (5) rows—14 (16) (16) sts.

Cast off.

TO MAKE UP THE SWEATER: Press work lightly on the wrong side, using a cool iron over a dry cloth. Overlap front shoulder edging over back and catch together at shoulder edge. Set in sleeves, then join sleeve and side seams. Add buttons.

Opposite *Sweater with Duck Motifs (page 73)*

Finger Puppet Sweaters

Illustrated on page 78

MEASUREMENTS	in centimetres *(and inches, in brackets)*		
To fit chest sizes	51 (20)	56 (22)	61 (24)
All round at underarms	54.5 (21½)	60 (23½)	65.5 (25½)
Side seam	18 (7)	20.5 (8)	22.5 (9)
Length	31 (12¼)	34 (13½)	37.5 (14¾)
Sleeve seam	24.5 (9½)	26.5 (10½)	28.5 (11¼)

MATERIALS: *Allow the following quantities in 50 g balls of Wendy Family Choice D.K.:* 3 *main for* 51 *cm and* 56 *cm sizes;* 3 *main for* 61 *cm size. For any one size: A pair each of No.* 8 (4 *mm) and No.* 10 (3¼ *mm) knitting needles; oddments of yarn in contrasting colours; thread for features; felt, lace, ribbon and wadding; a* 10 *cm (*4 *inch) slide fastener.*

TENSION: *Work at a tension of* 22 *stitches and* 28 *rows to measure* 10 × 10 *cm, over the stocking stitch, using No.* 8 (4 *mm) needles, to obtain measurements given above.*

ABBREVIATIONS: To be read before working: *K., knit plain; p., purl; st., stitch; tog., together; k.lb., k. into back of next st.; t.s.r., twisted single rib (k.lb. and p.* 1 *alternately); s.s., stocking st. (k. on right side and p. on wrong side); inc., increase (by working twice into next st.); k.* 2 *tog.b., k.* 2 *tog. through back of sts.; m.st., moss st.; dec., decrease (by taking* 2 *sts. tog.); br., brown; w., white; m., main; bl., blue; pk., pink; y., yellow.*

NOTE: *The instructions are given for the* 51 *cm (*20 *inch) chest size. Where they vary, work figures within first brackets for the* 56 *cm (*22 *inch) chest size; work figures within second brackets for the* 61 *cm (*24 *inch) chest size.*

CATS IN BASKET SWEATER

THE BACK: With No. 10 (3¼ mm) needles and m. cast on 60 (66) (72) sts. and work 14 rows in t.s.r.

Change to No. 8 (4 mm) needles and beginning with a k. row, s.s. 38 (44) (50) rows.

To shape raglan armholes: 1st and 2nd rows: Cast off 3 (4) (4) sts., s.s. to end.

3rd row: K. 2, k. 2 tog.b., k. until 4 sts. remain, k. 2 tog., k. 2.

4th row: P. to end.

Repeat 3rd and 4th rows, 16 (17) (19) times more.

Break yarn and leave remaining 20 (22) (24) sts. on a spare needle.

THE SLEEVES (both alike): With No. 10 (3¼ mm) needles and m. cast on 34 (36) (38) sts. and work 14 rows in t.s.r.

Change to No. 8 (4 mm) needles and working in s.s., inc. 1 st. each end of next row and the 8 (9) (10) following 6th rows—52 (56) (60) sts.

S.s. 7 rows.

To shape raglan sleeve top: Work as given for raglan armhole shaping on back when 12 sts. will remain.

Break yarn and leave sts. on safety pin.

THE FRONT: Work as given for back to armholes.

To shape raglan armholes: Work 1st to 4th armhole shaping rows of back.

Repeat 3rd and 4th rows, 10 (11) (13) times more, then 3rd row again—30 (32) (34) sts.

To divide for neck: Next row: P. 11 and leave on spare needle for right front neck, p. 8 (10) (12) and leave on a st. holder, p. to end and work on these last 11 sts. for left front neck.

The left front neck: Continue decreasing at raglan edge as before on next row and 4 following alternate rows, *at the same time*, dec. 1 st. at neck edge on the first 4 of these rows—2 sts.

P. 1 row, then k. remaining 2 sts. tog. and fasten off.

The right front neck: With right side facing, rejoin m. to inner end of sts. on spare needle and work as left front neck, to end.

THE NECK RIBBING: First join right raglan seams, then left sleeve to front only.

With No. 10 (3¼ mm) needles and m., rejoin yarn, and k. across 12 sts. at top of left sleeve, pick up and k. 10 sts. from row ends of left front neck, k. across 8 (10) (12) sts. at front, pick up and k. 10 sts. from row ends of right front neck, k. across 12 sts. from top of right sleeve, and finally, k. across 20 (22) (24) sts. of back—72 (76) (80) sts.

Work 7 rows in t.s.r. Cast off in rib.

TO MAKE UP THE SWEATER: Press lightly with a warm iron over a dry cloth. Join remaining raglan seam, leaving 10 cm free at neck edge. Join side and sleeve seams. Insert slide fastener.

THE BASKET: With No. 8 (4 mm) needles and y. cast on 10 sts.

1st (m.st.) row: *K. 1, p. 1; repeat from * to end.

2nd row: Inc., k. 1, * p. 1, k. 1; repeat from * to end.

3rd row: Inc., * p. 1, k. 1; repeat from * to end.

4th row: Inc., k. 1, * k. 1, p. 1; repeat from * to end.

5th row: Inc., * k. 1, p. 1; repeat from * to end.

Repeat 2nd to 5th rows, once, then 2nd and 3rd rows again—20 sts.

Work 4 rows straight.

Cast off. Sew to centre front of sweater beginning 1 cm up from top of ribbing. Embroider a y. handle in chain st., then using oddments embroider flowers each side in lazy daisy and straight sts.

THE SMALL CAT: The back: Using No. 10 (3¼ mm) needles and br. cast on 7 sts. and k. 14 rows, then s.s. 8 rows for head.

Break yarn and leave sts.

The front: Work as back, but using br. for 1st 6 rows, w. for next 14 rows and br. for final 2 rows.

The tail: With No. 10 (3¼ mm) needles and br. cast on 12 sts. then cast off k. wise.

TO COMPLETE: Join side seams. Run a thread through all top sts., draw up and fasten off. Stuff head lightly then tie lightly round at base of head. Sew tail to base of back. Cut 2 small ovals of br. felt and sew on for ears. Embroider features and whiskers with black thread.

THE LARGE CAT: Work as a small cat but using No. 8 (4 mm) needles throughout, and using black ovals of felt for eyes. Insert cats into basket.

TWINS IN PRAM SWEATER

THE SWEATER: Work as cats in basket sweater.
THE PRAM: With No. 8 (4 mm) needles and br. cast on 12 sts. and working in s.s., k. 1 row, then inc. 1 st. each end of the next 3 rows, then at end only of the next row—19 sts.

S.s. 5 rows, then cast off 11 sts. at beginning of next row—8 sts.

S.s. 6 rows, then dec. 1 st. at beginning of next row and following alternate row.

Work 1 row, then cast off remaining 6 sts.

Sew to front of sweater. With br. embroider wheels and handle in chain st., then using oddments embroider flowers and leaves in French knots and straight sts.

THE GIRL TWIN: The back: With No. 10 (3¼ mm) needles and w. work as back of small cat.

The front: Work as back but using w. for 1st 14 rows and pk. for last 8 rows.

Make up as for cat. Embroider hair with yellow, and eyes and mouth with cotton. Gather a short length of narrow lace and sew to join of head. Make and add a small bow at neck.

THE BOY TWIN: Work as girl twin but using bl. in place of w.

Make up as for girl twin, but using br. for hair and a 3 cm (1¼ inch) diameter circle of blue felt for hat. Tuck twins in pram.

FROGS SWEATER

THE SWEATER: Work back and sleeves as cats in basket sweater.

THE POCKET BACKS (2 alike): With No. 8 (4 mm) needles and m. cast on 12 sts. and s.s. 11 rows.

Break yarn and leave on a spare needle.

THE FRONT: With No. 10 (3¼ mm) needles and m. cast on 60 (66) (72) sts. and work 14 rows in t.s.r.

Change to No. 8 (4 mm) needles and beginning with a k. row., s.s. 2 rows. Join in w.

1st pattern row: K. 22 (25) (28) m., 16 w., 22 (25) (28) m.

2nd and 3rd rows: 21 (24) (27) m., 1 w., 16 m., 1 w., 21 (24) (27) m.

4th and 5th rows: 22 (25) (28) m., 1 w., 14 m., 1 w., 22 (25) (28) m.

6th row: 9 (12) (15) m., 13 w., 16 m., 13 w., 9 (12) (15) m.

7th and 8th rows: 8 (11) (14) m., 1 w., 42 m., 1 w., 8 (11) (14) m.

Break off w. and continue with m. only.

Work 1 row.

To divide for pockets: Next row: P. 9 (12) (15), * slip next 12 sts. on to st. holder and leave at right side of work and in their place p. across 12 sts. of one pocket back *, p. 18, repeat from * to * once, p. 9 (12) (15).

S.s. 26 (32) (38) rows.

Shape armholes and complete sweater as given for cats in basket sweater.

THE POCKET TOPS (2 alike): With wrong side facing, rejoin m. and using No. 8 (4 mm) needles, work 4 rows in t.s.r.

Cast off in rib. Sew down row ends on right side and pocket backs to wrong side.

THE FROGS: Work as small and large cats but using green throughout. Cut 2 small ovals of white felt and sew in place for eyes, then 2 smaller pieces in black and sew to lower sections of white felt. Embroider mouth with yellow thread. Cut 2 small triangles of green felt for hands, cut a "v" in one edge and sew opposite point to puppets. Embroider bullrushes and leaves either side of pockets. Insert frogs into pockets.

FOOTBALLERS SWEATER

THE SWEATER: Work as frogs sweater, but in m. throughout.

Embroider goal post round one pocket in w. chain st. and grass in straight sts.

FOOTBALLERS: With No. 10 (3¼ mm) needles and bl. cast on 14 sts. and s.s. 6 rows bl., 2 rows w., 2 rows bl., 2 rows w. and 6 rows pk.

Break yarn leaving an end. Run end through remaining sts., draw up and fasten off then join side seam. Stuff head lightly then tie tightly round at base of head. Embroider hair with br. and eyes and nose with thread. Cut a small badge shape in w. felt and sew on with coloured thread.

Make another footballer but using red instead of bl. Make a small pompon with br. for football. Place footballers and football in pockets.

Above and left *Finger Puppet Sweaters, including Cats in Basket Sweater (page 76), and Twins in Pram Sweater, Frogs Sweater and Footballers Sweater (page 77).*
Opposite *Sweater (page 80) and Dungarees (page 81)*

Sweater and Dungarees

Illustrated on page 79 and opposite

MEASUREMENTS	\multicolumn{6}{c}{*in centimetres (and inches, in brackets)*}					
To fit chest sizes	51	(20)	56	(22)	61	(24)
SWEATER						
All round at underarms	53	(20¾)	58	(22¾)	63	(24¾)
Side seam	19	(7½)	22.5	(8¾)	24	(9½)
Length	29	(11½)	33.5	(13¼)	36.5	(14¼)
Sleeve seam	23	(9)	26.5	(10¼)	30	(11¾)
DUNGAREES						
Length, from waist to ankle, including ribbing	43.5	(17)	51	(20)	58.5	(23)
Length, from crotch to ankle, including ribbing	25	(9¾)	30	(11¾)	35	(13¾)

MATERIALS: *Allow the following quantities in 50 g balls of Wendy Family Choice Double Knit: Sweater: 2 blue, 1 white for 51 cm size; 3 blue, 1 white for 56 cm size; 3 blue, 2 white for 61 cm size; a press fastener. Dungarees: 3 blue, 1 white for 51 cm size; 4 blue, 1 white for 56 cm size; 4 blue, 1 white for 61 cm size; 8 buttons. For any one size or garment: a pair each of No. 9 (3¾ mm) and No. 10 (3¼ mm) needles.*

TENSION: *Work at a tension of 24 stitches and 35 rows to measure 10 × 10 cm over the pattern, and 24 stitches and 32 rows to measure 10 × 10 cm over the stocking stitch, using No. 9 (3¾ mm) needles, to obtain measurements given above.*

ABBREVIATIONS: To be read before working: *K., knit plain; p., purl; st., stitch; tog., together; inc., increase (by working twice into next st.); dec., decrease (by working 2 stitches tog.); s.s., stocking st. (k. on right side and p. on wrong side); y.r.n., yarn round needle to make a st.; s.k.p.o., slip 1, k. 1, pass slipped st. over; single rib is k. 1 and p. 1 alternately; b., blue; w., white; nil, meaning nothing is worked here for this size.*

NOTE: *The instructions are given for the 51 cm (20 inch) size. Where they vary, work figures within first brackets for 56 cm (22 inch) size, and so on.*

THE SWEATER

Illustrated on page 81

THE BACK: With No. 10 (3¼ mm) needles and b. cast on 64 (70) (76) sts. and work 12 rows in single rib.

Change to No. 9 (3¾ mm) needles and work the 6-row pattern as follows:

1st to 4th rows: S.s. 4 rows b. Join in w.

5th and 6th rows: K. 2 rows in w.

Pattern a further 48 (60) (66) rows. ★★

To shape the raglan armholes: Cast off 3 sts. at beginning of next 2 rows, then dec. 1 st. each end of next row and then on the 16 (18) (20) following alternate rows—24 (26) (28) sts.

Work 1 row, then leave sts. on a spare needle.

THE FRONT: Work as back to ★★.

To shape the raglan armholes: Cast off 3 sts. at beginning of next 2 rows, then dec. 1 st. each end of next row and then on the 8 (10) (12) following alternate rows— 40 (42) (44) sts.

To divide for neck: Next row: Pattern 12 and leave these sts. on a safety pin for right half neck, pattern 16 (18) (20) and leave these sts. on a st. holder, pattern to end and work on these 12 sts. for left half neck.

The left half neck: Dec. 1 st. each end of next row, then on the 2 following alternate rows and then at armhole edge only on the 4 following alternate rows—2 sts.

Work 1 row, then k. 2 tog. and fasten off.

The right half neck: With right side of work facing, rejoin yarn to the 12 sts. left on safety pin and work as left half neck.

THE SLEEVES (both alike): With No. 10 (3¼ mm) needles and b. cast on 30 (32) (36) sts. and work 19 rows in single rib.

Inc. row: Rib 4 (2) (4), ★ inc., rib 2; repeat from ★ until 2 (nil) (2) sts. remain, rib 2 (nil) (2)—38 (42) (46) sts.

Change to No. 9 (3¾ mm) needles and, working in pattern as given for back, work 6 rows, then inc. 1 st. each end of next row and then on the 5 following 6th rows—50 (54) (58) sts. Pattern 23 (35) (47) rows.

To shape the raglan sleeve top: Work as raglan armhole shaping on back—10 sts.

Work 1 row, then leave sts.

THE NECK RIBBING: First join right sleeve to back and front, then left sleeve to front only. With right side of work facing and using No. 10 (3¼ mm) needles, rejoin b. and k. across 10 sts. of left sleeve, pick up and k. 15 sts. down left front neck, k. across 16 (18) (20) sts. at centre front, pick up and k. 15 sts. up right front neck, k. across 10 sts. of right sleeve, k. across 24 (26) (28) sts. of back, then finally cast on 4 sts. for placket—94 (98) (102) sts.

Work 6 rows in single rib. Cast off.

TO MAKE UP THE SWEATER: Press with a warm iron over a dry cloth. Join remaining raglan seam, leaving ribbing at neck free. Join side and sleeve seams. Close neck ribbing with a press fastener.

THE DUNGAREES
Illustrated on page 79

THE FRONT: The right leg: With No. 10 (3¼ mm) needles and b. cast on 16 (18) (18) sts. and work 11 rows in single rib, increasing 1 st. at the end of the last of these rows on the 61 cm size only—16 (18) (19) sts.

Inc. row: Inc. into each st. to end—32 (36) (38) sts.

Change to No. 9 (3¾ mm) needles and, beginning with a k. row, s.s. 70 (86) (102) rows. Leave sts. on a spare needle.

The left leg: Work as right leg, then continue as follows:

Next (joining) row: K. across 32 (36) (38) sts. of left leg, cast on 10 sts., k. across 32 (36) (38) sts. of right leg—74 (82) (86) sts.

Next row: All p.

To shape for crotch: 1st row: K. 31 (35) (37), s.k.p.o., k. 8, k. 2 tog., k. to end.

2nd and alternate rows: All p.

3rd row: K. 31 (35) (37), s.k.p.o., k. 6. k. 2 tog., k. to end.

5th row: K. 31 (35) (37), s.k.p.o., k. 4, k. 2 tog., k. to end.

7th row: K. 31 (35) (37), s.k.p.o., k. 2, k. 2 tog., k. to end.

9th row: K. 31 (35) (37), s.k.p.o., k. 2 tog., k. to end—64 (72) (76) sts.

S.s. 41 (49) (57) rows—s.s. 40 (48) (56) rows here when working front. ★★★

THE WAIST RIBBING: Change to No. 10 (3¼ mm) needles and work 2 rows in single rib.

1st buttonhole row: Rib 3, y.r.n. twice, k. 2 tog., rib until 5 sts. remain, p. 2 tog., y.r.n. twice, rib 3.

2nd buttonhole row: Rib to end, dropping extra loops off needle.

Rib 2 rows.

Work the 2 buttonhole rows once.

Next row: Cast off 8 sts., rib to end.

Next row: Cast off 9 sts., rib to end—47 (55) (59) sts.

THE BIB: Change to No. 9 (3¾ mm) needles and continue as follows:

1st row: K. 1, p. 1, k. 1, p. 2 tog., k. until 5 sts. remain, p. 2 tog., k. 1, p. 1, k. 1.

2nd row: P. 1, k. 1, p. 1, k. 1, p. until 4 sts. remain, k. 1, p. 1, k. 1, p. 1.

3rd row: Rib 4, k. until 4 sts. remain, rib 4.

4th row: Rib 4, p. until 4 sts. remain, rib 4. Repeat the last 4 rows, 6 (8) (9) times more—33 (37) (39) sts.

Work the 3rd and 4th rows, once.

Work the 1st and 2nd rows, once—31 (35) (37) sts.

Next row: K. 1, * p. 1, k. 1; repeat from * to end. **Next row:** P. 1, * k. 1, p. 1; repeat from * to end.

1st buttonhole row: K. 1, k. 2 tog., y.r.n. twice, p. 1, k. 1, k. 2 tog., y.r.n. twice, rib until 7 sts. remain, y.r.n. twice, p. 2 tog., k. 1, p. 1, y.r.n. twice, p. 2 tog., k. 1.

Rib 2 rows, dropping extra loops on the first of these rows. Cast off in rib.

THE BACK: Work as front to ★★★, noting variation.

1st and 2nd turning rows: P. until 8 sts. remain, turn, k. until 8 sts. remain, turn.

3rd and 4th turning rows: P. until 16 sts. remain, turn k. until 16 sts. remain, turn.

5th and 6th turning rows: P. until 24 sts. remain, turn, k. until 24 sts. remain, turn.

Next row: P. across all sts., turn and cast on 4 sts. placket—68 (76) (80) sts.

Next row: * K. 1, p. 1; repeat from * to end, turn and cast on 4 sts. for placket—72 (80) (84) sts.

Next row: * K. 1, p. 1; repeat from * to end. Rib a further 7 rows. Cast off in rib.

THE STRAPS (2 alike): With No. 10 (3¼ mm) needles and b. cast on 9 sts. and, beginning odd-numbered rows with k. 1, and even-numbered rows with p. 1, continue in single rib until work measures 26 (29) (33) cm in length. Cast off in rib.

THE POCKETS (2 alike): With No. 9 (3¾ mm) needles and b. cast on 20 sts. and work 24 rows in pattern as given for back of sweater.

Change to No. 10 (3¼ mm) needles and, continuing in b. only, k. 1 row, then work 2 rows in single rib. Cast off in rib.

TO MAKE UP THE DUNGAREES: Press as for sweater. Sew side seams and inside leg seams. Sew one end of each strap to inside of back waist ribbing, placing straps 6 (7) (8) cm apart. Sew 2 buttons on free end of each strap and 2 buttons on both plackets of back waist ribbing, to correspond with buttonholes. Sew one pocket on right front and on left back.

Above *Pink Lacy Sweater*

Pink Lacy Sweater

Illustrated opposite

MEASUREMENTS	in centimetres (and inches, in brackets)					
To fit chest sizes	51	(20)	56	(22)	61	(24)
All round at underarms	54	(21¼)	59	(23¼)	64.5	(25½)
Side seam	19	(7½)	23	(9)	25	(9¾)
Length	32	(12½)	37.5	(14¾)	41.5	(16¼)
Sleeve seam	18	(7)	22	(8½)	24	(9½)

MATERIALS: *Allow the following quantities in 40 g balls of Richard Poppleton Spoton Double Knitting: 4 for 51 cm size; 5 for 56 cm size; 6 for 61 cm size. For any one size: A pair each of No. 8 (4 mm) and No. 10 (3¼ mm) knitting needles; a cable needle.*

TENSION: *Work at a tension of 31 stitches and 29 rows to measure 10 × 10 cm, over the pattern slightly stretched, using No. 8 (4 mm) needles, to obtain the measurements given above.*

ABBREVIATIONS: To be read before working: *K., knit plain; p., purl; st., stitch; tog., together; dec., decrease (by working 2 sts. tog.); c.4f., cable 4 front (slip next 2 sts. on to cable needle and leave at front of work, k. 2, then k.2 from cable needle); up 1, pick up loop lying between needles and k. or p. into back of it; y.fwd., yarn forward to make a st.; s.k.p.o., slip 1, k. 1, pass slipped st. over; single rib is k. 1 and p. 1 alternately.*

NOTE: *Instructions are given for the 51 cm (20 inch) size. Where they vary, work figures within first brackets for the 56 cm (22 inch) size; work figures within second brackets for 61 cm (24 inch) size.*

THE BACK: With No. 10 (3¼ mm) needles cast on 68 (74) (82) sts. and work 13 rows in single rib.

Increase row: Rib 4 (3) (7), up 1, * rib 4, up 1; repeat from * 14 (16) (16) times, rib 4 (3) (7)—84 (92) (100) sts.

Change to No. 8 (4 mm) needles and work the 8-row pattern as follows:

1st row: P. 2, * k. 4, p. 3 (4) (5), k. 9, p. 3 (4) (5); repeat from * until 6 sts. remain, k. 4, p. 2.

2nd and alternate rows: K. 2, * p. 4, k. 3 (4) (5), p. 9, k. 3 (4) (5); repeat from * until 6 sts. remain, p. 4, k. 2.

3rd row: P. 2, * c.4f., p. 3 (4) (5), k. 4, y.fwd., s.k.p.o., k. 3, p. 3 (4) (5); repeat from * until 6 sts. remain, c.4f., p. 2.

5th row: P. 2, * k. 4, p. 3 (4) (5), k. 2, k. 2 tog., y.fwd., k. 1, y.fwd., s.k.p.o., k. 2, p. 3 (4) (5); repeat from * until 6 sts. remain, k. 4, p. 2.

7th row: P. 2, * c.4f., p. 3 (4) (5), k. 1, k. 2 tog., y.fwd., k. 3, y.fwd., s.k.p.o., k. 1, p. 3 (4) (5); repeat from * until 6 sts. remain, c.4f., p. 2.

8th row: As 2nd row.

Pattern a further 34 (46) (52) rows. **

To shape the raglan armholes: Cast off 4 (4) (5) sts. at beginning of next 2 rows, then dec. 1 st. each end of next row and then on the 12 (13) (17) following alternate rows—50 (56) (54) sts.

Work 1 row.

Dec. 1 st. each end of next 10 (12) (10) rows—30 (32) (34) sts.

Leave sts. on a spare needle.

THE FRONT: Work as back to **.

To shape the raglan armholes: Cast off 4 (4) (5) sts. at beginning of next 2 rows, then dec. 1 st. each end of next row and the 10 (11) (14) following alternate rows—54 (60) (60) sts.

To divide for neck: Next row: Pattern 20 (22) (21) and leave these sts. on a spare needle for right half neck, pattern 14 (16) (18) and leave these sts. on a st. holder, pattern to end and work on these 20 (22) (21) sts. for left half neck.

The left half neck: Dec. 1 st. at armhole edge on the next row, then on the 2 (2) (3) following alternate rows and then on the following 9 (11) (9) rows, *at the same time*, dec. 1 st. at neck edge on the 1st 6 of these rows—2 sts.

K. 2 tog. and fasten off.

The right half neck: With right side of work facing rejoin yarn to sts. on spare needle and work as left half neck, to end.

THE SLEEVES (both alike): With No. 10 (3¼ mm) needles cast on 36 (38) (40) sts. and work 11 rows in single rib.

Increase row: Rib 4 (3) (2), up 1, * rib 1, up 1; repeat from * until 4 (3) (2) sts. remain, rib to end—65 (71) (77) sts.

Change to No. 8 (4 mm) needles and work 42 (54) (60) rows in pattern as given for back.

To shape the sleeve top: Cast off 4 (4) (5) sts. at beginning of next 2 rows, then dec. 1 st. each end of next row and then on the 11 (12) (16) following alternate rows and then on the following 13 (15) (13) rows—7 sts.

Leave sts. on a safety pin.

THE NECK RIBBING: First join right raglan seams, then left sleeve to front only. With right side of work facing and using No. 10 (3¼ mm) needles, rejoin yarn and k. 7 sts. across left sleeve, pick up and k. 10 (12) (12) sts. down left half neck, k. 14 (16) (18) sts. across front, decreasing 2 sts. evenly across these sts., pick up and k. 10 (12) (12) sts. up right half neck, k. 7 sts. across right sleeve, then k. 30 (32) (34) sts. across back neck decreasing 2 sts. evenly across these sts.—74 (82) (86) sts.

Work 15 rows in single rib.

Cast off loosely in rib.

TO MAKE UP THE SWEATER: Do not press. Join remaining raglan seam, continuing seam across neck ribbing. Join sleeve and side seams. Fold neck ribbing in half to wrong side and lightly sew into place.

Sailor Dress

Illustrated on page 86

MEASUREMENTS	in centimetres (and inches, in brackets)			
To fit chest sizes	56	(22)	61	(24)
All round at lower edge	84	(33)	89.5	(35¼)
Side seam	25	(10)	27.5	(10¾)
Length	35	(13¾)	38.5	(15¼)
Sleeve seam	19.5	(7¾)	21	(8¼)

MATERIALS: *Allow the following quantities in 50 g balls of Hayfield Grampian Perle 4-ply: 2 main and 1 contrast for the 56 cm and 61 cm sizes. For either size: a pair each of No. 10 (3¼ mm) and No. 12 (2¾ mm) needles; 2 buttons.*

TENSION: *Work at a tension of 30 stitches and 35 rows to measure 10 × 10 cm over the broad rib pattern, and 18 rows to measure 5 cm in depth over the striped pattern, using No. 10 (3¼ mm) needles, to obtain the measurements given above.*

ABBREVIATIONS: To be read before working: *K., knit plain; p., purl; st., stitch; tog., together; inc., increase (by working twice into same st.); dec., decrease (by taking 2 sts. tog.); g.st., garter st. (k. plain on every row); single rib is k. 1 and p. 1 alternately; s.s., stocking st. (k. on the right side and p. on the wrong side); up 1, pick up loop lying between needles and k. or p. into back of it; s.k.p.o., slip 1, k. 1, pass slipped stitch over; m., main; c., contrast.*

NOTE: *The instructions are given for the 56 cm (22 inch) size. Where they vary, work the figures within brackets for 61 cm (26 inch) size.*

THE BACK: With 12 (2¾ mm) needles and m. cast on 126 (134) sts. and k. 6 rows.

Change to No. 10 (3¼ mm) needles.

1st row: K. 3 (7), * p. 1, k. 6; repeat from * until 4 (8) sts. remain, p. 1 k. 3 (7).

2nd row: P. 3 (7), * k. 1, p. 6; repeat from * until 4 (8) sts. remain, k. 1, p. 3 (7).

Pattern a further 79 (87) rows.

Next (dec.) row: P. 3 (5), * p. 2 tog.; repeat from * until 3 (5) sts. remain, p. to end—66 (72) sts.

Change to No. 12 (2¾ mm) needles and work 4 rows in single rib. **★★**

Change to No. 10 (3¼ mm) needles join in c. and work in following striped sequence.

With c., s.s. 10 rows. With m., k. 2 rows.

Continuing in the striped sequence, pattern a further 20 (24) rows.

To slope the shoulders: Cast off 11 (12) sts. at the beginning of each of the next 2 rows, then 10 (11) sts. at the beginning of each of the next 2 rows. Cast off 24 (26) sts.

THE FRONT: Work as back to **★★**.

Change to No. 10 (3¼ mm) needles.

With c., k. 1 row.

Divide sts. for front neck: Next row: With c., p. 33 (36) and leave these sts. on a spare needle for right half front, p. to end and work on these 33 (36) sts. for left half front.

The left half front: To shape the neck: Maintaining continuity of the striped sequence to match back, dec. 1 st. at neck edge on the next row and the 11 (12) following alternate rows—21 (23) sts.

Pattern 7 (9) rows—pattern 8 (10) rows here when working right half front.

To slope the shoulder: Cast off 11 (12) sts. at beginning of next row—10 (11) sts.

Work 1 row. Cast off.

The right half front: With right side of work facing, rejoin c. yarn to inner end of sts. on spare needle and work as given for left half front, noting variation.

THE SLEEVES (both alike): With No. 12 (2¾ mm) needles and m. cast on 34 (36) sts. and work 9 rows in single rib.

Next (increase) row: Rib 3 (4) * up 1, rib 9; repeat from * twice, up 1, rib 4 (5)—38 (40) sts.

Change to No. 10 (3¼ mm) needles and, working in the same striped sequence as given on back, pattern 2 rows.

Maintaining continuity of the striped sequence, inc. 1 st. at each end of the next row and the 11 (13) following 4th rows—62 (68) sts.

Pattern a further 17 (13) rows. Cast off.

THE INSET: With No. 10 (3¼ mm) needles and c. cast on 15 sts. and work 4 rows in g.st.

P. 1 row.

To shape sides: 1st row: S.k.p.o., k. until 2 sts. remain, k. 2 tog. **2nd row:** P.

Repeat the last 2 rows, 4 times, then the 1st row again—3 sts.

P. 1 row. Take 3 sts. tog. and fasten off.

THE COLLAR: With No. 10 (3¼ mm) needles and m. cast on 48 (50) sts. and work 38 rows in g.st.

Divide for neck: Next row: K. 12 and leave these sts. on a safety pin for 2nd side, cast off 24 (26) sts., k. to end and work on these 12 sts. for 1st side of collar.

The 1st side of collar: G.st. 24 (28) rows.

★★★ To shape the collar: 1st row: Dec., k. to end. **2nd row:** All k.

Repeat the last 2 rows, 8 times, then the 1st row again. Take 2 sts. tog. and fasten off.

The 2nd side of collar: With wrong side facing, rejoin m. to inner end of sts. on safety pin, cast off 9 sts. for opening, then k. 2.

Next row: K. 3, turn, cast on 9 sts.—12 sts.

G.st. 23 (27) rows. Work as given for 1st side of collar from **★★★** to end.

THE BOW: With No. 10 (3¼ mm) needles and c. cast on 40 sts. and g.st. 5 rows. Cast off.

TO MAKE UP THE DRESS: Press work lightly on the wrong side, using a warm iron over a dry cloth. Join left shoulder seam, then right shoulder seam for 2 cm ($\frac{3}{4}$ inch) from shoulder edge. Set in sleeves to row ends above rib on back and front, gathering sleeves lightly at shoulder seams to fit. Join sleeve and side seams. Sew cast off group at centre of collar to cast off group of back neck on the right side, then sew inner row ends of collar sides to shaped row ends of V-neck. Sew shaped edges of inset inside V-neck. Fold c. strip into a bow and secure by winding several strands of c. yarn round centre, then sew into position. Close shoulder opening on collar with a button and loop at shoulder edge, then close right shoulder seam with a button and loop in centre of opening.

Blue/White Sweater
Illustrated on page 87

MEASUREMENTS								
To fit chest sizes	56	(22)	61	(24)	66	(26)	71	(28)
All round at underarms	58.5	(23)	63	($24\frac{3}{4}$)	68	($26\frac{3}{4}$)	73	($28\frac{3}{4}$)
Side seam	19	($7\frac{1}{2}$)	21	($8\frac{1}{4}$)	23	(9)	25	($9\frac{3}{4}$)
Length	34	($13\frac{1}{2}$)	37.5	($14\frac{3}{4}$)	41	($16\frac{1}{4}$)	44.5	($17\frac{1}{2}$)
Sleeve seam	25.5	(10)	27.5	($10\frac{3}{4}$)	29.5	($11\frac{1}{2}$)	32	($12\frac{1}{2}$)

in centimetres (and inches, in brackets)

MATERIALS: *Allow the following quantities in 20 g balls of Wendy Peter Pan Darling Double Knit or Peter Pan Darling Dolly Mixtures Double Knit: 5 main and 2 contrast for the 56 cm size; 6 main and 2 contrast for the 61 cm size; 7 main and 3 contrast for the 66 cm size; 8 main and 4 contrast for the 71 cm size. For any one size: A pair each of No. 8 (4 mm) and No. 10 ($3\frac{1}{4}$ mm) knitting needles.*

TENSION: *Work at a tension of 25 stitches and 28 rows to measure 10 × 10 cm, over the stocking stitch, using No. 8 (4 mm) needles, to obtain the measurements given above.*

ABBREVIATIONS: To be read before working: K., knit plain; p., purl; st., stitch; tog., together; inc., increase *(by working twice into same st.)*; dec., decrease *(by working 2 sts. tog.)*; s.s., stocking st. *(k. on the right side and p. on the wrong side)*; single rib is k. 1 and p. 1 alternately; up 1, pick up loop lying between needles, then k. into back of it; m., main colour; c., contrast colour.

NOTE: *The instructions are given for the 56 cm (22 inch) size. Where they vary, work figures within the first brackets for the 61 cm (24 inch) size, and so on.*

THE BACK: With No. 10 ($3\frac{1}{4}$ mm) needles and m. cast on 73 (79) (85) (91) sts. and, beginning odd-numbered rows with k. 1 and even-numbered rows with p. 1, work 16 rows in single rib.

Change to No. 8 (4 mm) needles and work the 2-colour pattern, which is worked entirely in s.s. beginning with a k. row, so only the colour details are given.

1st and 2nd rows: All m.
3rd and 4th rows: All c.
5th and 6th rows: All m.
7th and 8th rows: 1 m., * 5 c., 1 m.; repeat from * to end.
9th row: 1 m., * 2 c., 1 m.; repeat from * to end.
10th row: 1 m., * 1 c., 3 m., 1 c., 1 m.; repeat from * to end.
11th row: As 9th row.

12th row: As 7th and 8th rows.
13th row: 2 m., * 3 c., 3 m.; repeat from * until 5 sts. remain, 3 c., 2 m.
14th row: 1 c., * 2 m., 1 c.; repeat from * to end.
15th row: 2 c., * 3 m., 3 c.; repeat from * until 5 sts. remain, 3 m., 2 c.
16th row: 3 c., * 1 m., 5 c.; repeat from * until 4 sts. remain, 1 m., 3 c. Break off m.
Continuing in c. only, s.s. 10 (16) (22) (28) rows.
Rejoin m. and work the 16th row back to 3rd row in that reverse order. Break off c. and continue with m. only.

To shape the armholes: Cast off 6 sts. at the beginning of each of the next 2 rows, then dec. 1 st. at each end of the next 6 (7) (8) (9) rows—49 (53) (57) (61) sts.
S.s. 28 (31) (34) (37) rows.

To slope the shoulders: Cast off 4 (5) (6) (6) sts. at the beginning of each of the next 2 rows and 5 (5) (6) (7) sts. at the beginning of the next 2 rows, and 5 (6) (6) (7) sts. at beginning of each of the following 2 rows.
Leave remaining 21 sts. on a spare needle.

THE FRONT: Work as given for back until armhole shaping has been completed.
S.s. 11 (12) (13) (14) rows.
Divide sts. for front neck: Next row: P. 18 (20) (22) (24) and leave these sts. on a spare needle for right front shoulder, p. 13 and leave these sts. on a st. holder for polo collar, p. to end and work on these 18 (20) (22) (24) sts. for left front shoulder.
The left front shoulder: To shape the neck: Dec. 1 st. at neck edge on each of the next 4 rows—14 (16) (18) (20) sts.
S.s. 12 (14) (16) (18) rows—s.s. 13 (15) (17) (19) rows here when working right front shoulder.
To slope the shoulder: Cast off 4 (5) (6) (6) sts. at the beginning of the next row, 5 (5) (6) (7) sts. on the next alternate row—5 (6) (6) (7) sts.
Work 1 row. Cast off.

Continued on page 87

Above and left *Sailor Dress (page 84)*
Opposite *Blue/White Sweater (page 85)*

The right front shoulder: With right side of work facing, rejoin yarn to inner end of sts. on spare needle and work as given for left front shoulder to end, noting variation.

THE SLEEVES: (both alike): With No. 10 (3¼ mm) needles and m. cast on 39 sts. and work 14 rows in rib as given for back.

Change to No. 8 (4 mm) needles and s.s. 6 rows.

Continuing in s.s., inc. 1 st. at each end of the next row and the 5 (7) (9) (11) following 6th rows—51 (55) (59) (63) sts.

S.s. 23 (17) (11) (5) rows.

To shape the sleeve top: Cast off 6 sts. at the beginning of each of the next 2 rows, then dec. 1 st. at each end of the next 3 (4) (2) (3) rows.

Work 2 rows, then dec. 1 st. at each end of the next row and the 7 (8) (10) (11) following 3rd rows.

Work 1 row. Cast off remaining 17 (17) (21) (21) sts.

THE POLO COLLAR: First join right shoulder seam. With right side of work facing and using No. 10 (3¼ mm) needles and m., pick up and k. 20 (22) (24) (26) sts. down left front neck edge, work across 13 sts. at centre front as follows: * k. 2, up 1; repeat from * 5 times, k. 1, pick up and k. 20 (22) (24) (26) sts. up right front neck edge, then work across the 21 sts. at back neck as follows: k. 1, * up 1, k. 3; repeat from * 5 times, up 1, k. 2—87 (91) (95) (99) sts.

Work 20 rows in rib as given for back. Break off m.

With c., k. 1 row, then rib a further 12 rows. Cast off in rib.

TO MAKE UP THE SWEATER: Press work lightly on the wrong side, using a warm iron. Join left shoulder seam, continuing seam across polo collar. Set in sleeves, then join sleeve and side seams.

Yellow Polo Neck Sweater

Illustrated on page 90

MEASUREMENTS	*in centimetres (and inches, in brackets)*					
To fit chest sizes	56	(22)	61	(24)	66	(26)
All round at underarms	59	(23¼)	63.5	(25)	67.5	(26½)
Side seam	21	(8¼)	23	(9)	26	(10¼)
Length	34	(13¼)	38	(15)	41.5	(16¼)
Sleeve seam	22	(8¾)	24.5	(9¾)	27	(10¾)

MATERIALS: *Allow the following quantities in 50 g balls of Robin Reward D.K.: 4 for the 56 cm and 61 cm sizes; 5 for the 66 cm size. For any one size: A pair each of No. 8 (4 mm) and No. 10 (3¼ mm) knitting needles; a cable needle.*

TENSION: *Work at a tension of 24 stitches and 32 rows to measure 10 × 10 cm, over the pattern, using No. 8 (4 mm) needles, to obtain the measurements given above.*

ABBREVIATIONS: To be read before working: *K., knit plain; p., purl; st., stitch; tog., together; dec., decrease (by working 2 sts. tog.); inc., increase (by working twice into same st.); tw. 2, twist 2 (slip next st. on to cable needle and leave at back of work, k. 1, then k. st. from cable needle); single rib is k. 1 and p. 1 alternately.*

NOTE: *The instructions are given for the 56 cm (22 inch) size. Where they vary, work figures within first brackets for the 61 cm (24 inch) size; work figures within second brackets for 66 cm (26 inch) size.*

THE BACK: With No. 10 (3¼ mm) needles cast on 71 (75) (81) sts. and, beginning odd-numbered rows with k. 1 and even-numbered rows with p. 1, work 14 rows in single rib, increasing 1 st. at the end of the last of these rows on the 61 cm size only—71 (76) (81) sts.

Change to No. 8 (4 mm) needles and work the 2-row pattern as follows:

1st row: K. 1, * p. 1, tw. 2, p. 1, k. 1; repeat from * to end.

2nd row: All p.

Pattern a further 52 (60) (68) rows.

To shape the raglan armholes: Keeping continuity of the pattern, cast off 3 sts. at the beginning of each of the next 2 rows **, then dec. 1 st. at each end of the next row and the 19 (21) (23) following alternate rows—25 (26) (27) sts.

Work 1 row. Leave these sts. on a spare needle.

THE FRONT: Work as given for back to **, then dec. 1 st. at each end of the next row and the 14 (16) (18) following alternate rows—35 (36) (37) sts.

To divide for neck: Next row: Pattern 12 and leave these sts. on a spare needle for right half neck, pattern 11 (12) (13) and leave these sts. on a st. holder, pattern to end and work on these 12 sts. for left half neck.

The left half neck: Dec. 1 st. at each end of the next row and the 4 following alternate rows—2 sts.

Work 2 tog.

Fasten off.

The right half neck: With right side of work facing, rejoin yarn to inner end of 12 sts. left on spare needle and work as given for left half neck.

THE SLEEVES (both alike): With No. 10 (3¼ mm) needles cast on 37 (41) (43) sts. and work 13 rows in rib as given on back.

Next (inc.) row: * Rib 8 (7) (4), inc.; repeat from * until 1 (1) (3) st(s). remain(s), rib 1 (1) (3)—41 (46) (51) sts.

Change to No. 8 (4 mm) needles and work 4 (8) (12) rows in pattern as given on back.

Maintaining continuity of the pattern, taking extra sts. into pattern as they occur, inc. 1 st. at each end of the next row and the 4 following 8th (10th) (12th) rows—51 (56) (61) sts.

Pattern a further 21 (17) (13) rows.

To shape the raglan sleeve top: Work exactly as given for raglan armhole shaping on back, when 5 (6) (7) sts. will remain.

Leave these sts. on a safety pin.

THE POLO COLLAR: First join right raglan seams, then left sleeve to front only. With right side of work facing, using No. 10 (3¼ mm) needles, k. across the 5 (6) (7) sts. of left sleeve, increasing 1 st. at the centre of these sts., pick up and k. 12 sts. down left side of neck, k. across the 11 (12) (13) sts. at centre front, increasing 2 sts. evenly across these sts., pick up and k. 12 sts. up right side of neck, k. across the 5 (6) (7) sts. of right sleeve, increasing 1 st. at the centre of these sts., and finally, work across back neck sts. as follows: k. 1 (2) (3), * inc., k. 3; repeat from * 5 times—80 (84) (88) sts.

Work 33 (35) (37) rows in single rib.

Cast off loosely in rib.

TO MAKE UP THE SWEATER: Press on the wrong side with a warm iron over a dry cloth. Join remaining raglan seam, continuing seam across polo collar. Join side and sleeve seams. Fold polo collar in half to right side.

Boy's Multicoloured Slipover

Illustrated on page 91

MEASUREMENTS	*in centimetres (and inches, in brackets)*		
To fit chest sizes	56 (22)	61 (24)	66 (26)
All round at underarms	61.5 ($24\frac{1}{4}$)	67 ($26\frac{1}{4}$)	72.5 ($28\frac{1}{2}$)
Side seam	26.5 ($10\frac{1}{2}$)	28.5 ($11\frac{1}{4}$)	30 ($11\frac{3}{4}$)
Length	41.5 ($16\frac{1}{4}$)	44.5 ($17\frac{1}{2}$)	47.5 ($18\frac{3}{4}$)

MATERIALS: *Allow the following quantities in 50 g balls of Pingouin Pingolaine 4-ply: 2 red, 2 yellow and 1 green for the 56 cm and 61 cm sizes; 3 red, 2 yellow and 1 green for the 66 cm size. For any one size: a pair each of No. 9 ($3\frac{3}{4}$ mm) and No. 12 ($2\frac{3}{4}$ mm) knitting needles.*

TENSION: *Work at a tension of 29 stitches and 32 rows, to measure 10 × 10 cm, over the stocking stitch, using No. 9 ($3\frac{3}{4}$ mm) needles, to obtain the measurements given above.*

ABBREVIATIONS: To be read before working: *K., knit plain; p., purl; st., stitch; tog., together; inc., increase (by working twice into next st.); dec., decrease (by taking 2 sts. tog.); s.s., stocking st. (k. on the right side and p. on the wrong side); single rib is k. 1 and p. 1 alternately; k. or p. 2 tog. b., (k. or p. 2 tog. through back of sts.); nil, meaning nothing is worked here for this size; r., red; y., yellow; gr., green.*

NOTE: *The instructions are given for the 56 cm (22 inch) size. Where they vary, work the figures within the first brackets for the 61 cm (24 inch) size; work the figures within the second brackets for the 66 cm (26 inch) size.*

THE BACK: With No. 12 ($2\frac{3}{4}$ mm) needles and r. cast on 89 (97) (105) sts. and, beginning odd-numbered rows with k. 1 and even-numbered rows with p. 1, work 20 rows in single rib.

Change to No. 9 ($3\frac{3}{4}$ mm) needles and beginning with a k. row, s.s. 4 rows.

Joining in and breaking off colours as required, work in pattern, which is worked entirely in s.s. beginning with a k. row so only the colour details are given.

1st row: 2 r., * 1 y., 3 r.; repeat from * until 3 sts. remain, 1 y., 2 r.

2nd row: 1 r., * 1 y., 1 r.; repeat from * to end.

3rd row: * 1 y., 1 r.; repeat from * until 1 st. remains, 1 y.

4th row: * 1 r., 3 y.; repeat from * until 1 st. remains, 1 r.

5th row: 2 y., * 1 gr., 3 y.; repeat from * until 3 sts. remain, 1 gr., 2 y.

6th row: * 1 y., 3 gr.; repeat from * until 1 st. remains, 1 y.

7th row: As 5th row.

8th row: All gr.

9th and 10th rows: 1 r., * 1 gr., 1 r.; repeat from * to end.

11th to 18th rows: As 8th row back to 1st row in that reverse order.

Repeat the last 22 rows twice, then the first 4 (10) (16) rows again. **

To shape the armholes: Cast off 6 sts. at the beginning of each of the next 2 rows—77 (85) (93) sts.

Pattern a further 40 (44) (48) rows.

To slope the shoulder: Cast off 7 (8) (9) sts. at the beginning of each of the next 2 rows, then 8 (9) (10) sts. at the beginning of each of the next 4 rows.

Leave remaining 31 (33) (35) sts. on a spare needle.

THE FRONT: Work as back to **.

To shape the armholes and divide for V-neck: 1st row: Cast off 6 sts., pattern to end.

2nd row: Cast off 6, pattern a further 35 (39) (43), p. 2 tog., and leave these 37 (41) (45) sts. on a spare needle for right half front, p. 1 and leave this st. on a safety pin, p. 2 tog., pattern to end and work on these 37 (41) (45) sts. for left half front.

The left half front: To shape the neck: Dec. 1 st. at neck edge on the next row and the 13 (14) (15) following 3rd rows—23 (26) (29) sts.

Pattern nil (1) (2) row(s)—pattern 1 (2) (3) row(s) here when working right half front.

To slope the shoulder: Cast off 7 (8) (9) sts. at the beginning of the next row, 8 (9) (10) sts. at the beginning of the following alternate row—8 (9) (10) sts.

Pattern 1 row. Cast off.

The right half front: With right side of work facing, rejoin yarn to inner end of sts. on spare needle and work as given for left half front to end, noting variation.

THE NECKBAND: First join right shoulder seam. With right side of work facing, using No. 12 ($2\frac{3}{4}$ mm) needles and r., pick up and k. 47 (51) (55) sts. down left front neck edge, k. the st. from safety pin, pick up and k. 47 (51) (55) sts. up right front neck edge and finally k. across the 31 (33) (35) sts. at back neck, increasing 1 st.—127 (137) (147) sts.

1st row: * K. 1, p. 1; repeat from * to within 2 sts. of centre st., p. 2 tog. b., p. 1, p. 2 tog., ** p. 1, k. 1; repeat from ** to end.

2nd row: Rib to within 2 sts. of centre front st., k. 2 tog., k. 1, k. 2 tog. b., rib to end.

Rib a further 7 rows, decreasing at each side of centre st. on every row. Cast off in rib decreasing as before.

THE ARMHOLE BORDERS (both alike): First join left shoulder seam, continuing seam across neckband. With right side of work facing and using No. 12 ($2\frac{3}{4}$ mm) needles and r., pick up and k. 80 (88) (96) sts. round armhole edge, leaving cast-off groups free. Work 9 rows in single rib. Cast off in rib.

TO MAKE UP THE SLIPOVER: Press work lightly on the wrong side, using a warm iron over a dry cloth. Join side seams. Sew row ends of armhole borders to cast off sts. at underarms.

Above *Yellow Polo Neck Sweater (page 88)*
Opposite *Multicoloured Slipover (page 89)*

Boy's Multicoloured Waistcoat

Illustrated on page 94

MEASUREMENTS	*in centimetres (and inches, in brackets)*					
To fit chest sizes	56	(22)	61	(24)	66	(26)
All round at underarms, fastened	60	(23½)	65	(25½)	70	(27½)
Side seam, including armhole ribbing	21.5	(8½)	23	(9)	25	(10)
Length	35	(13¾)	38	(15)	41.5	(16¼)

MATERIALS: *Allow the following quantities in 50 g balls of Sirdar Country Style D.K.: 1 parchment for 56 cm size; 2 parchment for 61 cm and 66 cm sizes. For any one size: a ball of the above yarn in russet and blue haze; a pair each of No. 8 (4 mm) and No. 9 (3¾ mm) knitting needles; 5 buttons.*

TENSION: *Work at a tension of 23 stitches and 28 rows to measure 10 × 10 cm, over the pattern, using No. 8 (4 mm) needles, to obtain measurements given above.*

ABBREVIATIONS: To be read before working: *K., knit plain; p., purl; st., stitch; dec., decrease (by working 2 sts. together); s.s., stocking st. (k. on right side and p. on wrong side); single rib is k. 1 and p. 1 alternately; m., main (parchment); r., russet; b., blue haze.*

NOTE: *The instructions are given for the 56 cm (22 inch) size. Where they vary, work figures within first brackets for 61 cm (24 inch) size; work figures within second brackets for 66 cm (26 inch) size.*

THE BACK AND FRONTS (worked in one piece to armholes): With No. 9 (3¾ mm) needles and m. cast on 132 (144) (156) sts. and work 16 rows in single rib.

Change to No. 8 (4 mm) needles.

Joining and breaking colours as required, work the pattern as follows, which is worked entirely in s.s., beginning with a k. row, so only the colour details are given.

1st to 4th rows: All m.
5th row: * 2 m., 2 r.; repeat from * to end.
6th row: * 2 r., 2 m.; repeat from * to end.
7th to 10th rows: All r.
11th and 12th rows: All b.
13th and 14th rows: All m.
15th and 16th rows: All b.
17th row: * 5 b., 1 m.; repeat from * to end.
18th row: * 2 m., 4 b.; repeat from * to end.
19th row: * 3 b., 3 m.; repeat from * to end.
20th row: * 4 m., 2 b.; repeat from * to end.
21st: * 1 b., 5 m.; repeat from * to end.
22nd and 23rd rows: All m.
24th to 26th rows: All b.
27th row: * 2 b., 2 r.; repeat from * to end.
28th row: * 2 r., 2 b.; repeat from * to end.
29th row: As 28th row.
30th row: As 27th row.
31st and 32nd rows: All b.
33rd row: * 1 m., 5 r.; repeat from * to end.
34th row: * 4 r., 2 m.; repeat from * to end.
35th row: * 3 m., 3 r.; repeat from * to end.
36th row: * 2 r., 4 m.; repeat from * to end.

37th row: * 5 m., 1 r.; repeat from * to end.
38th to 40th rows: All m.
The 5th to 40th rows form the pattern.
Work a further 1 (5) (11) row(s).
To divide for back and fronts: Next row: Pattern 29 (32) (35) and leave these sts. on a spare needle for left front, cast off 4, pattern 65 (71) (77) and leave these 66 (72) (78) sts. on a spare needle for back, cast off 4, pattern to end and work on these 29 (32) (35) sts. for right front.

The right front: To shape the armhole and shape front edge: Dec. 1 st. at front edge on next row, then on the 2 (3) (3) following 3rd rows, *at the same time*, dec. 1 st. at armhole edge on the 2nd, 4th, 6th (2nd, 4th, 6th, 8th) (2nd, 4th, 6th, 8th) of these rows—23 (24) (27) sts.

Work 2 rows, then dec. 1 st. at front edge of next row and then on the 8 (8) (9) following 3rd rows—14 (15) (17) sts. left on needle.

Pattern 3 (4) (5) rows—pattern 4 (5) (6) rows here when working left front.

To slope the shoulder: Cast off 7 (7) (8) sts. at beginning of next row—7 (8) (9) sts.

Pattern 1 row.

Cast off.

The back: With right side of work facing, rejoin yarn to sts. on spare needle, work 1 row, then dec. 1 st. each end of next row and on the 2 (3) (3) following alternate rows—60 (64) (70) sts.

Pattern 32 (34) (38) rows.

To slope the shoulders: Cast off 7 (7) (8) sts. at beginning of next 2 rows, then 7 (8) (9) sts. on the following 2 rows—32 (34) (36) sts.

Leave sts. on a spare needle until required for front border.

The left front: With right side of work facing, rejoin yarn to sts. on spare needle and work as right front, noting variation where indicated.

THE ARMHOLE BORDERS (both alike): With right side of work facing and using No. 9 (3¾ mm) needles rejoin m. and pick up and k. 74 (82) (90) sts. evenly all round armhole edge.

Work 6 rows in single rib.

Cast off in rib.

THE FRONT BORDER: First join shoulder seams, including armhole borders. With right side of work facing and using No. 9 (3¾ mm) needles, rejoin m. and pick up and k. 50 (58) (66) sts. up right front to first front dec., pick up and k. 34 (39) (44) sts. to shoulder, k. across 32 (34) (36) sts. across back neck, pick up and k. 34 (39) (44) sts. to first front dec., then pick up and k. 50 (58) (66) sts. to cast on edge—200 (228) (256) sts.

Work 4 rows in single rib.

1st buttonhole row: Rib 4 (6) (8), * cast off 2, rib 8 (9) (10); repeat from * 3 times, cast off 2, rib to end.

2nd buttonhole row: Rib to end, casting on 2 sts. over each group cast off on previous row.

Rib a further 2 rows.
Cast off in rib.

TO COMPLETE THE WAISTCOAT: Press with a warm iron over a dry cloth. Add buttons.

Cardigan, Sweater and Beret with a Nautical Theme

Illustrated on page 95

MEASUREMENTS								
To fit chest sizes	56	(22)	61	(24)	66	(26)	71	(28)
All round at underarms (sweater)	60	$(23\frac{1}{2})$	65	$(25\frac{1}{2})$	70	$(27\frac{1}{2})$	75	$(29\frac{1}{2})$
All round at underarms (cardigan)	58.5	(23)	63.5	(25)	68.5	(27)	73.5	(29)
Side seam	24.5	$(9\frac{1}{2})$	26.5	$(10\frac{1}{2})$	28	(11)	30	$(11\frac{3}{4})$
Length	36.5	$(14\frac{1}{4})$	39	$(15\frac{1}{4})$	41.5	$(16\frac{1}{4})$	44	$(17\frac{3}{4})$
Sleeve seam	25	$(9\frac{3}{4})$	27.5	$(10\frac{3}{4})$	30	$(11\frac{3}{4})$	32.5	$(12\frac{3}{4})$
Hat will fit an average head size.								

in centimetres (and inches, in brackets)

MATERIALS: *Allow the following quantities in 40 g balls of Sirdar Wash 'n' Wear Double Crepe: Sweater: 3 white each for 56 cm and 61 cm sizes; 4 white each for 66 cm and 71 cm sizes. For any one size: 1 ball each in blue and red; a pair each of No. 8 (4 mm) and No. 9 (3¾ mm) knitting needles; a size 4.00 crochet hook; 3 buttons. Cardigan: 3 white for 56 cm size; 4 white each for 61 cm, 66 cm and 71 cm sizes. For any one size: 1 ball each in blue and red; a pair each of No. 8 (4 mm) and No. 9 (3¾ mm) knitting needles; 6 buttons. Beret: 1 ball of white and a small ball of blue remaining from sweater; a pair each of No. 8 (4 mm) and No. 9 (3¾ mm) knitting needles.*

TENSION: *Work at a tension of 24 stitches and 31 rows to measure 10 × 10 cm, over the plain stocking st., using No. 8 (4 mm) needles, and 29 rows to measure 10 cm in depth, over the pattern, using No. 8 (4 mm) needles, to obtain measurements given above.*

ABBREVIATIONS: To be read before working: *K., knit plain; p., purl; st., stitch; tog., together; inc., increase (by working twice into next st.); dec., decrease (by working 2 sts. tog.); s.s., stocking st. (k. on the right side and p. on the wrong side); nil, meaning nothing is worked here for this size; d.c., double crochet; ch., chain; single rib is k. 1 and p. 1 alternately; w., white; bl., blue; r., red.*

NOTE: *The instructions are given for the 56 cm (22 inch) chest size. Where they vary, work figures within first brackets for 61 cm (24 inch) chest size; work figures within second brackets for 66 cm (26 inch) chest size, and so on.*

THE SWEATER

THE BACK: With No. 9 (3¾ mm) needles and w. cast on 72 (78) (84) (90) sts. and work 16 rows in single rib.

** Change to No. 8 (4 mm) needles and, beginning with a k. row, continue in pattern which is worked entirely in s.s., so only the colour details are given. Join in yarns when required and use separate balls of yarn for each boat.

1st to 6th rows: All with bl.**

7th row: * 3 bl., 3 w.; repeat from * to end.

8th row: * 4 w., 2 bl.; repeat from * to end.

9th and 10th rows: * 3 w., 3 bl.; repeat from * to end.

11th row: * 2 bl., 4 w., repeat from * to end.

12th to 14th rows: All with w.

15th row: 13 (16) (19) (22) w., * 5 bl., 16 w.; repeat from * ending last repeat with 12 (15) (18) (21) w.

16th row: 10 (13) (16) (19) w., * 8 bl., 13 w.; repeat from * ending last repeat with 12 (15) (18) (21) w.

17th row: 11 (14) (17) (20) w., * 11 bl., 10 w.; repeat from * ending last repeat with 8 (11) (14) (17) w.

18th row: 8 (11) (14) (17) w., * 3 bl., 3 w., 1 bl., 14 w.; repeat from * ending last repeat with 15 (18) (21) (24) w.

19th row: 15 (18) (21) (24) w., * 1 bl., 20 w.; repeat from * ending last repeat with 14 (17) (20) (23) w.

20th row: 5 (8) (11) (14) w., * 9 r., 1 bl., 1 w., 7 r., 3 w.; repeat from * ending last repeat with 7 (10) (13) (16) w.

21st row: 8 (11) (14) (17) w., * 6 r., 1 w., 1 bl., 8 r., 5 w.; repeat from * ending last repeat with 6 (9) (12) (15) w.

Continued on page 96

Above *Multicoloured Waistcoat (page 92)*

Opposite *Cardigan (page 96) and Beret (page 97) with a Nautical Theme*

22nd row: 7 (10) (13) (16) w., * 7 r., 1 bl., 1 w., 5 r., 7 w.; repeat from * ending last repeat with 9 (12) (15) (18) w.

23rd row: 10 (13) (16) (19) w., * 4 r., 1 w., 1 bl., 6 r., 9 w.; repeat from * ending last repeat with 8 (11) (14) (17) w.

24th row: 9 (12) (15) (18) w., * 5 r., 1 bl., 1 w., 3 r., 11 w.; repeat from * ending last repeat with 11 (14) (17) (20) w.

25th row: 12 (15) (18) (21) w., * 2 r., 1 w., 1 bl., 4 r., 13 w.; repeat from * ending last repeat with 10 (13) (16) (19) w.

26th row: 11 (14) (17) (20) w., * 3 r., 1 bl., 1 w., 1 r., 15 w.; repeat from * ending last repeat with 13 (16) (19) (22) w.

27th row: 15 (18) (21) (24) w., * 1 bl., 2 r., 18 w.; repeat from * ending last repeat with 12 (15) (18) (21) w.

28th row: 13 (16) (19) (22) w., * 1 r., 1 bl., 19 w.; repeat from * ending last repeat with 15 (18) (21) (24) w.

29th row: 15 (18) (21) (24) w., * 1 bl., 20 w.; repeat from * ending last repeat with 14 (17) (20) (23) w.

30th to 34th rows: All with w.

These 34 rows form the pattern. Pattern a further 34 rows, marking each end of 22nd (28th) (34th) (nil) row to denote end of side seams.

Continue in w. only and s.s. 22 (30) (38) (46) rows, marking each end of nil (nil) (nil) (6th) row to denote end of side seams for 71 cm size only.

To slope the shoulders: Cast off 11 (12) (13) (14) sts. at beginning of next 4 rows.

Break yarn and leave remaining 28 (30) (32) (34) sts. on a spare needle.

THE FRONT: Work as given for back until 15 (17) (17) (19) rows have been completed after markers.

To divide for neck: Next row: P. 22 (24) (26) (28) and leave these sts. on a spare needle for right half neck, p. 28 (30) (32) (34) and leave these sts. on a st. holder, p. to end and work on these last 22 (24) (26) (28) sts. for left half neck.

The left half neck: S.s. 18 (18) (20) (20) rows—read 19 (19) (21) (21) rows here when working right half neck.

To slope shoulder: Cast off 11 (12) (13) (14) sts. at beginning of next row.

Work 1 row, then cast off remaining 11 (12) (13) (14) sts.

The right half neck: With right side facing, rejoin yarn to inner end of sts. on spare needle and work as given for left half neck, noting variation.

THE SLEEVES: (2 alike): With No. 9 (3¾ mm) needles and w. cast on 38 (40) (42) (44) sts. and work 16 rows in single rib.

Change to No. 8 (4 mm) needles and, beginning with a k. row, s.s. 4 rows, then inc. 1 st. each end of next row and the 6 (7) (7) (8) following 8th rows—52 (56) (58) (62) sts.

S.s. 3 (3) (11) (11) rows.

Break off w., join in bl. and s.s. a further 6 rows. Cast off.

THE NECK RIBBING: First join right shoulder seam. With right side facing, rejoin w. and using No. 9 (3¾ mm) needles, pick up and k. 15 (15) (17) (17) sts. from row ends of left half neck, k. across 28 (30) (32) (34) sts. at centre front, pick up and k. 15 (15) (17) (17) sts. from row ends of right half neck, and finally, k. across 28 (30) (32) (34) sts. at back neck—86 (90) (98) (102) sts.

1st rib row: * P. 1, k. 1 *; repeat from * to * a further 20 (21) (23) (24) times, p. 1 and mark this st. for corner, k. 1, repeat from * to * 13 (14) (15) (16) times, p. 1 and mark this st. for corner, k. 1, repeat from * to * 7 (7) (8) (8) times.

2nd row: * Rib to within 2 sts. of marked st., p. 2 tog., k. marked st., p. 2 tog.; repeat from * once, rib to end.

3rd row: * Rib to within 2 sts. of marked st., k. 2 tog., p. marked st., k. 2 tog.; repeat from * once, rib to end.

Repeat 2nd and 3rd rows, once, then 2nd row again. Cast off in rib.

THE OPENING EDGING: Join left shoulder seam leaving seam open for 5 cm at neck edge.

With size 4.00 crochet hook, rejoin w. and work 32 d.c. all round shoulder opening including row ends of neck ribbing, turn.

Buttonhole row: 2 ch. for d.c., 1 d.c. in next d.c., 1 ch., miss 1 d.c., * 1 d.c. in each of next 4 d.c., 1 ch., miss 1 d.c.; repeat from * once, 1 d.c. in each d.c. to end. Fasten off.

TO MAKE UP THE SWEATER: Press with a warm iron over a dry cloth. Set in sleeves above markers, then join side and sleeve seams. Add buttons.

THE CARDIGAN

THE BACK AND SLEEVES: Work as given for back and sleeves of sweater.

THE LEFT FRONT: With No. 9 (3¾ mm) needles and w. cast on 38 (42) (44) (48) sts. and, beginning with p. 1, work 15 rows in single rib.

Next row: Rib 7 and leave these on a safety pin for button band, rib to end increasing 1 st. at end of row for the 1st and 3rd sizes only—32 (35) (38) (41) sts.

Work as for sweater back from ** to **.

7th row: * 3 bl., 3 w.; repeat from * until 2 (5) (2) (5) sts. remain, 2 bl. (3 bl., 2 w.) (2 bl.) (3 bl., 2 w.).

8th row: Nil (3) (nil) (3) w., 2 bl., * 4 w., 2 bl.; repeat from * to end.

9th row: * 3 w., 3 bl.; repeat from * until 2 (5) (2) (5) sts. remain, 2 w. (3 w., 2 bl.) (2 w.) (3 w., 2 bl.).

10th row: 2 bl. (2 w., 3 bl.) (2 bl.) (2 w., 3 bl.), * 3 w., 3 bl.; repeat from * to end.

11th row: * 2 bl., 4 w.; repeat from * until 2 (5) (2) (5) sts. remain, 2 bl., nil. (3) (nil) (3) w.

12th to 14th rows: All with w.

15th row: 16 (19) (22) (25) w., 5 bl., 11 w.

16th row: 9 w., 8 bl., 15 (18) (21) (24) w.

17th row: 14 (17) (20) (23) w., 11 bl., 7 w.

18th row: 7 w., 3 bl., 3 w., 1 bl., 18 (21) (24) (27) w.

19th row: 18 (21) (24) (27) w., 1 bl., 13 w.

20th row: 4 w., 9 r., 1 bl., 1 w., 7 r., 10 (13) (16) (19) w.

*** These 20 rows set position of the pattern for left front. Keeping continuity of pattern to match back, pattern a further 36 (42) (48) (54) rows. Mark *end*—read *beginning* here when working right front—of last row to denote end of side seam.

Pattern a further 15 (17) (17) (19) rows—pattern 16 (18) (18) (20) rows here when working right front.

To shape neck: Next row: Pattern 10 (11) (12) (13) and leave these sts. on a safety pin, pattern to end.

On 22 (24) (26) (28) sts., work 18 (18) (20) (20) rows.

To slope shoulder: Cast off 11 (12) (13) (14) sts. at beginning of next row.

Work 1 row, then cast off remaining 11 (12) (13) (14) sts.

THE RIGHT FRONT: With No. 9 (3¾ mm) needles and w. cast on 38 (42) (44) (48) sts. and work 15 rows in a single rib.

Next row: Inc. 1 (nil) (1) (nil), rib 31 (35) (37) (41), turn, leaving remaining 7 sts. on a safety pin for buttonhole band—32 (35) (38) (41) sts.

Work as given for sweater back from ** to **.

7th row: 2 w. (2 bl., 3 w.) (2 w.) (2 bl., 3 w.), * 3 bl., 3 w.; repeat from * to end.

8th row: * 4 w., 2 bl.; repeat from * until 2 (5) (2) (5) sts. remain, 2 w. (4 w., 1 bl.) (2 w.) (4 w., 1 bl.).

9th row: 2 bl. (2 w., 3 bl.) (2 bl.) (2 w., 3 bl.), * 3 w., 3 bl.; repeat from * to end.

10th row: * 3 w., 3 bl.; repeat from * until 2 (5) (2) (5) sts. remain, 2 w. (3 w., 2 bl.) (2 w.) (3 w., 2 bl.).

11th row: 2 w. (1 bl., 4 w.) (2 w.) (1 bl., 4 w.), * 2 bl., 4 w.; repeat from * to end.

12th to 14th rows: All with w.

15th row: 10 w., 5 bl., 17 (20) (23) (26) w.

16th row: 15 (18) (21) (24) w., 8 bl., 9 w.

17th row: 8 w., 11 bl., 13 (16) (19) (22) w.

18th row: 13 (16) (19) (22) w., 3 bl., 3 w., 1 bl., 12 w.

19th row: 12 w., 1 bl., 19 (22) (25) (28) w.

20th row: 10 (13) (16) (19) w., 9 r., 1 bl., 1 w., 7 r., 4 w.

Work as left front from *** to end, noting variations.

THE BUTTON BAND: With right side facing, rejoin w. and, using No. 9 (3¾ mm) needles, rib 7 sts. from safety pin on left front.

Work a further 67 (77) (87) (97) rows.

Break yarn and leave sts. on a safety pin.

THE BUTTONHOLE BAND: With wrong side facing, rejoin w. and, using No. 9 (3¾ mm) needles, rib across 7 sts. from safety pin on right front.

1st buttonhole row: Rib 2, cast off 2, rib to end.

2nd buttonhole row: Rib to end, casting on 2 sts. over those cast off on previous row.

Rib 12 (14) (16) (18) rows.

Repeat the last 14 (16) (18) (20) rows, 3 times, then the 2 buttonhole rows again.

Rib a further 10 (12) (14) (16) rows.

Do not break yarn.

THE NECK RIBBING: Join shoulder seams.

With right side facing, rib across buttonhole band sts., then k. across 10 (11) (12) (13) sts. from safety pin on right front, pick up and k. 15 (15) (17) (17) sts. from right front neck shaping, k. across back neck sts. decreasing 1 st., pick up and k. 15 (15) (17) (17) sts. from left front neck shaping, k. across 10 (11) (12) (13) sts. from safety pin on left front, and finally, rib across button band sts.—91 (95) (103) (107) sts.

1st rib row: * P. 1, k. 1 *; repeat from * to * 7 (8) (8) (9) times, p. 1 and mark this st. for corner, k. 1, repeat from * to * 28 (28) (32) (32) times, p. 1 and mark this st. for corner, * k. 1, p. 1; repeat from this * 7 (8) (8) (9) times.

Repeat 2nd and 3rd neck ribbing rows of sweater, twice, then 2nd row again, *at the same time*, make a buttonhole at right front edge as before on 1st and 2nd of these rows.

Cast off in rib.

TO MAKE UP THE CARDIGAN: Press as for sweater. Set in sleeves above markers, then join side and sleeve seams. Sew front bands into place. Add buttons.

THE BERET

TO MAKE: With No. 9 (3¾ mm) needles and w. cast on 92 sts. and single rib 2 rows with w., 2 rows with bl. and 2 rows with w.

Change to No. 8 (4 mm) needles and continue with w. as follows: **1st (inc.) row:** K. 1, * k. 8, inc.; repeat from * 9 times, k. 1—102 sts.

2nd, 3rd and 4th rows: P. 1 row, k. 1 row and p. 1 row.

5th (inc.) row: K. 1, * k. 9, inc.; repeat from * 9 times, k. 1—112 sts.

Repeat 2nd to 5th rows, 3 times more, working 1 st. extra between increases on each repeat of the 5th row—142 sts.

P. 1 row.

Drop w., join in bl. and s.s. 8 rows with bl.

Break off bl., take up w.

1st (dec.) row: K. 1, * k. 12, k. 2 tog.; repeat from * until 1 st. remains, k. 1—132 sts.

2nd row: P. to end.

3rd (dec.) row: K. 1, * k. 11, k. 2 tog.; repeat from * until 1 st. remains, k. 1—122 sts.

Repeat 2nd and 3rd rows, 10 times more, working 1 st. less between increases on each repeat of the 3rd row—22 sts.

P. 1 row.

Next row: * K. 2 tog.; repeat from * to end—11 sts.

Break yarn leaving an end. Run end through remaining sts., draw up and fasten off, then join seam. Finish top with a pompon.

Red Sweater with Train Motif

Illustrated opposite

MEASUREMENTS	*in centimetres (and inches, in brackets)*					
To fit chest sizes	61	(24)	66	(26)	71	(28)
All round at underarms	66	(26)	71	(28)	76	(30)
Side seam	21	(8¼)	23.5	(9¼)	26	(10¼)
Length	33	(13)	37	(14½)	40.5	(16)
Sleeve seam	26.5	(10¼)	30	(11¾)	33.5	(13¼)

MATERIALS: *Allow the following quantities in 50 g balls of Lister Motoravia Double Knitting:* 5 red for 61 cm size; 5 red for 66 cm size; 6 red for 71 cm size. For any one size: a small ball of the above yarn in white and green; a pair each of No. 9 (3¾ mm) and No. 11 (3 mm) knitting needles.

TENSION: *Work at a tension of 24 stitches and 33 rows to measure 10 × 10 cm, over the stocking stitch, using No. 9 (3¾ mm) needles, to obtain measurements given above.*

ABBREVIATIONS: To be read before working: *K., knit plain; p., purl; st., stitch; inc., increase (by working twice into same st.); dec., decrease (by working 2 sts. together); s.s., stocking st. (k. on the right side and p. on wrong side); r., red; w., white; g., green; single rib is k. 1 and p. 1 alternately.*

NOTE: *The instructions are given for the 61 cm size. Where they vary, work figures within first brackets for 66 cm size; work figures within second brackets for 71 cm size.*

THE BACK: With No. 11 (3 mm) needles and r. cast on 78 (84) (90) sts. and work 12 rows in single rib, increasing 1 st. at the end of the last of these rows—79 (85) (91) sts.
Change to No. 9 (3¾ mm) needles.**
Beginning with a k. row, s.s. 58 (66) (74) rows.
***To shape the armholes:** Cast off 4 sts. at beginning of next 2 rows, then dec. 1 st. each end of next 5 (6) (7) rows and then on the following alternate row—59 (63) (67) sts. ***
S.s. 27 (30) (33) rows.
To slope the shoulders: Cast off 8 (9) (9) sts. at beginning of next 2 rows, then 8 (8) (9) sts. on the following 2 rows—27 (29) (31) sts.
Leave sts. on a spare needle.

THE FRONT: Work as back to **.
Beginning with a k. row, s.s. 44 (52) (60) rows.
Joining in and breaking off colours as required, work the 12-row motif pattern as follows, which is worked entirely in s.s., beginning with a k. row, so only the colour details are given: **1st row:** 16 (19) (22) r., 2 g., 7 r., 2 g., 7 r., 2 g., 4 r., 2 g., 6 r., 2 g., 4 r., 2 g., 4 r., 2 g., 17 (20) (23) r.
2nd row: 16 (19) (22) r., 4 g., 2 r., 4 g., 2 r., 4 g., 4 r., 4 g., 2 r., 4 g., 5 r., 4 g., 5 r., 4 g., 15 (18) (21) r.
3rd row: 13 (16) (19) r., 17 w., 2 r., 12 w., 2 r., 18 w., 15 (18) (21) r.
4th row: 15 (18) (21) r., 51 w., 13 (16) (19) r.
5th row: As 3rd row.
6th row: 15 (18) (21) r., 18 w., 2 r., 12 w., 2 r., 17 w., 13 (16) (19) r.

7th row: 13 (16) (19) r., 2 w., 17 r., 6 w., 8 r., 17 w., 16 (19) (22) r.
8th row: 16 (19) (22) r., 3 w., 1 r., 2 w., 1 r., 2 w., 2 r., 2 w., 3 r., 1 w., 10 r., 4 w., 32 (35) (38) r.
9th row: 46 (49) (52) r., 1 w., 3 r., 2 w., 8 r., 3 w., 16 (19) (22) r.
10th row: 16 (19) (22) r., 3 w., 8 r., 2 w., 3 r., 1 w., 46 (49) (52) r.
11th row: 46 (49) (52) r., 6 w., 8 r., 3 w., 16 (19) (22) r.
12th row: 15 (18) (21) r., 5 w., 59 (62) (65) r.
Continuing in r. only, s.s. 2 rows, then work as back from *** to ***.
S.s. 18 (21) (24) rows.
To divide for neck: Next row: P. 20 (21) (22) and leave these sts. on a spare needle for right half neck, p. the next 19 (21) (23) and leave these sts. on a st. holder for polo collar, p. to end and work on these 20 (21) (22) sts. for left half neck.
The left half neck: Dec. 1 st. at neck edge on next row, then on the 3 following alternate rows—16 (17) (18) sts.
S.s. 1 row—s.s. 2 rows here when working right half neck.
To slope the shoulder: Cast off 8 (9) (9) sts. at beginning of next row—8 (8) (9) sts.
Work 1 row, then cast off.
The right half neck: With right side of work facing, rejoin yarn to sts. on spare needle and work as left half neck, noting variation.

THE SLEEVES (both alike): With No. 11 (3 mm) needles and r. cast on 32 (36) (40) sts. and work 21 rows in single rib.
Inc. row: * Rib 3, inc.; repeat from * to end—40 (45) (50) sts.
Change to No. 9 (3¾ mm) needles.
S.s. 4 rows, then inc. 1 st. each end of next row and then on the 6 (7) (7) following 5th rows—54 (61) (66) sts.
S.s. 29 (36) (48) rows.
To shape the sleeve top: Cast off 4 sts. at beginning of next 2 rows, 2 sts. on the following 12 (14) (16) rows, then 4 sts. on the next 2 rows—14 (17) (18) sts.
Cast off.

THE POLO COLLAR: First join right shoulder seam. With right side of work facing and using No. 11 (3 mm) needles, rejoin r. and pick up and k. 10 sts. down left half neck, k. 19 (21) (23) sts. across front, pick up and k. 10 sts. up right half neck, then k. 27 (29) (31) sts. across back neck—66 (70) (74) sts.
Work 8 rows in single rib.

Change to No. 9 (3¾ mm) needles and rib a further 22 rows.

Cast off in rib.

TO MAKE UP THE SWEATER: Press with a warm iron over a dry cloth. Join left shoulder seam, continuing seam across polo collar. Set in sleeves, then join sleeve and side seams.

Above *Red Sweater with Train Motif*

School Age Children

Tyrolean Cardigan

Illustrated opposite

MEASUREMENTS	*in centimetres (and inches, in brackets)*					
To fit chest sizes	61	(24)	66	(26)	71	(28)
All round at underarms	63.5	(25)	69	(27¼)	74.5	(29¼)
Side seam	20	(8)	22	(8½)	23	(9)
Length	34.5	(13½)	37	(14½)	39.5	(15½)
Sleeve seam	21	(8¼)	22.5	(8¾)	24	(9½)

MATERIALS: *Allow the following quantities in 50 g balls of Pingouin Confortable: 3 for the 61 cm size; 4 for the 66 cm size; 5 for the 71 cm size. For any one size: 1 ball each in 2 contrasting colours; oddments in contrasting colours for flowers; a pair each of No. 8 (4 mm) knitting needles; a size 3.50 crochet hook; 4 (5) (5) hooks and eyes.*

TENSION: *Work at a tension of 22 stitches and 28 rows to measure 10 × 10 cm, over the stocking stitch, 1 cable panel measures 5.5 cm (2¼ inches) in width, using No. 8 (4 mm) knitting needles to obtain the measurements given above.*

ABBREVIATIONS: To be read before working: *K., knit plain; p., purl; st., stitch; tog., together; dec., decrease (by working 2 sts. tog.); inc., increase (by working twice into next st.); s.s., stocking st. (k. on the right side and p. on the wrong side); c. 4f., cable 4 front (slip next 2 sts. on to a cable needle and leave at front of work, k. 2, then k. 2 from cable needle); c. 4b., cable 4 back (slip next 2 sts. on to a cable needle and leave at back of work, k. 2, then k. 2 from cable needle); d.c., double crochet; y.o.h., yarn over hook; ch., chain; m., main colour; 1st c.c., 1st contrast colour; 2nd c.c., 2nd contrast colour.*

NOTE: *The instructions are given for the 61 cm (24 inch) size. Where they vary, work the figures within the first brackets for the 66 cm (26 inch) size; work the figures within the second brackets for the 71 cm (28 inch) size.*

THE BACK: With No. 8 (4 mm) needles and m., cast on 71 (77) (83) sts. and work in pattern as follows:

Foundation row: P. 8 (10) (12), ★ k. 2, p. 4, k. 1, p. 4, k. 2 ★, p. 29 (31) (33); repeat from ★ to ★ once, p. 8 (10) (12).

1st row (right side): K. 8 (10) (12), ★ p. 2, k. 4, p. 1, k. 4, p. 2 ★, k. 29 (31) (33); repeat from ★ to ★ once, k. 8 (10) (12).

2nd and every following alternate row: P. 8 (10) (12), ★ k. 2, p. 4, k. 1, p. 4, k. 2, ★ p. 29 (31) (33); repeat from ★ to ★ once, p. 8 (10) (12).

3rd row: K. 8 (10) (12), ★ p. 2, c. 4f., p. 1, c. 4b., p. 2 ★, k. 29 (31) (33); repeat from ★ to ★ once, k. 8 (10) (12).

5th and 7th rows: As 1st row.

9th row: K. 8 (10) (12), ★ p. 2, c. 4b., p. 1, c. 4f., p. 2 ★, k. 29 (31) (33); repeat from ★ to ★ once, k. 8 (10) (12).

11th row: As 1st row.

12th row: As 2nd row.

These 12 rows form the pattern.

Pattern a further 42 (46) (50) rows.

To shape the armholes: Keeping the continuity of pattern, cast off 3 sts. at the beginning of the next 2 rows, then dec. 1 st. at each end of next row and 3 (4) (5) following alternate rows—57 (61) (65) sts.

Pattern a further 23 (25) (27) rows.

To slope the shoulders: Cast off 6 sts. at the beginning of the next 4 rows, then 5 (6) (7) sts. at the beginning of the next 2 rows—23 (25) (27) sts.

Cast off.

THE POCKET LININGS (make 2): With No. 8 (4 mm) needles and m. cast on 18 (18) (20) sts. and, beginning with a k. row, s.s 20 (24) (28) rows.

Next (inc.) row: K. 3 (3) (5), ★ inc., k. 4; repeat from ★ to end—21 (21) (23) sts.

Leave these sts. on a spare needles until required for fronts.

THE LEFT FRONT: With No. 8 (4 mm) needles and m. cast on 34 (37) (40) sts. and work as follows:

Foundation row: P. 13 (14) (15), k. 2, p. 4, k. 1, p. 4, k. 2, p. 8 (10) (12).

1st row (right side): K. 8 (10) (12), work from ★ to ★ on 1st row of back, k. 13 (14) (15).

2nd and every following alternate row: P. 13 (14) (15), k. 2, p. 4, k. 1, p. 4, k. 2, p. 8 (10) (12).

3rd row: K. 8 (10) (12), work from ★ to ★ on 3rd row of back, k. 13 (14) (15).

These 3 rows set the position for the left front.

Pattern a further 21 (25) (29) rows.

Next (pocket) row: K. 4 (6) (7), cast off the next 21 (21) (23) sts., then pattern to end of row.

Next row: P. 9 (10) (10), with wrong side of pocket lining facing, pattern across the 21 (21) (23) sts., pattern to end—34 (37) (40) sts.

Pattern 28 rows.

Continued on page 104

Opposite Tyrolean Cardigan

** To shape the armhole: Cast off 3 sts. at the beginning of the next row.

Pattern 1 row—omit this row when working right front.

Dec. 1 st. at armhole edge on the next row and the 3 (4) (5) following alternate rows—27 (29) (31) sts.

Pattern 14 rows—pattern 15 rows here when working right front.

To shape the neck: Cast off 4 (4) (5) sts. at the beginning of the next row.

Dec. 1 st. at neck edge on the next 4 rows, then dec. 1 st. at the same edge on the 2 (3) (3) following alternate rows—17 (18) (19) sts.

Pattern nil (nil) (2) rows.

To slope the shoulder: Cast off 6 sts. at the beginning of the next and following alternate row—5 (6) (7) sts.

Work 1 row. Cast off.

THE RIGHT FRONT: With No. 8 (4 mm) needles and m., cast on 34 (37) (40) sts. and work as follows:

Foundation row: P. 8 (10) (12), k. 2, p. 4, k. 1, p. 4, k. 2, p. 13 (14) (15).

1st row (right side): K. 13 (14) (15), work from * to * on 1st row of back, k. 8 (10) (12).

2nd and every following alternate row: P. 8 (10) (12), k. 2, p. 4, k. 1, p. 4, k. 2, p. 13 (14) (15).

3rd row: K. 13 (14) (15), work from * to * on 3rd row of back, k. 8 (10) (12).

These 3 rows set the position of the pattern for the right front.

Pattern a further 21 (25) (29) rows.

Next (pocket) row: Pattern 9 (10) (10), cast off the next 21 (21) (23) sts., pattern to end.

Next row: P. 4 (6) (7), with wrong side of pocket lining facing, pattern across the 21 (21) (23) sts., pattern to end—34 (37) (40) sts.

Pattern 29 rows.

Complete as given for left front from ** to end, noting variations.

THE SLEEVES: (both alike): With No. 8 (4 mm) needles and m., cast on 37 (39) (41) sts. and work as follows:

Foundation row: P. 12 (13) (14), k. 2, p. 4, k. 1, p. 4, k. 2, p. 12 (13) (14).

1st row (right side): K. 12 (13) (14), work from * to * on 1st row of back, k. 12 (13) (14).

2nd and every following alternate row: P. 12 (13) (14), k. 2, p. 4, k. 1, p. 4, k. 2, p. 12 (13) (14).

These 2 rows set the position of the pattern for the sleeves.

Keeping continuity of pattern and taking extra sts. into s.s. as they occur, pattern 4 rows.

Inc. 1 st. at each end of the next row and the 6 (7) (9) following 6th rows—51 (55) (61) sts.

Pattern a further 13 (11) (3) rows.

To shape the sleeve top: Cast off 3 sts. at the beginning of the next 2 rows, dec. 1 st. at the beginning of the next 16 (20) (24) rows, then dec. 1 st. at each end of the next 8 rows—13 (13) (15) sts.

Cast off.

TO MAKE UP THE CARDIGAN: Press on the wrong side with a cool iron over a dry cloth. Join shoulder seams. Set in sleeves. Join side and sleeve seams. Catch down pocket linings to wrong side of work.

The sleeve edgings (both alike): With No. 3.50 crochet hook and 1st c.c., work 30 (32) (34) d.c. evenly along lower edge of sleeve, join with a slip st. to 1st d.c.

Work a further 2 rounds of d.c. and fasten off.

Join in 2nd c.c. to 1st d.c. of previous round, * insert hook into next space between d.c.'s 2 rows down, draw yarn through and up to top of crochet edge, y.o.h., and draw through 2 loops, 1 ch., miss 2 d.c. of first row; repeat from * all round, join and fasten off.

The pocket edgings (both alike): With No. 3.50 crochet hook and 1st c.c., work 16 (16) (18) d.c. evenly along pocket edge and work as given for sleeve edgings.

The main edging: Join in 1st c.c. to lower edge of right front at side seam and with a 3.50 crochet hook, work a round of d.c.s evenly along lower edge, up right front, across back neck, down left front, across lower edge of left front and across back, working 3 d.c.s into each corner at lower edges and at neck edge.

Complete to match the sleeves and pocket edgings.

The crochet flowers: Using oddments of yarns, in various colours make flowers as follows:

Make 5 ch. and join with a slip st. to form a ring.

1st round: * 3 ch., 1 d.c. into ring *; repeat from * 5 times more and fasten off.

Sew a flower in centre of each cable as in photograph on page 103. With various colours make a french knot in the centre of each flower, embroider leaves in 2nd c.c. in lazy daisy st. as in photograph.

Sew on hooks and eyes. Catch down pocket edgings to right side.

Girl's Pink Cardigan with Collar

Illustrated on page 106

MEASUREMENTS	*in centimetres (and inches, in brackets)*					
To fit chest sizes	61	(24)	66	(26)	71	(28)
All round at underarms, fastened	65.5	(25¾)	69	(27¼)	72	(28¼)
Side seam	19.5	(7¾)	21	(8¼)	22	(8¾)
Length	35.5	(14)	37	(14½)	39	(15¼)
Sleeve seam	23	(9)	24.5	(9¾)	27	(10½)

MATERIALS: *Allow the following quantities in 50 g balls of Patons Beehive Double Knitting:* 4 *for* 61 *cm and* 66 *cm sizes;* 5 *for* 71 *cm size. For any one size: A pair each of No.* 8 (4 *mm) and No.* 10 (3¼ *mm) knitting needles;* 6 *buttons.*

TENSION: *Work at a tension of* 25 *stitches and* 33 *rows to measure* 10 × 10 *cm, over the pattern, using No.* 8 (4 *mm) needles, to obtain the measurements given above.*

ABBREVIATIONS: To be read before working: *K., knit plain; p., purl; st., stitch; tog., together; inc., increase (by working twice into same st.); dec., decrease (by working* 2 *sts. tog.); k.* 2 *tog.b., k.* 2 *tog. through back of sts.; y.fwd., yarn forward to make a st.; single rib is k.* 1 *and p.* 1 *alternately; nil, meaning nothing is worked here for this size.*

NOTE: *Instructions are given for the* 61 *cm (*24 *inch) size. Where they vary, work figures within the first brackets for the* 66 *cm (*26 *inch) size; work figures within the second brackets for the* 71 *cm (*28 *inch) size.*

THE BACK: With No. 10 (3¼ mm) needles cast on 81 (85) (89) sts. and, beginning odd-numbered rows with k. 1 and even-numbered rows with p. 1, work 14 rows in single rib.

Change to No. 8 (4 mm) needles and work the 6-row pattern as follows:

1st row: All k.
2nd row: All p.
P. 1, * k. 3, p. 1; repeat from * to end.
4th row: K. 2, * p. 1, k. 3; repeat from * until 3 sts. remain, p. 1, k. 2.
5th and 6th rows: As 3rd and 4th rows.
Pattern a further 44 (48) (52) rows.
To shape the raglan armholes: 1st and 2nd rows: Cast off 3 sts., pattern to end.
3rd row: K. 1, k. 2 tog.b., pattern until 3 sts. remain, k. 2 tog., k. 1.
4th row: P. 2, pattern until 2 sts. remain, p. 2.
Repeat 3rd and 4th rows, 24 (25) (26) times more—25 (27) (29) sts. Cast off.

THE LEFT FRONT: With No. 10 (3¼ mm) needles cast on 39 (41) (43) sts. and work 14 rows in rib as given for back.

Change to No. 8 (4 mm) needles and work the 6-row pattern as follows:

1st row: All k.
2nd row: All p. **
3rd row: P. 1, * k. 3, p. 1; repeat from * until 2 (nil) (2) sts. remain, k. 2 (nil) (2).

4th row: P. 1 (nil) (1), k. 3 (2) (3), * p. 1, k. 3; repeat from * until 3 sts. remain, p. 1, k. 2.
*** **5th and 6th rows:** As 3rd and 4th rows.
Pattern a further 44 (48) (52) rows—pattern 45 (49) (53) rows here when working right front.
To shape the raglan armhole: 1st row: Cast off 3 sts., pattern to end. ***
2nd row: Pattern to end.
3rd row: K. 1, k. 2 tog.b., pattern to end.
4th row: Pattern until 2 sts. remain, p. 2.
Repeat 3rd and 4th rows, 17 (18) (19) times more then 3rd row again—17 (18) (19) sts.
To shape the neck and continue shaping the armhole: Next row: Cast off 5 (6) (7) sts., pattern to end.
Dec. 1 st. at neck edge on the next 5 rows, *at the same time,* dec. 1 st. at armhole edge as before on the 1st of these rows, then on the 2 following alternate rows—4 sts.
Work 1 row, then dec. 1 st. at armhole edge as before on the next row and following alternate row—2 sts.
P. 2, then k. 2 tog. and fasten off.

THE RIGHT FRONT: Work as left front to **.
3rd row: K. 2 (nil) (2), p. 1, * k. 3, p. 1: repeat from * to end.
4th row: K. 2, * p. 1, k. 3; repeat from * until 1 (3) (1) st(s). remain(s), p. 1, k. nil (2) (nil).
Work as left front from *** to ***, noting variation.
2nd row: Pattern until 3 sts. remain, k. 2 tog., k. 1.
3rd row: P. 2, pattern to end.
Repeat 2nd and 3rd rows, 18 (19) (20) times more—17 (18) (19) sts.
To shape the neck and continue armhole shaping: Cast off 5 (6) (7) sts. at beginning of next row, then dec. 1 st. at neck edge on the following 5 rows, *at the same time,* dec. 1 st. at armhole edge on the 1st of these rows, then on the 2 following alternate rows—4 sts.
Dec. 1 st. at armhole edge as before on next row and following alternate row—2 sts.
P. 2, then k. 2 tog. and fasten off.

THE SLEEVES (both alike): With No. 10 (3¼ mm) needles cast on 41 sts. and work 16 rows in rib as given for back.
Change to No. 8 (4 mm) needles and work 6 rows in pattern as given for back.
Taking extra sts. into the pattern as they occur, inc. 1 st. each end of next row, the on the 9 (10) (11) following 5th rows—61 (63) (65) sts.
Pattern 8 (9) (10) rows.
To shape the raglan sleeve top: Work exactly as

given for raglan armhole shaping on back when 5 sts. will remain. Cast off.

THE COLLAR: With No. 10 (3¼ mm) needles cast on 29 (33) (37) sts.

Next row: Cast on 8 sts., * p. 1, k. 1; repeat from * until 1 st. remains, p. 1.

Keeping continuity of rib and taking extra sts. into the rib as they occur, cast on 8 sts. at beginning of next 5 rows—77 (81) (85) sts.

Rib 12 rows.

Dec. 1 st. each end of next 6 rows—65 (69) (73) sts. Break yarn.

With right side of work facing, rejoin yarn and pick up and k. 19 sts. along row ends of right hand side of shaped edge, rib across 65 (69) (73) sts. on needle, then pick up and k. 19 sts. along row ends of left hand side of shaped edge—103 (107) (111) sts.

Next row: K. 1, * p. 1, k. 1; repeat from * to end.

Next row: P. 1, * k. 1, p. 1; repeat from * to end.

Repeat the last 2 rows, twice more.

Cast off in rib.

THE BUTTONHOLE BAND: With No. 10 (3¼ mm) needles cast on 7 sts. and work 4 (6) (8) rows in rib as given for back.

Buttonhole row: Rib 3, y.fwd., rib 2 tog., rib 2.

Rib 19 rows.

Repeat the last 20 rows, 4 times then the buttonhole row again.

Rib 5 (7) (9) rows. Cast off in rib.

THE BUTTON BAND: Work as buttonhole band, omitting buttonholes.

TO MAKE UP THE CARDIGAN: Do not press. Join raglan seams, then join sleeve and side seams. Sew on front bands, add buttons. Placing right side of collar to wrong side of work, sew on collar with a flat seam, including tops of front bands.

Left *Pink Cardigan with Collar (page 105)*

Boy's Cardigan with Dog Motifs

Illustrated opposite and on page 110

MEASUREMENTS	*in centimetres (and inches, in brackets)*					
To fit chest sizes	61	(24)	66	(26)	71	(28)
All round at underarms, fastened	63	(24¾)	68	(26¾)	73	(28¾)
Side seam	24.5	(9¾)	26.5	(10½)	29	(11½)
Length	37.5	(14¾)	41	(16¼)	44.5	(17½)
Sleeve seam	24.5	(9¾)	26.5	(10½)	29	(11½)

MATERIALS: *Allow the following quantities in 40 g balls of Argyll Top 20 D.K.: 3 brown, 1 natural and 1 red for 61 cm size; 4 brown, 1 natural and 1 red for 66 cm size; 4 brown, 2 natural and 1 red for 71 cm size. For any one size: A pair each of No. 8 (4 mm) and No. 10 (3¼ mm) knitting needles; 5 buttons.*

TENSION: *Work at a tension of 23 stitches and 28 rows to measure 10 × 10 cm, over the stocking stitch, using No. 8 (4 mm) needles, to obtain the measurements given above.*

ABBREVIATIONS: To be read before working: *K., knit plain; p., purl; st., stitch; inc., increase (by working twice into same st.); dec., decrease (by working 2 sts. together); s.s., stocking st. (k. on the right side and p. on the wrong side); b., brown; n., natural; r., red; single rib is k. 1 and p. 1 alternately; nil, meaning nothing is worked here for this size.*

NOTE: *The instructions are given for the 61 cm (24 inch) size. Where they vary, work figures within first brackets for 66 cm (26 inch) size; work figures within second brackets for 71 cm (28 inch) size.*

THE BACK: With No. 10 (3¼ mm) needles and b. cast on 72 (78) (84) sts. and work 14 rows in single rib.

Change to No. 8 (4 mm) needles and, beginning with a k. row, s.s. 56 (62) (68) rows.

To shape the armholes: Cast off 5 sts. at beginning of next 2 rows, then dec. 1 st. each end of next row, then on the 3 (4) (5) following alternate rows—54 (58) (62) sts.

S.s. 23 (25) (27) rows.

To slope the shoulders: Cast off 8 (8) (9) sts. at beginning of next 2 rows, then 7 (8) (8) sts. on the following 2 rows—24 (26) (28) sts.

Cast off.

THE LEFT FRONT: With No. 10 (3¼ mm) needles and b. cast on 41 (43) (47) sts. and, beginning odd-numbered rows with k. 1 and even-numbered rows with p. 1, work 4 rows in single rib.

1st buttonhole row: Rib until 5 sts. remain, cast off 2, rib to end.

2nd buttonhole row: Rib to end, casting on 2 sts. over those cast off on previous row.

Rib 7 rows.

Next row: Rib 7, and leave these sts. on a safety pin, rib to end, increasing 1 st. at end of this row for the 66 cm size only—34 (37) (40) sts.

** Change to No. 8 (4 mm) needles.

Joining in and breaking off colours as required, work the 5-row border pattern, which is worked entirely in s.s., so only the colour details are given.**

1st row: Nil (2) (3) n., * 1 r., 5 n.; repeat from * until 4 (5) (1) st(s). remain(s), 1 r., 3 (4) (nil) n.

2nd row: 2 (3) (nil) n., 3 (3) (2) b., * 3 n., 3 b.; repeat from * until 5 (1) (2) st(s). remain(s), 3 (1) (2) n., 2 (nil) (nil) b.

3rd row: 1 (nil) (1) n., * 2 b., 1 n.; repeat from * until nil (1) (nil) st. remains, nil (1) (nil) b.

4th row: 2 (3) (nil) b., 3 (3) (2) n., * 3 b., 3 n.; repeat from * until 5 (1) (2) st(s). remain(s), 3 (1) (2) b., 2 (nil) (nil) n.

5th row: 3 (5) (nil) n., * 1 b., 5 n.; repeat from * until 1 (2) (4) st(s). remain(s), 1 b., nil (1) (3) n.

*** S.s. 7 (9) (11) rows with n.—s.s. 8 (10) (12) rows here when working right front.

Work the 35-row dog-motif pattern:

1st row: 6 (8) (9) n., 11 b., 4 n., 6 b., 7 (8) (10) n.

2nd row: 7 (8) (10) n., 6 b., 4 n., 11 b., 6 (8) (9) n.

3rd row: 5 (7) (8) n., 11 b., 4 n., 6 b., 8 (9) (11) n.

4th row: 9 (10) (12) n., 5 b., 6 n., 9 b., 5 (7) (8) n.

5th row: 4 (6) (7) n., 11 b., 4 n., 6 b., 9 (10) (12) n.

6th row: 9 (10) (12) n., 6 b., 3 n., 12 b., 4 (6) (7) n.

7th row: 4 (6) (7) n., 11 b., 1 n., 9 b., 9 (10) (12) n.

8th row: 9 (10) (12) n., 10 b., 2 n., 9 b., 4 (6) (7) n.

9th row: 4 (6) (7) n., 8 b., 1 n., 12 b., 9 (10) (12) n.

10th row: 9 (10) (12) n., 22 b., 3 (5) (6) n.

11th row: 3 (5) (6) n., 22 b., 9 (10) (12) n.

12th and 13th rows: As 10th and 11th rows.

14th row: As 10th row.

15th row: 2 (4) (5) n., 23 b., 9 (10) (12) n.

16th row: 9 (10) (12) n., 23 b., 2 (4) (5) n.

17th row: 1 (3) (4) n., 5 b., 2 n., 14 b., 3 r., 9 (10) (12) n.

18th row: 9 (10) (12) n., 4 r., 10 b., 6 n., 4 b., 1 (3) (4) n.

19th row: 1 (3) (4) n., 3 b., 10 n., 6 b., 2 r., 3 b., 9 (10) (12) n.

20th row: 6 (7) (9) n., 7 b., 2 r., 2 b., 14 n., 2 b., 1 (3) (4) n.

21st row: 1 (3) (4) n., 2 b., 1 n., 2 b., 12 n., 2 r., 11 b., 3 (4) (6) n.

22nd row: 2 (3) (5) n., 13 b., 1 r., 11 n., 3 b., 1 n., 2 b., 1 (3) (4) n.

23rd row: 1 (3) (4) n., 2 b., 2 n., 2 b., 12 n., 11 b., 2 r., 2 (3) (5) n.

24th row: 2 (3) (5) n., 13 b., 12 n., 2 b., 2 n., 2 b., 1 (3) (4) n.

25th row: 1 (3) (4) n., 6 b., 12 n., 13 b., 2 (3) (5) n.

26th row: 1 (2) (4) n., 1 r., 2 n., 11 b., 13 n., 4 b., 2 (4) (5) n.

27th row: 3 (5) (6) n., 2 b., 14 n., 10 b., 5 (6) (8) n.

28th row: 6 (7) (9) n., 1 b., 1 n., 7 b., 19 (21) (22) n.

29th row: 19 (21) (22) n., 9 b., 6 (7) (9) n.

30th row: 6 (7) (9) n., 9 b., 3 n., 1 b., 15 (17) (18) n.

31st row: 15 (17) (18) n., 2 b., 1 n., 9 b., 3 n., 1 b., 3 (4) (6) n.

32nd row: 3 (4) (6) n., 2 b., 1 n., 13 b., 15 (17) (18) n.

33rd row: 15 (17) (18) n., 6 b., 4 n., 6 b., 3 (4) (6) n.

34th row: 4 (5) (7) n., 4 b., 6 n., 4 b., 16 (18) (19) n.

35th row: 27 (29) (30) n., 2 b., 5 (6) (8) n.

Break off b. and r. and continuing in n. only, s.s. 3 (7) (11) rows—s.s. 2 (6) (10) rows here when working right front.

To shape the front: Dec. 1 st. at neck edge on next row, then on the following 4th row—32 (35) (38) sts.

Work 1 row—work 2 rows here when working right front.

To shape the armhole and continue front shaping: Cast off 5 sts. at beginning of next row, work 1 row—omit this row when working right front—then dec. 1 st. at armhole edge on next row, then on the 3 (4) (5) following alternate rows, *at the same time*, dec. 1 st. at front edge on 4th row from previous front dec., then on the 7 (8) (9) following 4th rows—15 (16) (17) sts.

S.s. 1 row—s.s. 2 rows here when working right front.

To slope the shoulder: Cast off 8 (8) (9) sts. at beginning of next row—7 (8) (8) sts.

Work 1 row, then cast off.

THE RIGHT FRONT: With No. 10 (3¼ mm) needles and b. cast on 41 (43) (47) sts. and, beginning odd-numbered rows with k. 1 and even-numbered rows with p. 1, work 13 rows in single rib.

Next row: Nil (inc.) (nil), rib until 7 sts. remain, turn and leave these sts. on a safety pin—34 (37) (40) sts.

Work as left front from ** to **.

1st row: 3 (4) (nil) n., * 1 r., 5 n.; repeat from * until 1 (3) (4) st(s). remain(s), 1 r., nil (2) (3) n.

This row sets the position for border pattern. Keeping continuity of pattern to match left front, work a further 4 rows.

Work as left front from ***, noting variations.

THE SLEEVES (both alike): With No. 10 (3¼ mm) needles and b. cast on 38 (40) (42) sts. and work 14 rows in single rib.

Change to No. 8 (4 mm) needles and, beginning with a k. row, s.s. 6 rows, then inc. 1 st. each end of next row, then on the 5 (6) (7) following 8th rows—50 (54) (58) sts.

S.s. 9 (7) (5) rows.

To shape the sleeve top: Cast off 5 sts. at beginning of next 2 rows, work 2 rows, then dec. 1 st. each end of next row, then the 3 (4) (5) following 4th rows—32 (34) (36) sts.

Work 1 row, then dec. 1 st. each end of next row, then on the 2 following alternate rows.

Work 1 row, then cast off 3 sts. at the beginning of the next following 4 rows—14 (16) (18) sts. Cast off.

THE BUTTONHOLE BAND: First join shoulder seams. With right side of work facing and using No. 10 (3¼ mm) needles, rejoin b. to 7 sts. on safety pin, and work 8 (10) (12) rows in single rib.

Work the 2 buttonhole rows as given for left front, then rib 16 (18) (20) rows.

Repeat the last 18 (20) (22) rows twice, then the 2 buttonhole rows again.

Continue to rib until band fits up left front and across to centre back neck, casting off in rib when correct length is assured.

THE BUTTON BAND: Work as buttonhole band, but rejoining yarn to wrong side of work and omitting buttonholes.

TO MAKE UP THE CARDIGAN: Press lightly with a warm iron over a dry cloth. Set in sleeves, then join sleeve and side seams. Sew front bands into position, joining cast off groups at centre back neck and placing last buttonhole level with first front dec. Add buttons.

Opposite *Cardigan with Dog Motifs (page 108)*   Below *Lacy Yellow Cardigan (page 112)*

Girl's Lacy Yellow Cardigan

Illustrated on page 111

MEASUREMENTS	*in centimetres (and inches, in brackets)*					
To fit chest sizes	61	(24)	66	(26)	71	(28)
All round at underarms, fastened	63	$(24\frac{3}{4})$	68	$(26\frac{3}{4})$	73	$(28\frac{3}{4})$
Side seam	21.5	$(8\frac{1}{2})$	24	$(9\frac{1}{2})$	26.5	$(10\frac{1}{2})$
Length	35.5	(14)	39.5	$(15\frac{1}{2})$	43	(17)
Sleeve seam	25	(10)	28	(11)	32	$(12\frac{1}{2})$

MATERIALS: *Allow the following quantities in 50 g balls of Patons Beehive Double Knitting:* 4 *for 61 cm and 66 cm sizes and 5 buttons;* 5 *for 71 cm size and 6 buttons. For any one size: A pair each of No. 9 ($3\frac{3}{4}$ mm) and No. 11 (3 mm) knitting needles.*

TENSION: *Work at a tension of 25 stitches and 34 rows to measure 10 × 10 cm, over the pattern, using No. 9 ($3\frac{3}{4}$ mm) needles, to obtain the measurements given above.*

ABBREVIATIONS: To be read before working: *K., knit plain; p., purl; st., stitch; tog., together; inc., increase (by working twice into next st.); dec., decrease (by working 2 sts. tog.); single rib is k. 1 and p. 1 alternately; y.fwd., yarn forward to make a st.; y.r.n., yarn round needle to make a st.; sl., slip; s.k.p.o., (sl. 1, k. 1, pass sl. st. over); p. 2 tog.b., p. 2 tog. through back of sts.; nil meaning nothing is worked here for this size.*

NOTE: *The instructions are given for the 61 cm (24 inch) size. Where they vary, work figures within first brackets for 66 cm (26 inch) size; work figures within second brackets for 71 cm (28 inch) size.*

THE BACK: With No. 11 (3 mm) needles cast on 79 (85) (91) sts. and, beginning odd-numbered rows with k. 1 and even-numbered rows with p. 1, work 14 rows in single rib.

Change to No. 9 ($3\frac{3}{4}$ mm) needles and work the 6-row pattern as follows:

1st row: K. 1, * y.fwd., s.k.p.o., k. 1, k. 2 tog., y.fwd., k. 1; repeat from * to end of row.

2nd row: P. 2, * y.r.n., p. 3 tog., y.r.n., p. 3; repeat from * ending last repeat with p. 2.

3rd row: All k.

4th row: P. 1, * p. 2 tog.b., y.r.n., p. 1, y.r.n., p. 2 tog., p. 1; repeat from * to end of row.

5th row: K. 2 tog., * y.fwd., k. 3, y.fwd., k. 3 tog.; repeat from * ending last repeat with k. 2 tog. instead of k. 3 tog.

6th row: All p.

These 6 rows form the pattern.

Pattern a further 54 (62) (70) rows.

To shape the armholes: Keeping continuity of pattern, cast off 3 (4) (5) sts. at the beginning of each of the next 2 rows, then dec. 1 st. at each end of the next row and the 5 following alternate rows—61 (65) (69) sts.

Pattern 29 (33) (37) rows.

To slope the shoulders: Cast off 6 (6) (7) sts. at the beginning of each of the next 4 rows and 6 (7) (6) sts. at the beginning of each of the following 2 rows.

Cast off remaining 25 (27) (29) sts.

THE LEFT FRONT: With No. 11 (3 mm) needles cast on 45 (47) (51) sts. and work 13 rows in rib as given for back.

Next row: Rib 8 and leave these sts. on a safety pin for button border, rib to end, increasing 1 st. at the end of row for the 66 cm size only—37 (40) (43) sts.

Change to No. 9 ($3\frac{3}{4}$ mm) needles.

1st row: K. 1, * y.fwd., s.k.p.o., k. 1, k. 2 tog., y.fwd., k. 1; repeat from * to end (until 3 sts. remain, y.fwd., s.k.p.o., k. 1) (to end).

2nd row: P. 2 (p. 2 tog., y.r.n., p. 3) (p. 2), * y.r.n., p. 3 tog., y.r.n., p. 3; repeat from * ending last repeat with p. 2.

These 2 rows set the position of the pattern for the left front. Keeping continuity of pattern to match back, work a further 58 (66) (74) rows.

To shape the armhole and slope front edge: Cast off 3 (4) (5) sts. at the beginning of the next row. Work 1 row, then dec. 1 st. at armhole edge on the next row and the 5 following alternate rows, *at the same time*, dec. 1 st. at front edge on the 1st of these rows, then on the 9 (10) (11) following 4th rows—18 (19) (20) sts.

** Pattern 5 rows—pattern 6 rows here when working right front.

To slope the shoulder: Cast off 6 (6) (7) sts. at the beginning of the next row and the following alternate row—6 (7) (6) sts.

Work 1 row, then cast off.

THE RIGHT FRONT: With No. 11 (3 mm) needles cast on 45 (47) (51) sts. and work 4 rows in rib as given for back.

1st buttonhole row: Rib 3, cast off 2, rib to end.

2nd buttonhole row: Rib to end, casting on 2 sts. over those cast off on previous row.

Rib a further 7 rows.

Next row: Nil (inc.) (nil), rib until 8 sts. remain, turn and leave sts. on a safety-pin for buttonhole border—37 (40) (43) sts.

Change to No. 9 ($3\frac{3}{4}$ mm) needles.

1st row: K. 1 (k. 1, k. 2 tog., y.fwd., k. 1) (k. 1), * y.fwd., s.k.p.o., k. 1, k. 2 tog., y.fwd., k. 1; repeat from * to end.

2nd row: P. 2, * y.r.n., p. 3 tog., y.r.n., p. 3; repeat from * ending last repeat with p. 2 (until 2 sts. remain, y.r.n., p. 2 tog.) (ending last repeat with p. 2).

These 2 rows set the position of the pattern for the right front. Keeping continuity of pattern to match back, work a further 58 (66) (74) rows.

To slope the front edge: Next row: Dec., pattern to end.

To shape the armhole and continue to slope front edge: Cast off 3 (4) (5) sts. at the beginning of the next row, then dec. 1 st. at armhole edge on the next row and the 5 following alternate rows, *at the same time*, dec. 1 st. at front edge on the 4th row from previous dec. and then on the 8 (9) (10) following 4th rows—18 (19) (20) sts.

Work as given for left front from ** to end, noting variation.

THE SLEEVES (both alike): With No. 11 (3 mm) needles cast on 41 (43) (45) sts. and work 13 (15) (15) rows in rib as on back.

Next (inc.) row: Rib 13 (4) (7), inc., * rib 13 (6) (9), inc.; repeat from * until 13 (3) (7) sts. remain, rib to end—43 (49) (49) sts.

Change to No. 9 (3¾ mm) needles and work 6 (12) (6) rows in pattern as on back.

Maintaining continuity of the pattern and taking extra sts. into the pattern as they occur, inc. 1 st. at each end of the next row and the 7 (7) (10) following 8th rows—59 (65) (71) sts.

Pattern 9 (11) (7) rows.

To shape the sleeve top: Cast off 3 (4) (5) sts. at the beginning of each of the next 2 rows, then dec. 1 st. at the beginning only of the following 14 (18) (22) rows—39 sts.

Cast off 2 sts. at the beginning of each of the next 8 rows, then cast off 3 sts. at the beginning of each of the following 2 rows.

Cast off remaining 17 sts.

THE BUTTONHOLE BORDER: With wrong side of work facing and using No. 11 (3 mm) needles, rejoin yarn to the 8 sts. on safety pin and rib 9 (11) (9) rows.

Work the 2 buttonhole rows as before, then rib 16 (18) (16) rows.

Repeat the last 18 (20) (18) rows, 2 (2) (3) times, then the 2 buttonhole rows again.

Continue in rib until border is long enough, when slightly stretched to fit up right front to centre back neck, casting off in rib when correct length is assured.

THE BUTTON BORDER: With the right side of work facing and using No. 11 (3 mm) needles, rejoin yarn to the 8 sts. on safety pin and work as given for buttonhole border, omitting buttonholes.

TO MAKE UP THE CARDIGAN: Do not press. Set in sleeves, then join sleeve and side seams. Join cast-on and cast-off edges of button and buttonhole borders, then sew borders in position. Add buttons.

Girl's Embroidered Yellow Cardigan

Illustrated on page 114

MEASUREMENTS			*in centimetres (and inches, in brackets)*					
To fit chest sizes	61	(24)	66	(26)	71	(28)	76	(30)
Side seam	27	(10½)	30	(11¾)	32	(12½)	33.5	(13¼)
Length	40	(15¾)	44.5	(17½)	48	(19)	51.5	(20¼)
Sleeve seam	28	(11)	31	(12¼)	34.5	(13½)	37.5	(14¾)

MATERIALS: *Allow the following quantities in 50 g balls of Richard Poppleton Emmerdale D.K.: 4 for 61 cm size; 4 for 66 cm size; 5 for 71 cm size; 6 for 76 cm size. For any one size: a pair each of No. 8 (4 mm) and No. 10 (3¼ mm) knitting needles; 7 buttons; a small ball of yarn in each of pink and green for embroidery; a cable needle.*

TENSION: *Work at a tension of 25 stitches and 31 rows to measure 10 × 10 cm, over the stocking stitch, using No. 8 (4 mm) needles, to obtain measurements given above.*

ABBREVIATIONS: To be read before working: *K., knit plain; p., purl; st., stitch; tog., together; inc., increase (by working twice into same st.); dec., decrease (by working 2 sts. tog.); s.s., stocking st. (k. on right side, p. on wrong side); c. 4 f., cable 4 front (slip next 2 sts. on to cable needle and leave at front of work, k. 2 then k. 2 from cable needle); c. 4 b., cable 4* back (slip next 2 sts. on to cable needle and leave at back of work, k. 2 then k. 2 from cable needle); single rib is k. 1 and p. 1 alternately; y.fwd., yarn forward to make a st.

NOTE: *The instructions are given for the 61 cm (24 inch) size. Where they vary, work figures within first brackets for 66 cm (26 inch) size; work figures within second brackets for 71 cm (28 inch) size, and so on.*

THE BACK: With No. 10 (3¼ mm) needles cast on 79 (85) (91) (97) sts. and, beginning odd-numbered rows with k. 1 and even-numbered rows with p. 1, work 14 rows in single rib.

Change to No. 8 (4 mm) needles and, beginning with a k. row, s.s. 72 (80) (86) (92) rows.

Continued on page 116

Opposite *Embroidered Yellow Cardigan (page 113)*

Above *Twin-set with Contrast Yolk: Cardigan (page 118)*

To shape the armholes: Cast off 5 sts. at beginning of next 2 rows, then dec. 1 st. each end of next row and the 5 (6) (6) (7) following alternate rows—57 (61) (67) (71) sts.

S.s. 23 (27) (31) (35) rows.

To slope the shoulders: Cast off 8 (9) (10) (11) sts. at beginning of next 4 rows—25 (25) (27) (27) sts.

Cast off.

THE LEFT FRONT: With No. 10 (3¼ mm) needles cast on 41 (43) (47) (51) sts. and work 14 rows in single rib, increasing 1 st. at each end of the last of these rows on the 61 cm, 66 cm and 71 cm sizes only—43 (45) (49) (51) sts.

Change to No. 8 (4 mm) needles and work the 4-row pattern as follows:**

1st row: K. 11 (12) (13) (14), p. 1, c. 4f., k. 2, p. 6 (6) (8) (8), c. 4f., k. 2, p. 1, k. 12 (13) (14) (15).

2nd row: P. 12 (13) (14) (15), k. 1, p. 6, k. 6 (6) (8) (8), p. 6, k. 1, p. 11 (12) (13) (14).

3rd row: K. 11 (12) (13) (14), p. 1, k. 2, c. 4b., p. 6 (6) (8) (8), k. 2, c. 4b., p. 1, k. 12 (13) (14) (15).

4th row: As 2nd row.

*** Pattern a further 68 (76) (82) (88) rows—pattern 69 (77) (83) (89) rows here when working right front.

To shape the armhole: Cast off 5 sts. at beginning of next row, work 1 row—omit this row when working right front—then dec. 1 st. at armhole edge on next row, then on the 5 (6) (6) (7) following alternate rows—32 (33) (37) (38) sts.

Pattern 6 (10) (14) (18) rows—pattern 7 (11) (15) (19) rows here when working right front.

To shape the neck: Cast off 5 sts. at beginning of next row and then on the 6 following alternate rows—20 (21) (25) (26) sts.

Pattern 3 rows.

To slope the shoulder: Cast off 10 (11) (13) (13) sts. at beginning of next row—10 (10) (12) (13) sts.

Work 1 row.

Cast off.

THE RIGHT FRONT: Work as left front to **.

1st row: K. 12 (13) (14) (15), p. 1, c. 4f., k. 2, p. 6 (6) (8) (8), c. 4f., k. 2, p. 1, k. 11 (12) (13) (14).

2nd row: P. 11 (12) (13) (14), k. 1, p. 6, k. 6 (6) (8) (8), p. 6, k. 1, p. 12 (13) (14) (15).

3rd row: K. 12 (13) (14) (15), p. 1, k. 2, c. 4b., p. 6 (6) (8) (8), k. 2, c. 4b., p. 1, k. 11 (12) (13) (14).

4th row: As 2nd row.

Work as left front from ***, noting variations.

THE SLEEVES (both alike): With No. 10 (3¼ mm) needles cast on 39 (41) (43) (45) sts. and work 14 rows in single rib, increasing 1 st. at the end of the last of these rows—40 (42) (44) (46) sts.

Change to No. 8 (4 mm) needles and work the 4-row pattern as follows.

1st row: K. 10 (11) (11) (12), p. 1 c. 4f., k. 2, p. 6 (6) (8) (8), c. 4f., k. 2, p. 1, k. 10 (11) (11) (12).

2nd row: P. 10 (11) (11) (12), k. 1, p. 6, k. 6 (6) (8) (8), p. 6, k. 1, p. 10 (11) (11) (12).

3rd row: K. 10 (11) (11) (12), p. 1, k. 2, c. 4b., p. 6 (6) (8) (8), k. 2, c. 4b., p. 1, k. 10 (11) (11) (12).

4th row: As 2nd row.

Continuing in pattern, inc. 1 st. each end of next row, then on the following 10th row.

Pattern 9 rows.

Continuing in s.s. only, inc. 1 st. each end of next row,

then on the 4 (5) (6) (7) following 10th rows—54 (58) (62) (66) sts.

S.s. 9 rows.

To shape the sleeve top: Cast off 5 sts. at beginning of next 2 rows, then dec. 1 st. each end, next row and then on the 7 (7) (7) (9) following alternate rows then on the 1 (2) (3) (3) following 4th rows—26 (28) (30) (30) sts.

Work 1 row, then cast off 4 sts. at beginning of next 4 rows—10 (12) (12) (14) sts.

Cast off.

THE COLLAR: With No. 10 (3¼ mm) needles cast on 63 (63) (67) (67) sts. and work 14 rows in rib as given on back.

Dec. 1 st. at beginning of next 2 rows, then cast off 2 sts. at beginning of next 2 rows, then 3 sts. on the following 2 rows—51 (51) (55) (55) sts.

Next row: Cast on 18 sts., k. to end.

Next row: Cast on 18 sts., p. to end—87 (87) (91) (91) sts.

S.s. 3 rows.

Next row: All k. to mark hemline.

Beginning with a k. row, s.s. 4 rows.

Cast off.

THE BUTTONHOLE BORDER: With No. 10 (3¼ mm) needles cast on 7 sts. and work 4 (6) (4) (4) rows in rib as given for back.

Buttonhole row: Rib 3, y.fwd., k. 2 tog., rib 2.

Rib 15 (17) (19) (21) rows.

Repeat the last 16 (18) (20) (22) rows, 5 times more, then the buttonhole row again.

Rib 5 rows. Cast off in rib.

THE BUTTON BAND: Work as buttonhole band, omitting buttonholes.

TO MAKE UP THE CARDIGAN: Press with a warm iron over a dry cloth. Join shoulder seams, set in sleeves, then join sleeve and side seams. Sew on front bands, then add buttons. Sew 18 st. cast on groups to row ends of collar. Fold collar to wrong side at hemline and st. into place. Sew cast on edge of collar round neck edge, leaving front bands free. With green, embroider daisies down each front and sleeve panel in lazy-daisy stitches, and pink centres.

Girl's Twin-set with Contrast Yoke

Illustrated on pages 115 and 119

MEASUREMENTS							*in centimetres (and inches, in brackets)*	
To fit chest sizes	61	(24)	66	(26)	71	(28)	76	(30)
Sweater								
All round at underarms	66.5	(26¼)	70.5	(27¾)	74.5	(29¼)	79	(31)
Side seam	28.5	(11¼)	30	(11¾)	31.5	(12½)	33.5	(13¼)
Length	44.5	(17½)	46	(18)	49	(19¼)	50.5	(20)
Sleeve seam	33.5	(13¼)	35	(13¾)	36.5	(14¼)	38.5	(15¼)
Cardigan								
All round at underarms, fastened	67	(26½)	72.5	(28½)	77.5	(30½)	83	(32¾)
Side seam	31	(12¼)	33	(13)	35	(13¾)	37	(14½)
Length	48	(18¾)	50	(19¾)	53.5	(21)	55.5	(22)
Sleeve seam	33.5	(13¼)	35.5	(14)	37.5	(14¾)	40	(15¾)

MATERIALS: *Allow the following quantities in 50 g balls of Lister Richmond for 4-ply knitting: 2 main shade for the 61 cm size; 3 main shade for the 66 cm and 71 cm sizes; 4 main shade for the 76 cm size. For any one size: A ball each of the above yarn in 2 contrasting shades; a pair each of No. 10 (3¼ mm) and No. 12 (2¾ mm) knitting needles.*

Cardigan: *Allow the following quantities in 50 g balls of Lister Richmond Double Knitting: 4 main shade for the 61 cm size; 5 main shade for the 66 cm and 71 cm sizes; 6 main shade for the 76 cm size. For any one size: A ball each of the above yarn in 2 contrasting shades; a pair each of No. 8 (4 mm) and No. 10 (3¼ mm) knitting needles; 7 buttons.*

TENSION: *Sweater: Work at a tension of 26 stitches to measure 9 cm width and 36 rows to measure 10 cm in depth over the stocking stitch, using No. 10 (3¼ mm) needles and 4-ply, to obtain the measurements given above. Cardigan: Work at a tension of 23 stitches and 29 rows to measure 10 × 10 cm, over the stocking stitch, using No. 8 (4 mm) needles and double knitting, to obtain the measurements given above.*

ABBREVIATIONS: To be read before working: *K., knit plain; p., purl; st., stitch; dec., decrease (by working 2 sts. together); inc., increase (by working twice into same st.); s.s., stocking st. (k. on the right side and p. on the wrong side); single rib is k. 1 and p. 1 alternately; nil, meaning nothing is worked here for this size; m., main shade; a., first contrast; b., second contrast.*

NOTE: *Instructions as given for the 61 cm (24 inch) size. Where they vary, work figures within the first brackets for the 66 cm (26 inch) size; work figures within second brackets for the 71 cm (28 inch) size, and so on.*

SWEATER

THE BACK: With No. 12 (2¾ mm) needles and m. cast on 96 (102) (108) (114) sts. and work 20 rows in single rib.

Change to No. 10 (3¼ mm) needles and s.s. 84 (90) (96) (102) rows.

Join in a. and s.s. a further 2 rows.

Mark each end of last row for side seams.

S.s. 2 rows, b., 2 rows m., 2 rows a. and 2 rows b.

Work the yoke pattern as follows, which is worked entirely in s.s. beginning with a k. row, so only the colour details are given. Join in and break off colours as required and twist yarns when changing colours to avoid a hole.

1st row: 2 b., * 3 m., 3 b.; repeat from * ending last repeat with 1 b. instead of 3 b.

2nd row: * 2 b., 1 m.; repeat from * to end.

3rd row: 2 m., * 3 b., 3 m.; repeat from * ending last repeat with 1 m.

4th row: 2 m., * 1 b., 5 m.; repeat from * ending last repeat with 3 m.

5th to 8th rows: S.s. 1 row m., 2 rows b., 1 row m.

9th row: * 1 a., 5 m.; repeat from * to end.

10th row: 1 a., * 3 m., 3 a.; repeat from * ending last repeat with 2 a.

11th row: As 9th row. **12th row:** All m.

13th row: 3 m., * 1 a., 5 m.; repeat from * ending last repeat with 2 m.

14th row: 1 m., * 3 a., 3 m.; repeat from * ending last repeat with 2 m.

15th row: As 13th row. **16th row:** all m.

17th to 19th rows: Repeat the 9th and 10th rows once, then the 9th row again.

20th to 22nd rows: S.s. 1 row m., 2 rows b.

These 22 rows form the yoke pattern. ******

Pattern a further 22 rows.

Break off a. and b. and continue in m. only.

S.s. a further 2 (2) (6) (6) rows.

To slope the shoulders: Cast off 16 (17) (18) (19) sts. at the beginning of each of the next 2 rows, then 17 (18) (19) (20) sts. at the beginning of each of the following 2 rows—30 (32) (34) (36) sts. Leave these sts.

THE FRONT: Work as given for back to ******.

Pattern a further 5 (5) (9) (9) rows.

To divide for neck: Next row: Pattern 37 (39) (41) (43) and leave these sts. on a spare needle for right half neck, pattern 22 (24) (26) (28) and leave these sts. on a st. holder, pattern to end and work on remaining 37 (39) (41) (43) sts. for left half neck.

Continued on page 118

The left half-neck: Keeping continuity of pattern, dec. 1 st. at neck edge of the next row and the 3 (3) (2) (2) following 4th rows—33 (35) (38) (40) sts.

Pattern 3 rows.

Break off a. and b. and continue in m. only.

Work 1 row, decreasing 1 st. at neck edge on the 71 cm and 76 cm sizes only—33 (35) (37) (39) sts.

S.s. a further 1 (1) (5) (5) row(s)—s.s. 2 (2) (6) (6) rows here when working right half neck.

To slope the shoulder: Cast off 16 (17) (18) (19) sts. at the beginning of the next row—17 (18) (19) (20) sts.

Work 1 row. Cast off.

The right half neck: With right side of work facing, rejoin appropriate yarn to inner end of the 37 (39) (41) (43) sts. left on spare needle and work as given for left half neck, noting variation.

THE SLEEVES (both alike): With No. 12 (2¾ mm) needles and c. cast on 48 (48) (54) (54) sts. and work 18 rows in single rib.

Change to No. 10 (3¼ mm) needles and s.s. 2 (2) (2) (8) rows.

Maintaining continuity of s.s., inc. 1 st. at each end of the next row and the 17 following 4th rows—84 (84) (90) (90) sts.

S.s. a further 18 (24) (30) (30) rows.

Join in b. and s.s. 2 rows, then s.s. 1 row m.

Work the 9th and 22nd rows of yoke pattern as given on back. Cast off with b.

THE NECKBAND: First join right shoulder seam. With right side of work facing, using No. 12 (2¾ mm) needles and c., pick up and k. 18 sts. down left side of neck, k. across the 22 (24) (26) (28) sts. at centre front, pick up and k. 18 sts. up right side of neck, and finally, k. across 30 (32) (34) (36) sts. at back neck—88 (92) (96) (100) sts.

Work 8 rows in single rib. Cast off.

TO MAKE UP THE SWEATER: Press with a warm iron over a damp cloth. Join left shoulder seam. Sew cast off edge of sleeves between markers on back and front. Join side and sleeve seams.

CARDIGAN

THE BACK: With No. 10 (3¼ mm) needles and m. cast on 78 (84) (90) (96) sts. and work 14 rows in single rib.

*** Change to No. 8 (4 mm) needles and s.s. 78 (84) (90) (96) rows. ***

Mark each end of last row for side seams.

Work the 1st to 22nd rows of yoke pattern as given on back of sweater, twice.

Break off a. and b. and continue in m. only.

S.s. a further 2 (2) (6) (6) rows.

To slope the shoulders: Cast off 13 (14) (15) (16) sts. at the beginning of next 2 rows, then 13 (14) (16) (17) sts. on following 2 rows—26 (28) (28) (30) sts. Leave these sts.

THE LEFT FRONT: With No. 10 (3¼ mm) needles and m. cast on 36 (38) (42) (44) sts. and work 14 rows in single rib, increasing 1 st. at end of last row on the 66 cm and 76 cm sizes only—36 (39) (42) (45) sts.

Work as given for back from *** to ***.

Mark end—read beginning here when working right front—of last row to denote end of side seam. ****

1st pattern row: 2 b., * 3 m., 3 b.; repeat from * until 4 (1) (4) (1) st(s). remain(s), 3 m., 1 b. (1 m.) (3 m., 1 b.) (1 m.).

2nd row: * 2 b., 1 m.; repeat from * to end.

***** These 2 rows set the position of the pattern. Keeping continuity of pattern to match back, pattern a further 31 (31) (35) (35) rows—pattern 30 (30) (34) (34) rows here when working right front.

To shape the neck: Next row: Cast off 4 (5) (5) (6) sts., pattern to end.

Pattern 1 row here when working right front.

Dec. 1 st. at neck edge on the next row and the 4 (4) (2) (2) following alternate rows—27 (29) (34) (36) sts.

S.s. 1 row.

Break off a. and b. and continue in m. only.

Dec. 1 st. at neck edge on the next row and the nil (nil) (2) (2) following alternate rows—26 (28) (31) (33) sts.

S.s. 1 row—s.s. 2 rows here when working right front.

To slope the shoulder: Cast off 13 (14) (15) (16) sts. at the beginning of the next row—13 (14) (16) (17) sts. Work 1 row. Cast off.

THE RIGHT FRONT: Work as given for left front to ****, noting variation.

1st pattern row: 2 b. (2 m., 3 b.) (2 b.) (2 m., 3 b.), * 3 m., 3 b.; repeat from * until 4 sts. remain, 3 m., 1 b.

2nd row: * 2 b., 1 m.; repeat from * to end.

Work as given for left front from ***** to end, noting variations.

THE SLEEVES (both alike): With No. 10 (3¼ mm) needles and m. cast on 38 (38) (42) (42) sts. and work 14 rows in single rib.

Change to No. 8 (4 mm) needles.

S.s. 6 (2) (2) (2) rows.

Maintaining continuity of s.s., inc. 1 st. at each end of the next row and the 16 (16) (17) (17) following 3rd (4th) (4th) (4th) rows—72 (72) (78) (78) sts.

S.s. a further 14 (8) (10) (16) rows.

Join in b. and s.s. 2 rows, then s.s. 1 row m.

Work the 9th to 22nd rows of yoke pattern as given on back of sweater.

Cast off loosely with b.

THE BUTTONHOLE BORDER: With No. 10 (3¼ mm) needles and m. cast on 8 sts. and work 4 (2) (2) (4) rows in single rib.

1st (buttonhole) row: Rib 3, cast off 2 sts., rib to end.

2nd (buttonhole) row: Rib to end, casting on 2 sts. over this cast off on previous row.

Rib a further 16 (18) (20) (20) rows.

Repeat the last 18 (20) (22) (22) rows, 4 times, then the 2 buttonhole rows again.

Rib a further 14 (12) (12) (16) rows.

Leave these sts. on a safety pin.

THE BUTTONHOLE BORDER: Work as given for buttonhole border, omitting buttonholes.

THE NECKBAND: First join shoulder seams. With right side of work facing, using No. 10 (3¼ mm) needles and m., rib across the 8 sts. of buttonhole border, pick up and k. 23 sts. up right side of neck, k. across the 26 (28) (28) (30) sts. at back neck, pick up and k. 23 sts. down left side of

neck and finally rib across the 8 sts. of button border—89 (90) (90) (92) sts.

Work 3 rows in single rib, then work the 2 buttonhole rows again.

Rib a further 2 rows. Cast off in rib.

TO MAKE UP THE CARDIGAN: Press as given for sweater. Sew cast off edge of sleeves between markers on back and fronts. Join side and sleeve seams. Sew on front borders. Add buttons.

Above *Twin-set with Contrast Yolk: Sweater (page 117)*

Pink Mohair Jersey

Illustrated on page 122

MEASUREMENTS	*in centimetres (and inches, in brackets)*					
To fit chest sizes	61	(24)	66–71	(26–28)	76	(30)
All round at underarms	67.5	(26½)	74	(29)	80.5	(31½)
Side seam	26	(10¼)	27.5	(10¾)	29	(11¼)
Length	38	(15)	41	(16)	44.5	(17½)
Sleeve seam	26	(10¼)	27.5	(10¾)	29	(11¼)

MATERIALS: *Allow the following quantities in 25 g balls of Wendy Mohair: 9 for the 61 cm and 66–71 cm sizes; 10 for the 76 cm size. For any one size: A pair each of No. 7 (4½ mm) and No. 8 (4 mm) knitting needles.*

TENSION: *Work at a tension of 18 stitches and 25 rows to measure 10 × 10 cm over the ridge pattern, using No. 7 (4½ mm) needles, to obtain the measurements given above.*

ABBREVIATIONS: To be read before working: *K., knit plain; p., purl; st., stitch; tog., together; sl., slip; dec., decrease (by working 2 sts. tog.); inc., increase (by working twice into same st.); p.s.s.o., pass sl. st. over; s.k.p.o., (sl. 1, k. 1, p.s.s.o.); y.fwd., yarn forward to make a st.; s.s., stocking st. (k. on the right side and p. on the wrong side); p. 2 s.s.o., pass 2 sl.sts. over; single rib is k. 1 and p. 1 alternately.*

NOTE: *The instructions are given for the 61 cm (24 inch) size. Where they vary, work the figures within first brackets for the 66–71 cm (26–28 inch) size, and so on.*

THE BACK: With No. 8 (4 mm) needles cast on 60 (66) (72) sts. and work 12 rows in single rib.

Change to No. 7 (4½ mm) needles: **

1st to 12th rows: —Beginning with a p. row, s.s. 12 rows.

13th to 16th rows: All k.

These 16 rows form the ridge pattern.

Pattern a further 39 (43) (47) rows.

*** To shape the armholes: Keeping continuity of the pattern, cast off 2 sts. at the beginning of each of the next 2 rows, then dec. 1 st. at each end of the next row and the 1 (2) (3) following alternate row(s)—52 (56) (60) sts. ***

Pattern a further 21 (23) (25) rows.

To slope the shoulders: Cast off 6 (7) (7) sts. at the beginning of each of the next 2 rows, then 7 (7) (8) sts. on the following 2 rows—26 (28) (30) sts. Leave these sts.

THE FRONT: Work as given for back to **.

1st row: All p.

2nd row: K. 18 (21) (24), * y.fwd., s.k.p.o., k. 1, k. 2 tog., y.fwd., k. 1; repeat from * 3 times, k. 18 (21) (24).

3rd row: As 1st row.

4th row: K. 19 (22) (25), * y.fwd., sl. 2 k.wise, k. 1, p. 2 s.s.o., y.fwd., k. 3; repeat from * 3 times, k. 17 (20) (23).

5th to 12th rows: Repeat the 1st to 4th rows, twice.

13th row: K. 18 (21) (24), p. 24, k. 18 (21) (24). **14th row:** As 2nd row.

15th row: As 13th row.

16th row: As 4th row.

These 16 rows form the pattern for the front. Pattern a further 39 (43) (47) rows.

Work as given for back from *** to ***.

Pattern a further 12 (14) (16) rows.

To divide for neck: Next row: Pattern 19 (20) (21) and leave these sts. on a spare needle for right half neck, pattern 14 (16) (18) and leave these sts. on a st. holder, pattern to end and work on these sts. for left half neck.

The left half neck: Dec. 1 st. at neck edge on each of next 6 rows—13 (14) (15) sts.

Pattern a further 2 rows—pattern 3 rows here when working right half neck.

To slope the shoulder: Cast off 6 (7) (7) sts. at beginning of the next row—7 (7) (8) sts.

Work 1 row. Cast off.

The right half neck: With right side of work facing, rejoin yarn to inner end of the 19 (20) (21) sts. left on spare needle and work as given for left half neck, noting variation.

THE SLEEVES (both alike): With No. 8 (4 mm) needles cast on 34 (36) (38) sts. and work 12 rows in rib.

Change to No. 7 (4½ mm) needles and work 9 rows in pattern as given on back.

Maintaining continuity of the pattern, and taking extra sts. into pattern as they occur, inc. 1 st. at each end of the next row and 2 (3) (3) following 8th rows—40 (44) (46) sts.

Pattern a further 29 (25) (29) rows.

To shape the sleeve top: Cast off 2 sts. at the beginning of the next 2 rows, then dec. 1 st. at each end of next row and the 1 (2) (3) following alternate row(s)—32 (34) (34) sts.

Work 1 (1) (3) row(s).

Cast off 3 sts. at the beginning of the next 6 (8) (8) rows—14 (10) (10) sts. Cast off.

THE NECKBAND: First join right shoulder seam. With right side of work facing, rejoin yarn and using No. 8 (4 mm) needles, pick up and k. 11 (12) (13) sts. down left side of front neck, k. across the 14 (16) (18) sts. at centre front, pick up and k. 11 (12) (13) sts. up right side of front neck, and finally, k. across the 26 (28) (30) sts. at back neck—62 (68) (74) sts.

Work 5 rows in single rib. Cast off in rib.

TO MAKE UP THE JERSEY: Press. Join left shoulder seam. Set in sleeves. Join side and sleeve seams.

Boy's Twist Stitch and Cable Sweater

Illustrated on page 123

MEASUREMENTS		*in centimetres (and inches, in brackets)*				
To fit chest sizes	61	(24)	66	(26)	71	(28)
Side seam	24	(9½)	26.5	(10½)	29	(11½)
Length	38.5	(15¼)	41.5	(16¼)	45.5	(18)
Sleeve seam	29	(11½)	32	(12½)	35.5	(14)

MATERIALS: *Allow the following quantities in 50 g balls of Sirdar Talisman D.K.: 5 for 61 cm size; 6 for 66 cm and 71 cm sizes. For any one size: A pair each of No. 8 (4 mm) and No. 9 (3¾ mm) knitting needles; a cable needle.*

TENSION: *Work at a tension of 24 stitches and 32 rows to measure 10 × 10 cm, over the twist pattern, using No. 8 (4 mm) needles, to obtain the measurements given above.*

ABBREVIATIONS: To be read before working: *K., knit plain; p., purl; st., stitch; tog., together; k. 1 b., k. into back of next st.; inc., increase (by working twice into next st.); dec., decrease (by working 2 sts. tog.); c. 4 f., cable 4 front (slip next 2 sts. on to cable needle and leave at front of work, k. 2, then k. 2 from cable needle); c. 4 b., cable 4 back (as c. 4 f. but leave cable needle at back of work); tw. rib, twist rib (k. 1 b. and p. 1 alternately).*

NOTE: *The instructions are given for the 61 cm (24 inch) chest size. Where they vary, work figures within the first brackets for the 66 cm (26 inch) chest size; work figures within second brackets for the 71 cm (28 inch) chest size.*

THE BACK: With No. 9 (3¾ mm) needles cast on 78 (84) (90) sts. and work 15 rows in tw. rib.

Inc. row: Tw. rib 8 (11) (14), inc., * rib 11, inc.; repeat from * 4 times, tw. rib to end—84 (90) (96) sts.

Change to No. 8 (4 mm) needles.

Foundation row (wrong side): K. 21 (24) (27), p. 42, k. 21 (24) (27).

1st pattern row (right side): P. 3, * k. 1 b., p. 2; repeat from * 5 (6) (7) times, for panel k. 42, ** p. 2, k. 1 b.; repeat from ** 5 (6) (7) times, p. 3.

2nd and every alternate row: K. 21 (24) (27), for panel p. 42, k. 21 (24) (27).

These 2 rows form the tw. pattern at each side.

Keeping continuity of the tw. pattern, continue centre panel as follows: **3rd row:** Tw. pattern 21 (24) (27), k. 9, c. 4 f., c. 4 b., k. 8, c. 4 f., c. 4 b., k. 9, tw. pattern 21 (24) (27).

5th row: As 1st row.

7th row: Tw. pattern 21 (24) (27), k. 1, * c. 4 b., c. 4 f., k. 8; repeat from * once, c. 4 b., c. 4 f., k. 1, tw. pattern 21 (24) (27).

9th row: As 1st row.

11th row: Tw. pattern 21 (24) (27), k. 1, * c. 4 f., c. 4 b., k. 8; repeat from * once, c. 4 f., c. 4 b., k. 1, tw. pattern 21 (24) (27).

13th row: As 1st row.

15th row: Tw. pattern 21 (24) (27), k. 9, c. 4 b., c. 4 f., k. 8, c. 4 b., c. 4 f., k. 9, tw. pattern 21 (24) (27).

16th row: As 2nd row.

These 16 rows form the pattern. Pattern a further 44 (52) (60) rows.

To shape armholes: Keeping continuity of the pattern, cast off 4 sts. at beginning of the next 2 rows, then dec. 1 st. each end of next row and the 2 (3) (4) following alternate rows—70 (74) (78) sts. ★★★

Pattern 35 (35) (37) rows.

To slope shoulders: Cast off 8 (9) (9) sts. at beginning of next 2 rows, then 9 (9) (10) sts. on following 2 rows.

Break yarn and leave remaining 36 (38) (40) sts. on spare needle.

THE FRONT: Work as given for back to ★★★.

Pattern 20 (20) (22) rows.

To divide for neck: Next row: Pattern 23 (24) (25) and leave on a spare needle for right half neck, p. 24 (26) (28) and leave on st. holder, pattern to end and work on these last 23 (24) (25) sts. for left half neck.

The left half neck: Dec. 1 st. at neck edge on each of next 6 rows—17 (18) (19) sts.

Pattern 8 rows—read pattern 9 rows here when working right half neck.

To slope shoulder: Cast off 8 (9) (9) sts. at beginning of next row.

Work 1 row, then cast off remaining 9 (9) (10) sts.

The right half neck: With right side facing, rejoin yarn to inner end of 23 (24) (25) sts. on spare needle and work as given for left half neck, noting variation.

THE SLEEVES (2 alike): With No. 9 (3¾ mm) needles cast on 44 (44) (46) sts. and work 16 rows in tw. rib, increasing 1 st. at end of last row on the 71 cm size only—44 (44) (47) sts.

Change to No. 8 (4 mm) needles.

Foundation row (wrong side): K. to end.

1st pattern row (right side): P. 2, * k. 1 b., p. 2; repeat from * to end.

2nd row: K. to end.

These 2 rows form the pattern for the sleeves. Pattern a further 4 rows.

Keeping continuity of the pattern and, working extra sts. into pattern as they occur, inc. 1 st. at each end of next row and the 8 (9) (10) following 8th rows—62 (64) (69) sts.

Pattern 5 (7) (9) rows.

To shape sleeve top: Work as given for armhole shaping on back—48 (48) (51) sts.

Work 1 row, then cast off 4 sts. at beginning of the next 10 rows.

Cast off remaining 8 (8) (11) sts.

Continued on page 123

Below *Pink Mohair Jersey (page 120)*

THE NECK RIBBING: First join right shoulder seam. With right side facing, rejoin yarn and using No. 9 (3¾ mm) needles, pick up and k. 16 sts. from row ends of left front neck shaping, k. across 24 (26) (28) sts. at centre front, pick up and k. 16 sts. from row ends of right front neck shaping, and finally, k. across 36 (38) (40) sts. at back neck—92 (96) (100) sts.

   Work 8 rows in tw. rib.

   Cast off in rib.

Above *Twist Stitch and Cable Sweater (page 121)*

TO MAKE UP THE SWEATER: Press lightly with a warm iron over a dry cloth. Join left shoulder seam, continuing seam across neck ribbing. Set in sleeves, then join side and sleeve seams.

Boy's Cricket Sweater

Illustrated on page 126

MEASUREMENTS

in centimetres (and inches, in brackets)

To fit chest sizes	61	(24)	66	(26)	71	(28)	76	(30)	81	(32)	86	(34)	91	(36)
All round at underarms	64	(25)	69	(27)	76	(30)	81	(32)	87.5	(34½)	92.5	(36½)	97	(38¼)
Side seam	26	(10¼)	28	(11)	30	(11¾)	32	(12½)	34	(13¼)	36	(14¼)	38	(15)
Length	41	(16)	44	(17¼)	46.5	(18¼)	50	(19¾)	52.5	(20¾)	55	(21¾)	58	(22¾)
Sleeve seam	30.5	(12)	32	(12½)	33	(13)	34.5	(13½)	36	(14¼)	37	(14½)	38.5	(15¼)

MATERIALS: *Allow the following quantities in* 100 g *balls of King Cole Big Value D.K.:* 2 *main for* 61 *cm size;* 3 *main for* 66 *cm,* 71 *cm and* 76 *cm sizes;* 4 *for* 81 *cm,* 86 *cm and* 91 *cm sizes. For any one size:* 1 *ball contrast; a pair each of No.* 8 (4 *mm) and No.* 11 (3 *mm) knitting needles; a set of* 4 *No.* 11 (3 *mm) double pointed needles.*

TENSION: *Work at a tension of* 24 *stitches and* 30 *rows to measure* 10 × 10 *cm, over the pattern, using No.* 8 (4 *mm) needles, to obtain measurements given above.*

ABBREVIATIONS: To be read before working: *K., knit plain; p., purl; st., stitch; tog., together; inc., increase (by working twice into next st.); dec., decrease (by taking* 2 *sts. tog.); k.* 2 *tog. b., k.* 2 *tog. through back of sts.; m., main; c., contrast; single rib is k.* 1 *and p.* 1 *alternately.*

NOTE: *The instructions are given for the* 61 *cm* (24 *inch) size. Where they vary, work figures within first brackets for the* 66 *cm* (26 *inch) size; work figures within second brackets for the* 71 *cm* (28 *inch) size, and so on.*

THE BACK: With No. 11 (3 mm) needles and m. cast on 77 (83) (91) (97) (105) (111) (117) sts. and, beginning odd-numbered rows with k. 1 and even-numbered rows with p. 1, work 7 rows in single rib.

Join in c. and, using double-pointed No. 11 (3 mm) needles, rib 1 row with c.

Return to beginning of row, take up m. and, using double-pointed No. 11 (3 mm) needles, rib 1 row with m.

Return to beginning of row, take up c. and, using double-pointed No. 11 (3 mm) needles, rib 1 row. Break off c., return to beginning of row, take up m. and, using No. 11 (3 mm) needles, rib a further 7 rows.

Change to No. 8 (4 mm) needles.

1st pattern row (wrong side): K. to end.

2nd row: K. 1, * p. 1, k. 1; repeat from * to end.**

These 2 rows form the pattern.

Pattern a further 59 (65) (71) (77) (83) (89) (95) rows.

To shape armholes: Cast off 5 (5) (6) (6) (7) (7) (7) sts. at beginning of next 2 rows, then dec. 1 st. each end of next row and the 3 (4) (5) (6) (6) (7) (8) following alternate rows—59 (63) (67) (71) (77) (81) (85) sts.

Pattern 31 (31) (31) (33) (35) (35) (35) rows.

To slope shoulders: Cast off 6 (6) (6) (6) (7) (7) (7) sts. at beginning of next 4 rows, then 5 (6) (7) (8) (8) (9) (10) sts. on the 2 following rows.

Break yarn and leave 25 (27) (29) (31) (33) (35) (37) sts. on a spare needle.

THE FRONT: Work as back to **.

These 2 rows form the pattern. Pattern a further 58 (64) (70) (76) (82) (88) (94) rows.

To divide for V-neck: Next row: Pattern 38 (41) (45) (48) (52) (55) (58) and leave on a spare needle for right half neck, pattern 1 and leave on a safety pin, pattern to end and work on these last 38 (41) (45) (48) (52) (55) (58) sts. for left half neck.

The left half neck: To shape armhole and neck: 1st row: Cast off 5 (5) (6) (6) (7) (7) (7), pattern until 2 sts. remain, dec.

Work 1 row.

★★★ Dec. 1 st. at armhole edge on next row and the 3 (4) (5) (6) (6) (7) (8) following alternate rows, *at the same time*, dec. 1 st. at neck edge on 2nd of these rows and the 10 (11) (12) (13) (14) (15) (16) following 3rd rows—17 (18) (19) (20) (22) (23) (24) sts.

Pattern 6 (5) (4) (5) (4) (3) (2) rows—pattern 7 (6) (5) (6) (5) (4) (3) rows here when working right half neck.

To slope shoulder: Cast off 6 (6) (6) (6) (7) (7) (7) sts. at beginning of next row and following alternate row.

Work 1 row, then cast off remaining 5 (6) (7) (8) (8) (9) (10) sts.

The right half neck: With right side of work facing, rejoin yarn to inner end of sts. on spare needle.

To shape armhole and neck: 1st row: Dec., pattern to end.

2nd row: Cast off 5 (5) (6) (6) (7) (7) (7) sts., pattern to end.

Work as left half neck from **★★★** to end.

THE SLEEVES (both alike): With No. 11 (3 mm) needles and m. cast on 37 (41) (45) (49) (51) (55) (59) sts. and work as back to **.

Pattern a further 3 rows.

Keeping continuity of pattern and working extra sts. into pattern as they occur, inc. 1 st. each end of next row and the 10 (9) (9) (9) (10) (9) (8) following 6th (6th) (6th) (6th) (6th) (8th) (8th) rows—59 (61) (65) (69) (73) (75) (77) sts.

Pattern 9 (19) (25) (27) (25) (27) (29) rows.

To shape sleeve top: Cast off 5 (5) (6) (6) (7) (7) (7) sts. at beginning of next 2 rows, then dec. 1 st. each end of the following 4 rows.

Work 1 row, then dec. 1 st. each end of next row and the 4 (5) (6) (8) (9) (10) (11) following alternate rows—29 sts.

Work 1 row.

Cast off 3 sts. at beginning of next 4 rows.

Cast off remaining 17 sts.

THE NECK RIBBING: First join both shoulder seams.

With right side facing, rejoin m. and, using 3 of the set of No. 11 (3 mm) needles, pick up and k. 40 (42) (44) (48) (50) (52) (54) sts. from row ends of left front neck shaping on to 1st needle, k. st. at centre front, pick up and k. 40 (42) (44) (48) (50) (52) (54) sts. from row ends of right front neck shaping on to 2nd needle and finally, k. across sts. at back neck on to 3rd needle—106 (112) (118) (128) (134) (140) (146) sts.

Using 4th needle work in rounds as follows: **1st round:** * K. 1, p. 1; repeat from * to within 2 sts. of centre front st., k. 2 tog.b., k. centre front st., k. 2 tog., ** p. 1, k. 1; repeat from ** until 1 st. remains. p. 1.

2nd round: Rib to within 2 sts. of centre front st., p. 2 tog., k. centre front st., p. 2 tog., rib to end.

Repeat 1st round once with c., repeat 2nd round once with m., repeat 1st round once with c., then finally repeat 2nd round then 1st round with m.

Cast off in rib.

TO MAKE UP THE SWEATER: Do not press. Set in sleeves, then join side and sleeve seams.

Multicoloured Sweater

Illustrated on page 127

MEASUREMENTS						
To fit chest sizes	61	(24)	66	(26)	71	(28)
All round at underarms	66	(26)	71	(28)	76	(30)
Side seam	25	(10)	28	(11)	30.5	(12)
Length	39.5	(15½)	44	(17¼)	48	(19)
Sleeve seam	29.5	(11¾)	32.5	(12¾)	35	(14)

MATERIALS: *Allow the following quantities in 50 g balls of Wendy Shetland Double Knit: 3 red for the 61 cm size; 4 red for the 66 cm and 71 cm sizes. For any one size: 2 balls in cream and 1 each in navy and green; a pair each of No. 8 (4 mm) and No. 10 (3¼ mm) knitting needles.*

TENSION: *Work at a tension of 24 stitches and 29 rows, to measure 10 × 10 cm, over the pattern, using No. 8 (4 mm) needles, to obtain the measurements given above.*

ABBREVIATIONS: To be read before working: *K., knit plain; p., purl; st., stitch; tog., together; inc., increase (by working twice into same st.); dec., decrease (by working 2 sts. tog.); single rib is k. 1 and p. 1 alternately; s.s., stocking st. (k. on the right side and p. on the wrong side); r., red; n., navy; c., cream; g., green.*

NOTE: *The instructions are given for the 61 cm (24 inch) size. Where they vary, work figures within first brackets for the 66 cm (26 inch) size; work figures within second brackets for the 71 cm (28 inch) size.*

THE BACK: With No. 10 (3¼ mm) needles and r. cast on 78 (84) (90) sts. and work 16 rows in single rib, increasing 1 st. at the end of the last row—79 (85) (91) sts.

Change to No. 8 (4 mm) needles and work in pattern, which is worked entirely in s.s. beginning with a k. row, so only the colour details are given. It is not necessary to weave in the yarns, but care should be taken to avoid drawing the yarn too tightly across back of work or it could become puckered.

With r., s.s. 2 rows.

Work 1st pattern band as follows:

1st row: 1 n., * 2 r., 1 n.; repeat from * to end.

2nd row: 2 r., * 3 n., 3 r.; repeat from * ending last repeat with 2 r.

3rd row: 1 c., * 2 n., 1 c.; repeat from * to end.

4th row: As 3rd row.

5th row: As 2nd row.

6th row: As 1st row.

With r., s.s. 4 (6) (8) rows.

Work 2nd pattern band as follows:

1st and 2nd rows: 2 r., * 3 g., 3 r.; repeat from * ending last repeat with 2 r.

3rd and 4th rows: 2 g., * 3 r., 3 g.; repeat from * ending last repeat with 2 g.

With r., s.s. 4 (6) (8) rows.

Work 3rd pattern band as follows:

1st row: 1 r., * 1 c., 1 r.; repeat from * to end.

2nd and 3rd rows: All c.

4th and 5th rows: 1 c., * 1 n., 1 c.; repeat from * to end.

6th row: 3 c., * 1 r., 5 c.; repeat from * ending last repeat with 3 c.

7th row: 2 c., * 3 r., 3 c.; repeat from * ending last repeat with 2 c.

8th to 12th rows: As 6th row back to 2nd row in that reverse order.

Continued on page 128

Above *Cricket Sweater* (page 124)   Opposite *Multicoloured Sweater* (page 125)

With r., s.s. 4 (6) (8) rows.

For 4th pattern band: Work 4 rows of 2nd pattern band. With r., s.s. 4 (6) (8) rows.

The last 42 (50)(58) rows form the repeat of the pattern.

Maintaining continuity of the pattern, work a further 14 rows. Continuing in r. only when repeat of pattern has been completed, work as follows: **

To shape the raglan armholes: Cast off 4 sts. at the beginning of each of the next 2 rows, then dec. 1 st. at each end of the next row and the 19 (21)(23) following alternate rows.

Work 1 row. Leave remaining 31 (33)(35) sts. on a spare needle.

THE FRONT: Work as given for back to **.

To shape the raglan armholes: Cast off 4 sts. at the beginning of each of the next 2 rows, then dec. 1 st. at each end of the next row and the 11 (13)(15) following alternate rows—47 (49)(51) sts.

Divide sts. for front neck: **Next row:** Pattern 16 and leave these sts. on a spare needle for right front shoulder, pattern 15 (17)(19) and leave these sts. on a st. holder for neckband, pattern to end and work on these 16 sts. for left front shoulder.

The left front shoulder: Dec. 1 st. at each end of the next row and the 5 following alternate rows—4 sts.

Work 1 row, then dec. 1 st. at armhole edge only on the next row and the following alternate row.

Work 1 row.

Take remaining 2 sts. tog. and fasten off.

The right front shoulder: With right side of work facing, rejoin yarn to inner end of sts. on spare needle and work as given for left front shoulder, to end.

THE SLEEVES (both alike): With No. 10 (3¼ mm) needles and r. cast on 38 (42)(46) sts. and work 27 rows in single rib.

Next (increase) row: Rib 3, * inc., rib 1; repeat from * until 3 sts. remain, inc., rib 2—55 (61)(67) sts.

Change to No. 8 (4 mm) needles and work 60 (68)(76) rows in pattern and colour sequence as given for back.

To shape the raglan sleeve top: Work as given for raglan shaping on back when 7 (9)(11) sts. will remain. Leave sts. on a spare needle.

THE NECKBAND: First join right raglan seams, then left sleeve to front only. With right side of work facing and using No. 10 (3¼mm) needles and r., k. across the 7 (9)(11) sts. at top of left sleeve, pick up and k. 14 sts. down left front neck edge, k. across the 15 (17)(19) sts. at centre front, pick up and k. 14 sts. up right front neck edge, k. across the 7 (9)(11) sts. at top of right sleeve, then k. across the 31 (33) (35) sts. at back neck—88 (96)(104) sts.

Work 20 rows in single rib. Cast off loosely in rib.

TO MAKE UP THE SWEATER: Press work lightly on the wrong side, using a warm iron over a dry cloth. Join remaining raglan seam, continuing seam across neckband. Join sleeve and side seams. Fold neckband in half to wrong side and slip st. in place on the inside.

Girl's White Sweater with Cable

Illustrated on page 130

MEASUREMENTS						
To fit chest sizes	61	(24)	66	(26)	71	(28)
All round at underarms	65	(25½)	71	(28)	76	(30)
Side seam	23	(9)	24.5	(9¾)	26	(10¼)
Length	35	(13¾)	38	(15)	41	(16¼)
Sleeve seam	22.5	(8¾)	24	(9½)	26	(10¼)

in centimetres (and inches, in brackets)

MATERIALS: *Allow the following quantities in 40 g balls of Argyll Double Knitting Crystals: 3 for the 61 cm size; 4 for the 66 cm and 71 cm sizes. For any one size: A ball of the above yarn in a contrasting shade for embroidery; a pair of No. 8 (4 mm) and No. 10 (3¼ mm) knitting needles; a cable needle; 5 buttons.*

TENSION: *Work at a tension of 22 stitches and 27 rows to measure 10 × 10 cm, over the reverse stocking stitch, using No. 8 (4 mm) needles, to obtain the measurements given above.*

ABBREVIATIONS: To be read before working: *K., knit plain; p., purl; st., stitch; tog., together; dec., decrease (by working 2 sts. tog.); y.fwd., yarn forward to make a st.; inc., increase (by working twice into same st.); up 1, pick up*

loop lying between needles and k. or p. into back of it; r.s.s., reverse stocking st. (p. on the right side and k. on the wrong side); c. 8 b., cable 8 back (slip next 4 sts. on to cable needle and leave at back of work, k. 4, then k. 4 from cable needle); c. 8 f., cable 8 front (as c. 8 b., but leave sts. at front of work); double rib is k. 2 and p. 2 alternately; nil, meaning nothing is worked here for this size.

NOTE: *The instructions are given for the 61 cm (24 inch) size. Where they vary, work figures within first brackets for the 66 cm (26 inch) size; work figures within second brackets for 71 cm (28 inch) size.*

THE BACK: With No. 10 (3¼mm) needles cast on 62 (68) (72) sts. and work as follows:

1st row: K. 2 (nil) (nil), * p. 2, k. 2; repeat from * to end.

2nd row: * P. 2, k. 2; repeat from * until 2 (nil) (nil) sts. remain, p. 2 (nil) (nil).

Repeat the last 2 rows, 4 times more, then the 1st of these rows again. **

Next (increase) row: Rib 4 (7) (3), * up 1, rib 6; repeat from * until 4 (7) (3) sts. remain, up 1, rib 4 (7) (3)—72 (78) (84) sts.

Change to No. 8 (4 mm) needles and, beginning with a p. row, r.s.s. 52 (56) (60) rows.

To shape the armholes: Cast off 4 (5) (6) sts. at the beginning of each of the next 2 rows, then dec. 1 st. at each end of the next 2 rows, then dec. 1 st. at each end of the 2 following alternate rows—56 (60) (64) sts.

R.s.s. a further 20 (24) (28) rows.

To slope the shoulders: Cast off 8 (8) (9) sts. at the beginning of each of the next 2 rows, then 8 (9) (9) sts. at the beginning of each of the following 2 rows—24 (26) (28) sts.

Leave these sts. on a spare needle.

THE FRONT: Work as given for back to **.

Next (increase) row: Rib 5 (8) (6), * up 1, rib 4; repeat from * until 5 (8) (6) sts. remain, up 1, rib 5 (8) (6)—76 (82) (88) sts.

Change to No. 8 (4 mm) needles and work in pattern as follows:

1st row: P. 30 (33) (36), k. 16, p. 30 (33) (36).

2nd row: K. 30 (33) (36), p. 16, k. 30 (33) (36).

3rd row: P. 30 (33) (36), c. 8 b., c. 8 f., p. 30 (33) (36).

4th row: As 2nd row.

5th to 10th rows: Repeat 1st and 2nd row, 3 times more.

These 10 rows form the pattern. Pattern a further 42 (46) (50) rows.

To shape the armholes: Keeping continuity of the pattern, cast off 4 (5) (6) sts. at the beginning of each of the next 2 rows, then dec. 1 st. at each end of the next 2 rows, then dec. 1 st. at each end of the 2 following alternate rows—60 (64) (68) sts.

Pattern a further 5 (9) (13) rows.

To divide for neck: Next row: Pattern 26 (27) (28) and leave these sts. on a spare needle for right half neck, pattern 8 (10) (12) and leave these sts. on a st. holder, pattern to end, and work on these 26 (27) (28) sts. for left half neck.

The left half neck: Dec. 1 st. at neck edge on each of the next 6 rows, then on the 4 following alternate rows—16 (17) (18) sts.

Pattern 1 row here when working right half neck.

To slope the shoulder: Cast off 8 (8) (9) sts. at the beginning of the next row—8 (9) (9) sts.

Work 1 row. Cast off.

The right half neck: With right side of work facing, rejoin yarn to inner end of the 26 (27) (28) sts. left on spare needle and work as given for left half neck, noting variation.

THE SLEEVES (both alike): With No. 10 (3¼ mm) needles cast on 36 (38) (40) sts. and work as follows:

1st row: K. nil (2) (nil), * p. 2, k. 2; repeat from * to end.

2nd row: * P. 2, k. 2; repeat from * until nil (2) (nil) sts. remain, p. nil (2) (nil).

Repeat the last 2 rows, 3 times more.

Change to No. 8 (4 mm) needles and, beginning with a p. row, r.s.s. 2 rows.

Inc. and work in r.s.s., 1 st. at each end of the next row and the 11 following 4th rows—60 (62) (64) sts.

R.s.s. a further 7 (11) (15) rows.

To shape the sleeve top: Cast off 4 (5) (6) sts. at the beginning of each of the next 2 rows, then dec. 1 st. at the beginning of each of the next 6 (14) (22) rows—46 (38) (30) sts.

Dec. 1 st. at each end of the next 16 (12) (8) rows—14 sts. Cast off.

THE NECKBAND: First join right shoulder seam

With right side of the work facing, using No. 10 (3¼ mm) needles, pick up and k. 15 sts. down left side of neck, k. across the 8 (10) (12) sts. at centre front, pick up and k. 15 sts. up right side of neck, and finally, k. across the 24 (26) (28) sts. at back neck—62 (66) (70) sts.

Beginning odd-numbered rows with p. 2 and even-numbered rows with k. 2, work 7 rows in double rib.

Cast off loosely in rib.

THE BUTTONHOLE EDGING: With right side of work facing, using No. 10 (3¼ mm) needles, pick up and k. 22 (22) (24) sts. evenly along left front shoulder edge and row ends of neckband, then work as follows:

1st row: * P. 2, k. 2; repeat from * until 2 (2) (nil) sts. remain, p. 2 (2) (nil).

2nd row: * K. 2 (2) (nil), * p. 2, k. 2; repeat from * to end.

Next (buttonhole) row: Rib 2, * k. 2 tog., y.fwd., rib 2; repeat from * 3 times more, k. 2 tog., y.fwd., rib 2 (2) (4).

Rib a further 2 rows.

Cast off in rib.

THE BUTTON EDGING: With right side of work facing, using No. 10 (3¼ mm) needles, pick up and k. 22 (22) (24) sts. evenly along left back shoulder edge and neckband, then k. 1 row.

Cast off.

TO MAKE UP THE JUMPER: Press with a cool iron over a dry cloth. Overlap row ends of buttonhole edging over left back shoulder and catch down. Set in sleeves. Join side and sleeve seams. Sew on buttons. Embroider in lazy daisy sts. between cables as in photograph on page 130.

Opposite *White Sweater with Cable* (page *128*)
Below *Sweater with Dutch Figures* (page *132*)

Sweater with Dutch Figures

Illustrated on page 131

MEASUREMENTS		*in centimetres (and inches, in brackets)*						
To fit chest sizes	61	(24)	66	(26)	71	(28)	76	(30)
All round at underarms	63.5	(25)	68.5	(27)	74	(29¼)	79	(31)
Side seam	22.5	(9)	24	(9½)	25	(10)	26	(10¼)
Length	34	(13½)	36.5	(14½)	39	(15½)	41.5	(16½)
Sleeve seam	31	(12¼)	32.5	(13)	33.5	(13¼)	34	(13½)

MATERIALS: *Allow the following quantities in 50 g balls of Wendy Family Choice Double Knit: 3 main, 1 red and 1 blue for the 61 cm size; 4 main, 1 red and 1 blue for the 66 cm size; 4 main, 1 red and 1 blue for the 71 cm size; 5 main, 1 red and 1 blue for the 76 cm size. For any one size: A ball each of the above yarn in beige, pink and brown; a pair each of No. 9 (3¾ mm) and No. 11 (3 mm) knitting needles.*

TENSION: *Work at a tension of 23 stitches and 26 rows to measure 10 × 10 cm over the pattern, and 33 rows to measure 10 cm in depth, over the plain stocking stitch, using No. 9 (3¾ mm) needles, to obtain the measurements given above.*

ABBREVIATIONS: To be read before working: *K., knit plain; p., purl; st., stitch; tog., together; dec., decrease (by working 2 sts. tog.); inc., increase (by working twice into same st.); s.s., stocking st. (k. on the right side and p. on the wrong side); s.k.p.o., (slip 1, k. 1, pass slipped st. over); single rib is k. 1 and p. 1 alternately; nil, meaning nothing is worked here for this size; m., main colour; bl., blue; r., red; pk., pink; bg., beige; br., brown.*

THE BACK: With No. 11 (3 mm) needles and m. cast on 72 (78) (84) (90) sts. and work 16 rows in single rib, increasing 1 st. at the end of the last of these rows—73 (79) (85) (91) sts.

Change to No. 9 (3¾ mm) needles and, beginning with a k. row, s.s. 2 rows.

Work in pattern as follows, which is worked entirely in s.s. beginning with a k. row, so only the colour details are given, joining in and breaking off colours as required and twisting yarns when changing colours to avoid a hole.

1st to 4th rows: 1 m., * 2 bl., 1 m.; repeat from * to end.

5th row: 1 m., * 5 bl., 1 m.; repeat from * to end.

6th row: 2 m., * 3 bl., 3 m.; repeat from * ending last repeat with 2 m.

7th row: As 6th row, but using r. instead of bl.

8th row: As 6th row, but using bg. instead of bl.

9th row: 1 pk., * 5 r., 1 pk.; repeat from * to end.

10th row: 3 m., * 1 pk., 5 m.; repeat from * ending last repeat with 3m.

11th row: As 10th row, but using br. instead of pk.

12th to 14th rows: All m.

15th row: As 1st to 4th rows, but using bg. instead of bl.

16th and 17th rows: 2 m., * 1 bg., 1 m., 1 bg., 3 m.; repeat from * ending last repeat with 2 m.

18th and 19th rows: As 5th row, but using r. instead of bl.

20th row: As 6th row, but using r. instead of bl.

21st row: As 10th row, but using bl. instead of pk.

22nd row: As 6th row.

23rd row: As 9th row, but using bl. instead of r.

24th and 25th rows: As 10th and 11th rows.

26th and 28th rows: All m.

The last 28 rows form the pattern. Pattern a further 12 rows.

Break off pk., bg., r., bl. and br. and continue in m. only. Beginning with a k. row, s.s. 6 (10) (14) (18) rows.

To shape the raglan armholes: Cast off 4 (4) (5) (5) sts. at the beginning of each of the next 2 rows.

Next row: K. 1, s.k.p.o., work until 3 sts. remain, k. 2 tog., k. 1.

Next row: All p. **

Repeat the last 2 rows, 16 (18) (20) (22) times more—31 (33) (33) (35) sts.

Leave these sts. on a spare needle.

THE FRONT: Work as given for back to **.

Repeat the last 2 rows, 8 (10) (12) (14) times, then the 1st of these rows again—45 (47) (47) (49) sts.

To divide for neck: Next row: P. 15 and leave these sts. on a spare needle for right half neck, p. 15 (17) (17) (19) and leave these sts. on a st. holder, p. to end and work on these last 15 sts. for left half neck.

The left half neck: Dec. 1 st. at neck edge on the next row and the 5 following alternate rows, *at the same time,* dec. 1 st. at armhole edge as before on the first of these rows and the 6 following alternate rows—2 sts.

P. 2 tog. and fasten off.

The right half neck: With right side of work facing, rejoin yarn to inner end of the 15 sts. left on spare needle and work as given for left half neck.

THE SLEEVES (both alike): With No. 11 (3 mm) needles and m. cast on 34 (38) (38) (42) sts. and work 29 rows in single rib.

Next (inc.) row: Rib 3, * inc., rib 1; repeat from * until 1 st. remains, rib 1—49 (55) (55) (61) sts.

Change to No. 9 (3¾ mm) needles and, beginning with a k. row, s.s. 2 rows, then work the first 26 rows of pattern as given on back.

Break off pk., bg., r., bl., and br., and continue in m. only.

Inc. 1 st. at each end of the next row and the nil (nil) (3) (3) following 6th rows—51 (57) (63) (69) sts.

S.s. a further 37 (41) (27) (31) rows.

To shape the raglan sleeve top: Work exactly as given for raglan armhole shaping on back, when 9 (11) (11) (13) sts. will remain.

Leave these sts. on a safety pin.

THE NECKBAND: First join right raglan seams, then left sleeve to front only. With right side of work facing, using No. 11 (3 mm) needles and m., k. across the 9 (11) (11) (13) sts. of left sleeve, pick up and k. 14 sts. down left side of neck, k. across the 15 (17) (17) (19) sts. at centre front, pick up and k. 14 sts. up right side of neck, k. across the 9 (11) (11) (13) sts. of right sleeve, and finally, k. across the 31 (33) (33) (35) sts. at back neck—92 (100) (100) (108) sts.

Work 24 rows in single rib.
Cast off loosely in rib.

TO MAKE UP THE SWEATER: Press with a cool iron over a dry cloth. Join remaining raglan seam, continuing across neckband. Join side and sleeve seams, taking care to match pattern. Fold neckband in half to wrong side and slip st. in place.

Striped Sweater with Hat and Scarf

Illustrated on page 134

MEASUREMENTS						
	in centimetres (and inches, in brackets)					
To fit chest sizes	66	(26)	71 to 76	(28 to 30)	81	(32)
All round at underarms	71.5	(28¼)	78	(30¾)	85	(33½)
Side seam	32	(12½)	33.5	(13¼)	35	(13¾)
Length	48	(19)	50	(19¾)	52	(20½)
Sleeve seam	34	(13½)	35.5	(14)	37	(14½)

The hat will fit an average head and the scarf will measure 148 cm (58¼ inches), excluding fringe.

MATERIALS: *Allow the following quantities in 50 g balls of Wendy Family Choice Double Knit: 8 royal blue, 2 red and 1 yellow for the 66 cm size; 8 royal blue, 2 red and 1 yellow for the 71 cm to 76 cm size; 9 royal blue, 2 red and 2 yellow for the 81 cm size. For any one size: a pair each of No. 9 (3¾ mm), No. 10 (3¼ mm) and No. 7 (4½ mm) knitting needles.*

TENSION: *Work at a tension of 23 stitches and 29 rows to measure 10 × 10 cm, over the pattern, using No. 9 (3¾ mm) needles and 27 rows to measure 10 cm in depth, using No. 7 (4½ mm) needles, to obtain the measurements given above.*

ABBREVIATIONS: To be read before working: *K., knit plain; p., purl; st., stitch; tog., together; dec., decrease (by working 2 sts. tog.); inc., increase (by working twice into next st.); single rib is k. 1 and p. 1 alternately; nil, meaning nothing is worked here for this size; r.b., royal blue; r., red; y., yellow.*

NOTE: *The instructions are given for the 66 cm (26 inch) size. Where they vary, work the figures within the first brackets for the 71 cm to 76 cm (28 inch to 30 inch) size; work the figures within the second brackets for the 81 cm (32 inch) size.*

THE JUMPER

BACK AND FRONT ALIKE: With No. 10 (3¼ mm) needles and r.b., cast on 82 (90) (98) sts. and work 20 rows in single rib.

Change to No. 9 (3¾ mm) needles and work in pattern as follows:

1st row: K.
2nd row: P.
3rd row: K. 2, * p. 2, k. 2; repeat from * to end.
4th row: P. 2, * k. 2, p. 2; repeat from * to end.
5th and 6th rows: As 1st and 2nd rows.
7th row: As 4th row.
8th row: As 3rd row.
These 8 rows form the pattern.
Repeat the last 8 rows, once more.
With y., pattern 4 rows.
With r.b., pattern 4 rows.
With r., pattern 8 rows.
These 32 rows form the stripe sequence.
Keeping continuity of the pattern and stripe sequence, pattern a further 44 (48) (52) rows.

Opposite *Striped Sweater (page 133) with Hat and Scarf (page 136)*

Above *Lacy Waistcoat (page 137)*

Mark each end of last row with a coloured thread to denote end of side seams.

Pattern a further 30 (32) (34) rows.

Change to No. 10 (3¼ mm) needles.

With r.b., repeat the 3rd and 4th pattern rows, 10 times. Cast off in rib pattern.

THE SLEEVES (both alike): With No. 10 (3¼ mm) needles and r.b., cast on 38 (42) (44) sts. and work 25 rows in single rib.

Next (inc.) row: Rib 2 (4) (2), * inc., rib 2; repeat from * until nil (2) (nil) sts. remain, rib nil (2) (nil)—50 (54) (58) sts.

Change to No. 9 (3¾ mm) needles and working in pattern and stripe sequence as given for back and front, pattern 4 rows.

Keeping continuity of pattern and stripe sequence, taking extra sts. into pattern as they occur, inc. 1 st. at each end of the next row and the 10 (9) (9) following 6th rows—72 (74) (78) sts.

Pattern 11 (21) (25) rows.

Cast off.

TO MAKE UP THE JUMPER: Press with a cool iron over a dry cloth. Join the first 21 (22) (23) sts. of cast-off group for shoulder seams. Set in sleeves between markers on back and front. Join side and sleeve seams.

THE HAT

TO MAKE: With No. 10 (3¼ mm) needles and r.b., cast on 92 sts. and work 9 rows in single rib.

Change to No. 9 (3¾ mm) needles.

Next (inc.) row: * Rib 2, inc.; repeat from * until 2 sts. remain, rib to end—122 sts.

With r.b., work 8 rows in pattern as given for back and front.

With y., pattern 4 rows.

With r.b., pattern 4 rows.

With r., pattern 8 rows.

With r.b., k. 1 row.

Next row: With r.b., p. 2, * k. 2, p. 2; repeat from * to end.

Next row: With r.b., k. 2, * p. 2, k. 2; repeat from * to end.

Repeat the last 2 rows, 4 times more, then the 1st of these rows again.

1st (dec.) row: K. 2, * p. 2 tog., k. 2; repeat from * to end—92 sts.

2nd row: P. 2, * k. 1, p. 2; repeat from * to end.

3rd row: K. 2, * p. 1, k. 2; repeat from * to end.

4th row: As 2nd row.

5th (dec.) row: K. 2, * k. 2 tog., k. 1; repeat from * to end—62 sts.

6th row: P.

7th (dec.) row: K. 2 tog., all across row—31 sts.

8th row: P.

9th row: K. 1, * k. 2 tog.; repeat from * to end—16 sts.

10th row: P. 2, * p. 2 tog.; repeat from * to end—9 sts.

Break off yarn, leaving a long end, thread this through remaining sts., draw up tightly and fasten off securely.

TO MAKE UP THE HAT: Press lightly with a cool iron over a dry cloth. Join back seam.

THE SCARF

TO MAKE: With No. 7 (4½ mm) needles and r.b., cast on 58 sts. and work 32 rows in pattern and stripe sequence as given for back and front.

Continuing in r.b. only, pattern a further 336 rows.

With r., pattern 8 rows.

With r.b., pattern 4 rows.

With y., pattern 4 rows.

With r.b., pattern 16 rows. Cast off.

TO MAKE UP THE SCARF: Press lightly with a cool iron over a dry cloth. Fold scarf in half lengthwise and join side seam, then join short edges. With 6 strands of r.b. yarn 15 cm (6 inches) in length work fringe along short edges of scarf.

Girl's Lacy Waistcoat

Illustrated on page 135

MEASUREMENTS	*in centimetres (and inches, in brackets)*		
To fit chest sizes	66 (26)	71 (28)	76 (30)
Side seam, including armhole edging	25.6 (10½)	30.5 (12)	34.5 (13½)
Length	42 (16½)	50 (19¾)	58 (22¾)

MATERIALS: *Allow the following quantities in 50 g balls of Wendy Monaco: 3 for 66 cm size; 4 for 71 cm and 76 cm sizes. For any one size: a pair each of No. 2 (7 mm) and No. 6 (5 mm) knitting needles; sizes 3.50 and 5.00 crochet hooks.*

TENSION: *Work at a tension of 12 stitches and 20 rows to measure 10 × 10 cm, over the pattern, using No. 2 (7 mm) needles, to obtain measurements given above.*

ABBREVIATIONS: To be read before working: *K., knit plain; st., stitch; tog., together; dec., decrease (by working 2 sts. tog.); y.fwd., yarn forward to make a st.; g.st., garter stitch (k. plain on every row); ch., chain; d.c., double crochet; tr., treble.*

NOTE: *The instructions are given for the 66 cm size (26 inch) size. Where they vary, work figures within first brackets for 71 cm (28 inch) size; work figures within second brackets for 76 cm (30 inch) size.*

THE BACK: With No. 6 (5 mm) needles cast on 44 (48) (52) sts.
** G.st. 8 rows.
Eyelet row: K. 1, * y.fwd., k. 2 tog.; repeat from * until 1 st. remains, k. 1.
G.st. a further 8 rows.
Change to No. 2 (7 mm) needles and work the 4-row pattern as follows: **1st and 2nd rows:** K. 1, * y.fwd., k. 2 tog.; repeat from * until 1 st. remains, k. 1.
3rd and 4th rows: All k. **
Pattern a further 36 (44) (52) rows.
To shape the armholes: Cast off 2 sts. at beginning of next 2 rows, then dec. 1 st. each end of following 4 rows—32 (36) (40) sts.
Pattern 22 (30) (38) rows.
To slope the shoulders: Cast off 5 (6) (6) sts. at beginning of next 2 rows, then 5 (5) (6) sts. on the following 2 rows—12 (14) (16) sts.
Cast off.

THE LEFT FRONT: With No. 6 (5 mm) needles cast on 22 (24) (26) sts. and work as back from ** to **.
Pattern a further 2 rows.
To shape the front edge: Dec. 1 st. at end—read beginning here when working right front—of the next row, then on the 4 (5) (6) following 8th rows—17 (18) (19) sts.
Pattern 1 row—pattern 2 rows here when working right front.
To shape the armhole: Cast off 2 sts. at beginning of next row, pattern 1 row—omit this row when working right front—then dec. 1 st. at armhole edge on the following 4 rows.

Dec. 1 st. at front edge on the following row—10 (11) (12) sts.
Pattern 21 (29) (37) rows—pattern 22 (30) (38) rows here when working right front.
To slope the shoulder: Cast off 5 (6) (6) sts. at beginning of next row—5 (5) (6) sts.
Pattern 1 row.
Cast off.

THE RIGHT FRONT: Work as left front, noting variations.

THE ARMHOLE EDGINGS (both alike): First join shoulder seams. With right side of work facing and using size 3.50 crochet hook, rejoin yarn to underarm and work picot row as follows: 1 ch. * 1 d.c. into each of next 3 sts. or row ends, 3 ch., 1 d.c. into base of 3 ch.; repeat from * all round armhole edge.
Fasten off.

THE MAIN EDGING: First join side seams. With right side of work facing rejoin yarn to lower right front and work picot row as given for armhole edging up right front, across back neck and down left front.
Fasten off.

THE TIE: Using 2 strands of yarn tog. and size 5.00 hook make a length of chain to measure 150 cm (59 inches). Thread through eyelet row at waist. With size 3.50 hook make 3 ch. and join into a ring with a slip st., 3 ch. for first tr., 11 tr. into ring, join with a slip st. to top of first tr. Make another circle in the same way and attach to ends of tie.

Finishing Touches

SEWING IN A SLIDE FASTENER

Lay the pieces of the garment in position on the flat (they should have been pressed if so instructed on the ball band). First pin and then tack the slide fastener into place. With the wrong side of the work facing you, back stitch close to the zip teeth using ordinary thread. Finally slip stitch the outer edges of the fastener flat to the garment.

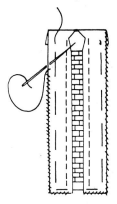

MAKING A FRINGE

Cut several strands of yarn of equal length, place them together and fold in half. Insert a crochet hook into the edge of the fabric and draw the looped ends of the strands through the fabric, thread the cut ends through the loops and draw up tightly to form the fringe. Repeat along the edge at regular intervals.

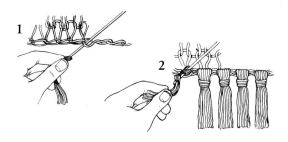

MAKING A POMPON

Cut two circles of card approximately the size of the pompon required, and cut a circle from the centre of each. Using several strands of yarn together, bind the cards together, taking the strands through the centre hole and round the outer edge until the card is covered and the centre hole if filled. Cut through the outer edges of the yarn, insert a thread between the cards and tie tightly round the centre. Remove the cards and trim the pompon to shape and size.

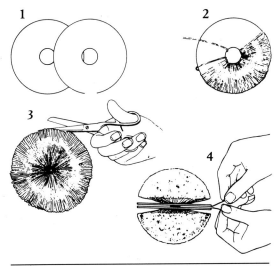

Knitting Needle Conversion Chart

ENGLISH	METRIC
14	2mm
13	$2\frac{1}{4}$mm
12	$2\frac{3}{4}$mm
11	3mm
10	$3\frac{1}{4}$mm
9	$3\frac{3}{4}$mm
8	4mm
7	$4\frac{1}{2}$mm
6	5mm
5	$5\frac{1}{2}$mm
4	6mm
3	$6\frac{1}{2}$mm
2	7mm
1	$7\frac{1}{2}$mm
0	8mm
00	9mm
000	10mm

Useful Addresses

For details of local stockists please write directly to the appropriate manufacturer at the address below:

Emu Wools,
Leeds Road,
Greengates,
Bradford,
W. Yorks.

Tel: Bradford 614031

Lister/Lee Hand Knitting Wools,
P.O. Box 37,
Whiteoak Mills,
Westgate,
Wakefield,
W. Yorks.

Tel: 0924 375311

3 Suisses,
Marlborough House,
Welford Road,
Leicester, LB2 7AA.

Tel: 0533 554713

Pingouin Knitting Yarns,
7–11 Lexington Street,
London, W.1.

Tel: 01 439 8891

Phildar (UK) Ltd.,
4 Gambrel Road,
Westgate Industrial Estate,
Northampton, NN5 5NF.

Tel: 0604 58311

Sirdar Wools,
Sirdar Press Office
   (Suite 507),
16 Berkeley Street,
London, W.1.

Tel: 01 499 0768

Wendy Wools Ltd.,
325 City Road,
London, E.C.1.

Tel: 01 837 7991

KingCole,
R.J. Cole Ltd.,
Rhone Mills,
Sun Street,
Keighley.

Tel: 0535 605249

Ladyship Wools,
Scarborough Mills,
Halifax,
W. Yorks.

Tel: 0422 58433

Argyll Wools,
P.O. Box 15,
Priestley Mills,
Pudsey,
W. Yorkshire, LS28 9LD.

Tel: 0532 558411

Patons & Baldwins,
16 St George Street,
London, W.1.

Tel: 01 493 4477

Robin Wools,
Golley Slater
   & Partners Ltd.,
42 Drury Lane,
London, W.C.2.

Tel: 01 240 5131

H.G. Twilley Ltd.,
Roman Mills,
Stamford,
Lincs.

Tel: 0780 52661

J. & P. Coats,
155 St. Vincent,
Glasgow,
Scotland.

Tel: 041 221 8711

Index

Page numbers in italics refer to illustrations